THE EMPEROR
WALLY LEWIS

Adrian McGregor is a writer with wide experience on Australian newspapers. He has a BA from the University of Queensland where he tutored in journalism for many years and has won several journalism prizes, including a National Press Club award for best sporting feature. His trail-blazing bestseller *King Wally* created a new readership for rugby league books. It was followed by the popular *Wally and the Broncos* (1989). His biography of Greg Chappell (new edition 1990) has been acclaimed as one of the finest contemporary contributions to the history of cricket. His account of the 1990 Kangaroos tour of England, *Simply the Best* (1991), was described as the Rugby League book of the year.

THE EMPEROR WALLY LEWIS

Adrian McGregor

University of Queensland Press

First published 1993 by University of Queensland Press
Box 42, St Lucia, Queensland 4067 Australia

© Adrian McGregor 1993

This book is copyright. Apart from any fair dealing
for the purposes of private study, research, criticism
or review, as permitted under the Copyright Act, no
part may be reproduced by any process without written
permission. Enquiries should be made to the publisher.

Typeset by University of Queensland Press
Printed in Australia by McPherson's Printing Group, Victoria

Distributed in the USA and Canada by
International Specialized Book Services, Inc.,
5804 N.E. Hassalo Street, Portland, Oregon 97213-3640

Cataloguing in Publication Data
National Library of Australia

McGregor, Adrian.
 Wally Lewis : the emperor.

 Includes index.

 I. Lewis, Wally, 1959-   . 2. Rugby League football players —
 Australia — Biography. I. Title.

796.3338

ISBN 0 7022 2493 6
ISBN 0 7022 2585 1 (special hardback)

Contents

Preface   *vii*

1   Who is King Wally?   *1*
2   Rorke's Drift   *12*
3   The Big Leap   *25*
4   Sacked!   *36*
5   Whispers and Rumours   *49*
6   Losing Geno   *65*
7   Cut From the Club   *80*
8   A Medical Dispute   *94*
9   Money Matters   *107*
10   Sun, Surf and Seagulls   *118*
11   Track and Field   *133*
12   Jamie-Lee Lewis   *149*
13   Bronzed Aussie   *164*
14   Exit the Emperor   *178*
15   Jacqui — Proud Partner   *188*
16   The Greatest Ever   *197*

Wally Lewis Picks His Players   *212*
Career Statistics   *220*
Index   *222*

Preface

The Emperor — Wally Lewis is the third and final book in my Wally Lewis biographical trilogy. The first, *King Wally*, covered his childhood to the end of 1986. The second, *Wally and the Broncos*, incorporated the years 1987-88. *The Emperor — Wally Lewis* takes up the story in 1989 and concludes four years later with his retirement from football at the end of 1992.

This has been by far the most difficult of the three books to write. To begin with, the topics were sensitive — the succession of heartbreaks which plagued Lewis' final playing years, the first being his sacking as captain of the Brisbane Broncos. The same questions which were levelled at the Broncos club then have had to be covered in this book as well. How much of a sportsman's private life belongs to his club? How much of his private life belongs in this book? Since the Broncos chose to make Lewis' off-field behaviour an issue, I have addressed these matters, while not compounding the original invasion of the Lewis family's privacy.

When I approached Broncos coach Wayne Bennett to talk about the Lewis years he courteously, but firmly, declined. "I haven't talked about it before and I don't want to now," he said. "The club has put all that behind us and we have both gone our different directions." Club manager John Ribot and trainer Kevin Giles followed suit. I was informed that Bennett subsequently discussed my prospective book with the Broncos board of directors and requested that they respect his decision.

All this is understandable and demonstrates the degree of trauma that the Lewis saga inflicted upon the Broncos. It meant, however, that I was not able to corroborate some controversial material which emerged in my conversations with Lewis. It is a matter of regret that Wayne Bennett chose to forfeit the opportunity to put his side of the story in this book.

There are many people who were helpful in providing insights into the Lewis character, but especially I would like to thank his wife Jacqueline. As often as not it is her recollection which provides the narrative for events which Wally could be excused for wanting to forget.

Second to Jacqui comes his current manager Peter Hickey, a shrewd observer of the Lewis personality and a loyal business adviser. Others deserving thanks include Lewis' testimonial accountant Bruce Hatcher, old friends Peter O'Callaghan, Brian Canavan and David Fordham, and Seagulls executive, Ron Morris.

For the background to the events described here I readily acknowledge the reports of Sydney and Brisbane rugby league print journalists, match coverages by both Channel 9 and 10 in NSW and Queensland, *Rugby League Week* magazine, the newspaper libraries of John Fairfax Group Pty Ltd and News Ltd in Sydney and, in Brisbane, the library of the now defunct Brisbane *Sun*, as well as the photographic library of Queensland Newspapers Pty Ltd. I am indebted once more to Helen King for her transcription and reading services, and to Clare Hoey for tightening the manuscript, as I had hoped. I have Malcolm Andrews to thank for the statistics of Wally's playing career as well as Max and Reet Howell and Peter Hastie's book *State of Origin*.

This is the final story of Lewis' career as a player. I know of no other Australian sportsman, Bradman excluded, who has had three books written about him during his active playing career. Wally Lewis came to so dominate rugby league that it was said he was bigger than the game. Perhaps posterity will be able to judge why the 1980s produced a phenomenon like him. This book reveals what happened in his final tumultuous seasons. I do not say I have the key to the enigma of the Lewis personality, but after writing this book I feel I know him better than ever before. If I can convey that understanding here then some justice will have been done to a man who gave a lot and deserved better than he got.

1
Who Is King Wally?

In February 1989 a British journalist who had flown into Brisbane was intrigued, on his journey from the airport, to see in every roadside newsagency, a Sunday newspaper poster proclaiming: "Possum Bites King Wally". Had some visiting African royal been mauled by a rogue marsupial in a zoo?

A year later, the Queensland minister for Sport asked his press secretary, who had recently returned from many years in South-east Asia, to compose a press release about King Wally. "Who is King Wally?" she innocently inquired. Computer screens blinked, photocopiers stalled and the tea urn boiled over.

Another year on, during the Lions international convention in Brisbane, overseas delegates were impressed that Prime Minister Hawke, Premier Goss and Lord Mayor Soorley were among the VIPs welcoming them. "And your King as well?" they inquired expectantly. No, it was explained, Australia had no king. But, they insisted, they had read about him every day since they had arrived — King Wally!

In the late 1980s if you didn't know who King Wally was you had to be either foreigners or Australians overseas for a decade. Those visiting Lions had it right about reading a King Wally newspaper story every day. In the first six months of 1990 the Brisbane *Courier* and *Sunday Mail* newspapers averaged two stories per day about Wally Lewis. They carried 406 stories or columns about him in that time, topping Treasurer Paul Keating (405) and Lord Mayor Sallyanne Atkinson (349). "Kylie Minogue rated a mere 123 and Princess Diana and the Queen weren't even into three figures," wrote *Courier-*

Mail journalist Paul Malone. Only Prime Minister Bob Hawke and Premier Wayne Goss exceeded Wally in volume of publicity, but they achieved theirs with the assistance of vast government media departments pumping out press releases by mail, fax and on teleprinters. Wally was a one-man band, generating nearly every news item from his own inexhaustible bag of controversies.

He was so famous a new Australian edition of the *Collins English Dictionary* recognised him under "K" for King Wally, on the same page as an assortment of English kings and Elvis Presley. He was so well known that newspapers even ran photographs of Lewis lookalikes. "Is this King Wally queuing up outside a Moscow food store?" ran one picture caption. "Recognise this chap?" ran another, under a photograph of a portrait of a balding English gent painted by Australian Tom Roberts in England in 1920. When I showed them to Wally he laughed. "We do have one thing in common — receding hairlines."

During a week in which Lewis, unusually, made few headlines, *Courier-Mail* sports columnist Wayne Smith wrote an ironic piece about summoning an electrician to check out his WAM (Wally Alert Machine). Told that the WAM was functioning perfectly Smith could scarcely accept the staggering implications — "Wally was no longer doing anything controversial!!!"

In Sydney, in the *Sunday Telegraph*, after a saturation week of Lewis headlines, sportswriter Mike Colman wrote, in humorous Damon Runyon vein, how having drunk 42 cups of morning coffee, he'd worked out his Wally Lewis story for the day. Then his boss dropped the bombshell — forget Wally. "Forget Wally?" wrote Colman. "Anything which took Wally off the back page was bound to have enormous repercussions. Not just on me. Not just on rugby league, but on life itself. The whole box and dice. The whole darn shooting match!"

Fan mail addressed to "King Wally, Queensland" was never a problem to the Brisbane Post Office; they simply monitored his changes of address. The Lewis name, or his royal title, was so widely recognised that when he won celebrity car races his picture took the front page, relegating the Grand Prix winner to the sports section. Newspaper editors knew that if they had a story — any story — about Wally, their news problems for the day were solved.

Hence the headline, "Possum Bites King Wally". The Brisbane

Broncos were at a training camp in the Australian Army's land warfare centre in the jungles of the Gold Coast hinterland. Wally's tent companions were Gene Miles, Greg Dowling and Allan Langer, who all knew from the previous season's camp that the Broncos nutritionist Holly Frail would restrict them to a boring diet of pure health foods.

"I loaded up with all the chocolates, barbequed chips, cans of Coke and rubbish food I thought we could sneak in," said Wally gleefully. "I saw a few guys from the other tents eyeing off our stock so I had it well hidden in the tent. I was asleep in the middle of the night when I heard this rustling in my bag. I immediately thought, 'Those other bastards are into our feed.' So I waited a moment, jumped out of bed in the dark and dived onto my bag and this enormous bloody great possum came leaping out at my head. I just about shit myself, climbed up the side of the tent and screamed like a big sheila. The other blokes woke up and pissed themselves laughing."

On this light-hearted note Wally began the 1989 football season. He was 28, captain of Australia, Queensland and the all-star, though not yet all-conquering Broncos rugby league team. No longer as quick as in his youth, he was nevertheless at a stage where his natural talent and strength combined with his knowledge and experience to make him as formidable as he had ever been in his illustrious career.

In March 1989, the Adidas World Ratings named him still the world's best five-eighth, the only footballer selected in every world team since the inception of the rankings. With 55 votes he polled the top figure for any position. The official NSW *Rugby League Yearbook* named Wally as one of the top five players from the previous season.

Former Australian Test selector Ernie Hammerton, choosing his best Australian team over the previous two decades, named Lewis at five-eighth, nudging Bobby Fulton into the centres. From the modern era only Lewis, Peter Sterling (half) and Michael O'Connor (wing) made Hammerton's team of champions. To top it off Hammerton appointed Lewis captain of this team too.

Wally was in fine fettle. In January 1989, he had undergone a small operation to re-position the 20 cm steel nail inserted in his right forearm, broken in the World Cup final against New Zealand in October 1988. The nail had worked slightly loose, restricting his wrist movement. Wally enjoyed the innovative training methods employed by Broncos coach Wayne Bennett, with whom he had forged a strong bond after their three years together as captain and coach respectively of the State of Origin team — 1986-88 — and their inaugural Broncos year.

Wally loved the Broncos. He was being paid well to play in the Sydney premiership, surrounded by State of Origin team-mates, including his close friend Gene "Geno" Miles and long-time friend Greg Dowling. Gene, having transferred from centre to second row, had reversed his decision to retire from representative football. This move delighted Wally, who had always thought his friend had retired prematurely. For 1989 the Broncos bought three more of Wally's State of Origin team-mates — Peter Jackson and Sam Backo from Canberra and Tony Currie from Canterbury. Though foremost of this elite, Wally felt among friends.

The Broncos clubhouse at Red Hill, an inner Brisbane suburb, was ideal for Wally, close to the city's business centre and only 15 minutes drive from the Mt Coot-tha television studios where he worked as a sports presenter for Channel 10. He always returned to the club after matches, win or lose, and stayed longer than most. His wife Jacqui would drop their two boys at her mother's and return to join him for a meal. The Lewises were such regulars that Jacqui came to know the waitresses equally as well as the players. Playing with the Broncos was a fitting climax to Wally's long career and if he, Geno and Greg all retired at the end of 1990 as they had discussed, whether they won the Sydney premiership or not, Wally would be content to go.

Although the Broncos had been disappointed with seventh placing in 1988, their 1989 pre-season favouritism at 4-1 was not entirely misplaced. They had, it seemed, talent to burn. However, coach Wayne Bennett sent a flicker of concern through the Old Guard players when he chose the team for the opening Panasonic Cup round. He awarded the hooking spot to novice Kerrod Walters over the incumbent Australian hooker Greg "Turtle" Conescu, who had played all three Tests against Great Britain the previous year. Wally recalled, "Turtle got man-of-the-match in one pre-season game and played strongly in the other. Kerrod was sharp and used to get the team on the front foot, no doubt, but nobody in their wildest dreams expected the Test hooker to be replaced by a reserve grader." Bennett's choice signalled to everyone that reputations meant little — Bennett was going with the future.

Wally played his first match on 11 March 1989, the last pre-season game. He walked slowly onto Lang Park midway through the second half, his right forearm protected by a heavy bandage. That morning he still had not been able to flatten his palm on the ground in a push-up though it had been six months since he broke his arm. "In the first tackle I got a few tingles through it," he said. "So I thought, here goes, and I really went into the next tackle. Nothing. I didn't think about it then for the rest of the game."

For the opening premiership match, lock Terry Matterson was out injured and Bennett immediately transferred Wally to lock, just as a temporary measure. "I don't need Wally to play lock in this club," said Bennett. Famous last words. Wally was unperturbed because in those early years Bronco positions were often covered by stopgap moves and he was prepared to change positions to help.

If Lewis was not always at the centre of all on-field drama he was never far from it. In that opening match Penrith fullback Neil Baker was flattened in a tackle and felt pins and needles shoot along his limbs. Wally was first to him, yelled to the referee to stop the game, held Baker's head still and called for a stretcher. "He had this awful look of fear in his eyes," said Wally. "I told him not to panic and he'd be all right."

Fortunately Baker escaped injury but he didn't forget Wally. "Everyone knows he is a great player but he's a gentleman as well," said Baker. "It just showed the other side of the man. I can't speak highly enough of him. I went up after the game and personally thanked him."

However in the very next match Lewis' reputation looked like declining from gentleman to thug. He was sent off by referee Greg McCallum for using his forearm while fending off a tackle by Manly-Warringah's Glenn Ryan at Brookvale Oval. Lewis thus earned the dubious distinction of becoming the first Bronco ever to be sent off. Wally explained the intricacies of his fend to me. "Try walking along and rolling your head around," he said. "You soon veer off in one direction. When blokes come in for the tackle, you try to push them off by moving their heads because once you do that their balance is gone."

In ducking Wally's fend Ryan copped an elbow. It was an accident, but this was Sydney football. Ryan dropped to the ground as though poleaxed. "Elbow, elbow!" bellowed the crowd. Wally's good friend Paul "Fatty" Vautin appealed to referee McCallum, "Oh c'mon sir, that's got to be a penalty?" As soon as McCallum blew his whistle and beckoned him, Wally knew, "This bastard's going to send me off." And he did. Vautin exclaimed softly, "Oh turn it up!" Wally glanced across. Fatty shook his head apologetically. He was only after a penalty. Wally was hooted every step to the dressing room where he showered and changed. At half-time he told Bennett he hadn't done anything wrong. Bennett nodded and agreed.

Wally was despondent but rationalised it to himself that he was in Sydney now where he had to accept this type of thing. Yet 12 indignant men can often overcome 13 complacent opponents and the Broncos eased Wally's guilt by defeating Manly 22-18. As the final siren sounded Wally saw Glenn Ryan sitting on the sideline. He walked over and said, "Glenn, listen mate, if I got you it was an accident, I didn't mean to elbow you." Ryan replied, "I know you didn't, I was just looking for a penalty." To Wally's surprise Ryan added, "If you want me to come up to the judiciary, I'll let them know what happened."

Others were also mobilising in Wally's defence. In Brisbane, friend and workmate David Fordham, Channel 10's senior football journalist, rang Broncos manager John Ribot asking him to delay the Lewis hearing until Fordham could get videotape evidence together. He retrieved film footage of Wally scoring tries in Great Britain in 1986 and against Manly in the Broncos' very first match in 1988. In each try, he noted, Lewis kept changing the ball from side to side, brushing aside tacklers with an open hand, just as he had attempted upon Ryan.

At the midweek hearing McCallum delivered his charge, and Wally prompted Ribot, "Ask McCallum what he saw." McCallum duly raised his arm to show a clenched fist fend. Wally nudged Ribot and whispered, "We're home and hosed." Wally rose and told the hearing in his best bush lawyer manner, "You've heard the evidence that says my hand was clenched, can we go to our video straight away please?" Ribot produced their video of open palm fends and the case was as good as over. But with rugby league judiciaries it is unwise to take chances.

"We have one more piece of evidence," said Wally and played his trump. "Would you call Glenn Ryan?" The Manly forward conceded he had not been badly hurt in the incident but that his trainer had told him to go to the head-bin for ten minutes. Ryan said that, though he was not supposed to admit it, he was looking for a penalty. After Lewis was exonerated he and Ribot took Ryan for a drink at the NSW Leagues Club, a curious case of the loyalty which exists between players in opposition to officialdom, which includes referees.

Wally had been alarmed that a guilty verdict would tarnish his reputation, and damage his image as national, state and club captain. He valued all those. *Rugby League Week* reported that after the Manly match, Glenn Ryan was signing autographs when a cheeky youngster offered, "I hope Wally breaks his arm." Ryan chastised the boy. "Hey, don't you dare say that, not about anybody and not about Wally. We need him to captain Australia."

Self-inflicted controversy continued to dog Lewis when the May 1989 edition of *Penthouse* magazine was published carrying his allegations that Balmain players were arch sledgers. In a frank interview, in which much of his colourful cursing was faithfully reproduced, Wally was quoted: "They'd call you a cat and a faggot and tell you you can't play and spit on you and all that sort of shit." Wally admitted to me that it was his own fault for being so naive in the interview. "I should have had more brains," he said. When next he spoke to Australian Rugby League (ARL) chairman, Ken Arthurson, Wally explained he had used the word "spit" figuratively rather than literally. Arthurson told him he had to be more careful when he wasn't talking to regular rugby league journalists. He could be talking to someone just looking for headlines.

It took only one month for Wally's allegations to rebound upon him with terrible irony. The Broncos played the Gold Coast Giants, as they were then known, in a local derby at Lang Park. The Giants had a tough, garrulous prop named Jim Cowell from North Queensland, who had moved to Redcliffe in Brisbane before eventually transferring to the Gold Coast. When Wally joined Gene Miles at Wynnum in 1984, Gene recounted how he'd occasionally clashed with Cowell in the Townsville competition. "I'm never going to be president of the Jim Cowell fan club and vice versa," Gene used to say. Thus Wally had been well primed for Cowell when Wynnum travelled to Mackay for a match against North Queensland in the old State league days. Referee Barry Gomersall sent Cowell off in that match after his repeated clashes with Lewis and Miles.

In 1987 Wynnum had played Redcliffe and that time both Cowell and Miles had been sent off after a fiery set-to. Said Wally, "We replayed it on video 100 times and Gene used to say, 'You know how we say if there's a blue about to start you never make the mistake of throwing the first punch if you're on the bottom? Well, watch this.' And Geno was underneath and he's gone whack! up at Cowell and Cowell's hammered him. I laughed because Geno would say, 'Look at me. I'm blocking all his punches with my head. Have a look at this. Every one of them.' "

Greg Dowling knew all about Cowell. "I give credit to Jimmy because he fought for his teams and he was never afraid to take the big names on," said Greg, "but he did go overboard a few times in his career." At Lang Park in 1989 against the Gold Coast Giants it was Dowling's turn. He had the ball and a brawl developed after he was hit with a late tackle. Wally rushed in to assist Dowling; Cowell was nearby. In the heat old animosities surfaced and Cowell hurled the type of abuse Wally had objected to in his criticism of Balmain — "cat", "faggot", "your missus" and so on. Wally spat at Cowell in contempt and Cowell spat back. Cats indeed, but Cowell and Lewis had not exchanged a blow.

"As soon as I did it, I knew I'd done the wrong thing," said Wally. "The anger lasted one or two seconds. It was the only way I could think of reacting at the time." Why didn't he punch Cowell? "I don't agree with it," said Wally. "My dad never encouraged that sort of thing. He used to say, 'You've got some sort of ability, don't waste the chance to display it.' " Afterwards it was suggested that Wally reacted to an insult about his receding hairline, likening him to Elton John. Wally shook his head. No, it was a remark about his missus, he said.

Dowling, who was in the thick of the action, said only Wally would have heard the abuse. "Wally will defend himself and his team, but he's not a bluer," he explained. "Sometimes on the field you lose all sense of proportion. It was caught on national television and being Wally Lewis, you can't do it."

Such are the contradictory moral codes of Anglo-Saxon sport that if Wally had KO'd Cowell he couldn't have been in worse disgrace. The incident was not technically foul play and was not reported by referee Eddie Ward, but with each passing day the furore gathered momentum. Two days after the match the scenes were replayed on television. It was almost impossible to pick up the incident at normal speed, but presented with a frame-by-frame barrage, the NSW Rugby League (NSWRL) cited both players for bringing the game into disrepute. Each pleaded guilty; Lewis as instigator was fined $2000, Cowell $1000. The media went for Wally's jugular. "I thought I must have assassinated the prime minister by the Sydney headlines," said Wally.

The *Daily Telegraph* ran an editorial which began: "Rugby League fans must be shaking their heads in disbelief at the lenient sentence handed out to Wally Lewis yesterday." Roy Masters in the *Sydney Morning Herald* called the decision to fine Lewis "hypocritical discipline". Two weeks later cartoonists were still lampooning Lewis. And at the second State of Origin match in Sydney on June 14 — nearly three weeks later — jokers in the crowd were photographed wearing cardboard masks with "Wally Golly Guard" scrawled on them.

ARL chief Ken Arthurson at first could not believe the spitting accusation. Once again, so soon after the *Penthouse* interview, his loyalty to Lewis was being tested. When he eventually spoke to Wally he told him that he was disappointed. "There's a time and place for everything and a right way to behave," he said. However the saga was unlikely to cost Wally the Australian captaincy. Peter Frilingos in the *Daily Mirror* drew closer to the mark when he wrote, "The real victim of the affair is not the game's image but Lewis himself."

That's how Wally felt. Interrogating him about the incident I said I'd heard that his old Valleys coach, Ross Strudwick, had employed the spit knowing an opponent would then throw a punch and draw a penalty. Wally shook his head. Then I reminded him how once, at high school, when another schoolboy had made a derogatory remark about his girlfriend's figure, Wally had spat at him. "Just schoolboy stuff," he said. I said it was the first time in all our conversations I sensed he did not really want to talk about an issue. "No, it's not that," he replied and sighed. "I can remember thinking to myself at the time, I was disappointed not so much over what happened, but what I'd brought myself down over. Just an insult. You don't get the opportunity to live your life over again, but if I ever did, that's one thing I would change. Unfortunately these things happen, otherwise the world would be a nicer place."

Wally wrote a column in the *Sun-Herald* in Sydney on 4 June, apologising to the rugby league public. The *Daily Telegraph* editorial and Roy Masters had both lashed out at Lewis for the bad influence his action could have upon children. That week a padded envelope addressed to "King Wally" arrived at the Broncos clubhouse. Inside was $4.17 in loose change and a letter from six-year-old Brendan Lukas of Concord in Sydney. "Dear King Wally, I heard about what you did and you can keep some of my money to pay." Said Jacqui Lewis, "He knew he'd done wrong. But he treasured that letter."

At the halfway mark of the season the Broncos had won nine of their eleven premiership matches but Wally's form had been patchy until round nine. It was 14 May, just over a week before the first State of Origin. He led the Broncos to a 36-2 mauling of Easts at the Sydney Football Stadium and earned from coach Bennett the praise, "When he captains the team like that he adds a whole new dimension to our performance."

Lewis admitted that Bennett had "got into his ear" about the lazy football he had been playing. Wally's explanation was that, subsconsciously, he had in mind 1988, when the side faded towards the end of the season. "I thought, 'Don't peak too early,' because I always seemed to hit top form right in the middle of the year," he said. "I'm not sure whether I told myself to hang back in the game, because it was obvious with the staff we had on board — Geno, Alfie [Langer] and TC [Tony Currie] — they could all win a game on their own. But it didn't work out that way."

Bennett was demanding more and more that Wally play to the patterns established in training. "I used to ask him, 'Do you mind if I do this?' and he'd say it was OK as long as it worked. So if it worked it was the right option, if it didn't it was the wrong option. That's a pretty fine line. If a chip-kick succeeded it was good, if it didn't you'd get a kick in the arse." However Bennett said Wally's dedication to training was better than he had ever known.

The Broncos lost their last match, at the season's halfway mark, against St George, on a field churned into a quagmire by torrential rain, but it would be fair to say that most of the players' minds were focused upon an exciting prospect three days ahead — the Panasonic Cup final they had reached against Illawarra. It would be the Broncos' first final. Brisbane was buzzing with expectation. After the disappointment of the club's debut season this was what the city was waiting for — first glories. The special pleasure for Brisbane was the confidence everyone felt in Wally. Having him as leader meant conversations about the match dwelt upon the special magic he could produce if the result was in the balance. Queenslanders trusted Wally with their hopes and dreams. It was a special affection they had for him and it was a measure of his greatness that he rarely disappointed them.

2
Rorke's Drift

When Wally Lewis looks back on the matches played in the nine weeks between 23 May and 24 July 1989, he will remember them as being close to the best series of representative matches in his already brilliant career. The period embraced the Panasonic Cup, the State of Origin series and the Kangaroo tour of New Zealand. As captain, Lewis led from the front, with courage and distinction.

He missed the Broncos' first round Panasonic Cup win over Canberra but he was omnipresent in Townsville for a quarter-final against Parramatta. Before the match Wayne Bennett called another of his interminable team meetings. Said Wally, "Paul Vautin used to joke that when Bennett coached us in State of Origin he held more meetings than the AJC Spring carnival." The players studied the Parramatta line-up, understrength principally because captain and wizard, Peter Sterling, was injured. Then they ran their tape across the rest of the teams in the competition and suddenly grew excited. To take out a cup in only their second season — what a coup! The players decided, "We can win this. We have to. We've got the team." They made an unspoken pact — the Brisbane Broncos would be 1989 Panasonic Cup champions.

Parramatta were one of Sydney's most popular travelling teams, especially in Townsville where players wore similar blue and gold jerseys. As well, the Broncos boasted two of Townsville's favourite sons, Gene Miles and Greg Dowling, and the double bill at the Townsville Sports Reserve drew 16,000 people, the largest ever Queensland rugby league crowd outside Brisbane. Wally sparkled, scoring his side's first two tries to overwhelm Parramatta 42-6. "He's playing well and making my job a lot easier," confirmed Bennett afterwards — his usual oblique form of compliment. To Wally privately he said, "You're obviously feeling happy at the moment." It was Bennett's belief that happiness in a player's personal life was essential to good football.

Next stop was Bathurst, for a semi-final against Souths, joint table leaders; they held the premiership's best defensive record. The Broncos paused long enough to spoil that, demolishing them 24-4 in a performance which had critics comparing them with Jack Gibson's great Parramatta sides of the early 1980s. The Bathurst night was so icy the showers in the change rooms ran tepid. Players put their boots back on, picked up their bags, and raced over the ground and across the highway, into their hotel and steaming hot showers. Wally's concern that night was the NSWRL board meeting being held in the team's hotel to consider how to penalise him for his spitting offence at Lang Park. The resulting $2000 fine was harsh by rugby league standards but lenient in terms of penalties in the world outside football. In Queensland there are two contemporary legal precedents of people convicted of spitting being given three month jail sentences.

Rarely has a rugby league match polarised the Sydney sporting public like the 1989 cup final between the Broncos and the Illawarra Steelers. Queensland had gone one up in the State of Origin series and now six of those Queensland canetoads — Wally Lewis, Gene Miles, Allan Langer, Tony Currie, Michael Hancock and Kerrod Walters — were descending upon the south disguised as Broncos. Further, the Broncos were much more closely identified as representing the north than was the composite Origin side with its contingent of Sydney club players.

The Broncos boasted a team with match experience totalling 69 Tests and 77 State of Origins. The Steelers had two Test players, but they were both Poms — Andy Gregory at half and Steve Hampson at fullback. The Broncos had five players — Lewis, Miles, Dowling, Peter Jackson and Joe Kilroy — who had played in the Combined Brisbane side which took out the Panasonic Cup in 1984. The Steelers had names — Rod Wishart, Brett Rodwell, Dean Schifilliti and Ian Russell — but it would be a few years before they lifted Illawarra into the premiership semi-finals.

Other contrasts added spice to the final. The Broncos were seen as silvertails, the Steelers as blue-collar workers, so it was the princes versus the paupers. The Broncos were top of the table, while the Steelers were near the bottom. Because of their attacking flair and suspect defence the Broncos were dubbed show ponies, while the Steelers, who had conceded only 12 points en route to the final, were depicted as tough pit ponies. The Broncos were the villains as surely as if they had worn moustaches, canes, top-hats and tails onto the field.

More than 50 buses brought Steelers fans to Parramatta Stadium that evening to join a Sydney crowd which had taken the south coast team to their hearts. They booed the Broncos as they ran out and raised "King Golly" signs to remind Wally his spitting was not forgotten.

When the Broncos led 16-0 early in the second quarter their 5-2 on favouritism seemed good odds indeed. However the Steelers were every bit as excited to be in this final as the Broncos were and, fired by Pommy gamecock Andy Gregory, they fought back. The Broncos tired and clung to a mere 16-14 lead at the end of the third quarter.

Wally had long admired Gregory. "He was a hard bastard but great to play against," said Wally. "He'd try to pull your ears off, elbow your head and break your nose in the first tackle and at the end of the game he'd be the first to come across and shake your hand, thank you for the game and offer to buy you a pint. A terrific bloke. I loved talking to him even though he was one of those Pommies who talk in shorthand." Gregory led by example and the young Steelers followed.

Twelve minutes from full-time, with Illawarra in full cry, Wally dug in, having made 15 second half tackles already. His sixteenth almost defied the theory of relativity. Fullback Steve Hampson chimed in at full ahead. Wally bent low and braced himself. He was much the heavier man but Hampson's mass was increased by his velocity. In the ensuing collision Wally exploded, converting Hampson's acceleration into an equal and opposite reaction — backwards. He lifted the English star a metre into the air and drove him flat on his back.

Such bravura fills hearts and souls alike. The Steelers' charge faltered, the Broncos recovered their poise and ran out 22-20 victors. Greg Dowling and Brett Le Man hoisted Wally to their shoulders, the signal for 17,000 fans to give vent to their disbelief at being

Hundreds more cheered their arrival at the Broncos clubhouse at Red Hill where the players partied on before adjourning to a city nightspot. Wally crawled into bed at 3 a.m.

The Sydney media didn't intend to let the northern infidels escape that cheaply. In the middle of the clubhouse celebrations most of the Broncos climbed on the stage and, at a signal from Wally, chorused that as far as the Steelers supporters were concerned, "Winners can laugh and losers can kiss our arse," and they all simultaneously turned and pointed humorously at their backsides. Said Greg Dowling, "We were all in that, me, Alfie. Even Wayne Bennett was up there. We all said to Wally, 'Yeah, let's do it, let's give it to them.'"

All four national television channels had their cameras aimed at the stage. David Fordham of Channel 10 told me he turned to his cameraman and said, "We won't use that." But, he said, the ABC broadcast it, so everyone had to follow. It was news, in Sydney especially. Inevitably complaints were phoned in to the NSWRL. General manager John Quayle sensibly adopted the Fordham approach, which was that what the Broncos did in front of their own supporters, in their own clubhouse, should not be a news event.

The Broncos' celebrations were shortlived. Even on the night of the victory, coach Bennett was putting the win into graphic perspective. "Yes, I'm pleased," he said. "But I'd swap 14 of these for a premiership." The match was Tuesday night, they celebrated Wednesday night and on Thursday evening it was back to training. Jacqui Lewis detected a tinge of resignation among the players. "It was the club's first big prize but we really didn't have time to enjoy it as we should have," she said. "It was a high point and then suddenly it was all back to work again." Wally understood the imperatives. Bennett had made up his mind when he got to training that the Cup was all over, and the Broncos were there to concentrate on the next premiership match.

For the moment, however, Wally and his State of Origin boys had to deal with the Blues in the second match of the series, in Sydney. They had good reason to be confident, having routed NSW 36-6 at Lang Park. That winning margin eclipsed the previous record of 43-22 in 1983. The win did not surprise Wally; the magnitude did. Queensland, under Bennett, had whitewashed NSW, coached by John Peard, 3-0 in the 1988 series. NSW were now asking miracles from new coach Jack Gibson. After Bennett retired from Origin denied a fairytale ending. Howls rose upon boos which were heaped upon insults. Wally tweaked their noses. As he was handed the Panasonic Cup he turned with an enormous smile and baited the mob, lifting the trophy high in exaggerated triumph. "When Wally gave it to them I didn't mind one iota," Tony Currie told me. Greg Dowling agreed that they had won it fair and square. It was Dowling's exclamation, "Get that up ya, wankers!" which was picked up by a Sydney radio station microphone.

The crowd's venom shocked Jacqui Lewis and her young brother Bruce, who were sitting in the stands. Jacqui remembered it as a crazy night. Her brother said, "I haven't been in this place for ten years and I'm not coming back. Thank God we're here in the dark." He was worried Jacqui was going to get into a fight.

Channel 10 and stadium announcers, Ian Maurice and Graeme Hughes, went with the flow. "Winners can smile," said Hughes over the loudspeakers, "but of course an outstanding performance from the Steelers to come back in the Cup of 1989." Maurice agreed. "One of the all-time great finals and Illawarra can be justly proud of their efforts tonight, a marvellous achievement."

The Broncos, expecting some praise themselves, heard all that, their faces reflecting their anger. Later Hughes, introducing the man-of-the match award for Andy Gregory, referred to the Steelers as "moral victors, probably". That was too much for Billy J. Smith, calling the match for Queensland viewers on the same television channel. He cut in, "Everyone has said it's a great performance from Illawarra but I do believe this is the moment for the Broncos and it should be their moment only, but anyway …"

The Broncos retreated to the change rooms where Ken Arthurson, forever the secretary-general of rugby league peace, approached Wally and apologised for the crowd's deplorable behaviour. "I was embarrassed and humiliated," he told Wally. The Broncos raced through their showers, into the bus to the airport, and onto their chartered plane. Once on board they unleashed their joy at possessing their first ever major trophy — and the winner's cheque of $87,500. "It was just the most incredibly happy atmosphere on the plane," said Jacqui Lewis. "And it got even better when we landed." The Brisbane terminal was packed with nearly a thousand wellwishers, fans who'd watched the match and been inspired to drive to the airport, even though it was close to midnight when the team arrived.

coaching Queensland had reappointed Arthur Beetson who had not lost a series between 1981 and 1984, and whose win-loss match record was 7-3.

"We were all sorry to lose Bennett," said Wally. "But when Arthur arrived it was like having one of the boys back — it was like a reunion. The washover from Wayne was that a little of our young men's tomfoolery and mucking around had been replaced by professionalism. Those of us — like Gene, Mal Meninga and myself — who knew Arthur from 1984, were five years older and wiser. And the young blokes, like Mick Hancock, Alfie Langer and Kerrod Walters, for the first time in their life they had a chance to be involved with one of the biggest names in rugby league history. They walked in and suddenly it was, 'Wow, Arthur Beetson, a legend, here we go!' "

Wally ran his eye over the NSW side and saw a team arranged by Jack Gibson, rather than selected on experience. Bradley Clyde and Laurie Daley were only 19, and the entire run-on team had only 36 Origins between them — 22 if Garry Jack's 14 appearances were subtracted. Queensland totalled 137 Origin matches — four times as many — and Origins were no place for those wet behind the ears. But what Wally noticed most was the absence of two names he admired, as people and players, as much as any in his career — Peter Sterling and Wayne Pearce.

"The greatest thing in my life, apart from my family, was representative football," Wally told me. "My wife knew exactly how much pride I took in playing for Australia. She never asked me to step down, in fact she said she got just as much pleasure out of it as I did." Wally didn't agree with the rule which banned Sterling and Pearce from Origin football simply because they were not available for the subsequent three week Kangaroo tour of New Zealand. Exemptions should have been made for players with their outstanding records of service to Australia, he thought.

More to the point, NSW were weakened by the pair's absence. Wally got to know them both on the 1982 Kangaroo tour to the UK. In those days "Junior" Pearce was light years ahead of everyone in the swing towards good diet and fitness. Wally, who lagged in the rear, laughed at the memory of the contrast. "It only took me ten years but today I don't think there would be too much difference in what we eat," he said. Wally felt that with Pearce gone NSW had lost a certain mongrel dog attitude. "You always knew with Junior that no matter whether he was 20 points up or down, he still wanted to win just as much," he said. "That's the way he played. For sheer determination, there wasn't a much better player in the game."

Sterling was one of the greatest players Wally had ever seen. "Steve Mortimer actually had better success in State of Origins than Sterlo and I pay credit to 'Turvey' [Mortimer] for that," he said. "He liked winning Origins so much he was like a Queenslander in a Blues jumper. But if I'm asked for my best ever player I come up with three or four and Sterlo's always one of them." On the 1982 UK tour Wally found the young half stayed in the company of his Parramatta team-mate Ray Price. "But in 1986 he was my vice-captain and we got on real well," said Wally. "A funny bloke, Sterlo. He doesn't mind spending a bit of time with himself — going to the races or casino alone. I can relate to that myself, but he was a good mixer as well."

Despite the Blues' apparent inexperience Queensland were wary of the known NSW dangers. One Queensland tactic was to attack the suspect defence of winger John "Chicka" Ferguson. "By the same token we probably spent a third of our defensive talk about how to stop Chicka because he was so unpredictable with the ball," said Wally. "So elusive. He'd step eight times and he wouldn't have moved off a five cent piece." Like Michael Hancock? "Mmm," said Wally. "Mick uses his strength more, Chicka basically kept in mid-air!"

At the Broncos, Chris Johns' selection for NSW was the signal for much leg-pulling at training. "It was no-one-talks-to-Johnsie," said Wally. "We just brushed him. Same with Terry Matterson in the third game. They were the only two NSW Origin blokes in the club. Johnsie would come up at training and talk to you just to make you ignore him. Bennett always insisted on strict discipline, but during the session every time the backline ran I'd throw a long ball past Johnsie to cut him out. He'd be trying not to laugh so that Bennett wouldn't notice, but the next time he'd say, 'Throw me the bloody ball, will you!' We'd smile and carry on as before. After that first Origin he was a shattered man. Whenever he lost we used to give it to him. He finally did win one, his fifth Origin, and then he made sure everyone knew."

Queensland led NSW 14-9 in Origin matches, having won the last five in a row, yet the NSW TAB, acting on pre-Origin instincts, had given Queensland 6.5 points start. Occasionally a champion team ascends to an absolute peak — where motivation, combination, youth and experience blend into a sublime performance. Such was the Queensland team on a still night on 23 May 1989, before a sellout crowd of 32,000 at Lang Park. The Queenslanders seemed nerveless but poor Laurie Daley reminded everyone what a pressure-filled forum Lang Park is at Origin time. A penalty kick dead in front, 15 metres out, and he missed.

When the final score, 36-6, was posted, Wally didn't rate as man-of-the-match. That rightly belonged to Martin Bella, a nose from Allan Langer. Then there were Mal Meninga's 16 points, including two tries. But a good judge, ARL chief Ken Arthurson, had his own view. "Without taking anything away from Martin Bella, I thought Wally Lewis was magnificent," he said. "He might just be the greatest player I've ever seen."

Wally's memory of that night was Queensland's sweet combination. "The 1984 Origin team was a hell of a team," he said. "But I'd need some convincing that it was a better side than this one." He was soon to witness just how good it really was.

Before the first Origin, Wally had told Ray Martin on the "Midday Show" that too much hatred was being generated around the Origin series. "The players don't hate each other, they respect each other," Wally said. When it was suggested Queensland had abetted this hate by endlessly depicting NSW as cockroaches Wally got annoyed. The real culprits were the NSW television producers of the Origin series, he told me. "They wanted us to dress up in camouflage uniforms and throw hand grenades," he said. "They wanted a real battle but I refused. I wouldn't be in that sort of commercial. I said, 'I'm playing football, I'm not in a war.' " Yet by the end of the second Origin the injured in the Queensland dressing room might have been casualties in a front-line hospital station.

With five team changes, NSW was a different proposition at the Sydney Football Stadium. Queensland's confidence was dented in the eighteenth minute when Allan Langer slipped awkwardly and let out a yelp. "Probably three or four times in a game you hear blokes yell like that and you just hope it's not serious," said Wally. It was a faint hope. Langer had fractured his shinbone. He could not even stand up. Play eddied around him until two trainers clasped hands to carry him off. Michael Hagan came on. "That eased my mind, Mick's such a talented bloke," said Wally. "I looked at him and his eyes were a bit glassy from nerves. It's hard for replacements, they have to fit in immediately with the speed of play. They don't get a chance to find a second wind. I said, 'You'll be right, mate.' And he sort of nodded. 'I'm here.' "

Queensland led 6-0 but within five minutes Gary Belcher spilt a bomb and Laurie Daley, with snake eyes and the opportunism of a fox, pounced to level the scores 6-6. A moment later Mal Meninga called anxiously to Wally, "Gator, I'm gone!" Wally, hassled, replied, "Mate, can you just hang on a minute?" Then Mal turned his face and Wally saw the big centre's right eye was swollen almost closed. Meninga walked to the sideline and Dale Shearer ran on.

"Again, I wasn't too upset because Dale was so capable," said Wally. "We lost something in size but neither of the NSW centres, Daley and Ettingshausen, were giants of men."

Queensland's fears about Chicka Ferguson proved true when the winger split Wally and Tony Currie, two normally reliable defenders, and dashed 50 metres. In the cover defending melee Michael Hancock rose, holding his shoulder gingerly. He'd dislocated his collarbone. Concerned about being a weakness in defence, Hancock told Wally he'd better go off. Wally knew about shoulder joints; he'd popped both his in his time. "Mick, stay on!" ordered Wally. Wally was trying to lead his team, call plays, take the kicks, attack and defend while computing positional changes to cover the injuries. It was to become his greatest captain's knock.

He could not afford to have three backs off. If Hancock did go, Wally could play centre and push Dale Shearer to the wing, but the two remaining replacements, Trevor Gillmeister and Gary Coyne, were forwards. Then Wally had it. Pull Geno out of the second row, where coach Beetson preferred him, and put him into centres, where Wally thought he should play anyway. Make a virtue out of misfortune.

Just before half-time Paul Vautin emerged from a tackle with his left arm hanging uselessly. "He didn't say anything but the only times I've seen Fatty react like that to tackles, he'd busted something," said Wally. In fact he had a dislocated elbow.

Amid all this, NSW attacked remorselessly, urged on by a crowd of 40,000 whose hopes for the Blues rose with every Maroon casualty. The first half ended with Michael Hancock punching clear a chip-kick into the in-goal and clutching his shoulder in agony.

Wally surveyed his troops in the break. Gillmeister would replace Vautin. "Fatty was the soul of Queensland, but I knew Gillie would go out and smash the NSW forwards," Wally said. Studying faces around the benches, he realised their confidence was ebbing. "They were staring at the obvious — we'd lost three senior players and in any other match Mick Hancock would be off too," he said. Langer had his leg in an air-splint, Meninga was packing ice on his closed eye, Vautin had his arm in a sling, and Hancock looked glum.

Beetson was trying to create calm, pursuing the orthodox line — don't worry about it fellas. Wally felt a sense of frustration at the team's ill luck. For the first and only time Wally interrupted the great Artie. "Instead of feeling sorry for ourselves, have a look at these blokes," he fumed, pointing to the injured. "We haven't come down here to get these blokes busted up and go back losing, have we? That's going to really hurt them. If we're sitting back having a drink tonight and we've wrapped up the series, at least they'll feel it's been worth it. Now let's get out there!"

He kept it up right down the tunnel onto the field, refusing to let despondency set in. Nor did it, because Queensland scored next, a 70-metre movement begun by Kerrod Walters, traversing seven players, and ending with Kerrod diving under the posts; 12-6 Queensland. The stadium crowd was stunned — just like when Jeff Fenech was knocked out by Azumah Nelson.

A minute later Hancock's shoulder proved too much even for his youthful courage. He came out of a tackle with a look of agony and departed. Gary Coyne came on and Queensland's bench was empty. With 22 minutes left, Bob Lindner limped noticeably after an innocuous tackle on Greg Alexander. "He didn't know what was wrong, he was just in pain," said Wally. "I asked him to stay in line and knock over anything that came his way." Lindner did better, moving up in line, hammering away, limping back into position.

NSW came roaring back. The crowd were being shown an epic performance, with the close score, the high standard of play, and the ebb and flow of field positions. Origin football is of consistently grand proportions but this looked like being the Origin equivalent of Rorke's Drift, the 1914 Test epic in which Great Britain defeated Australia despite being reduced by injury to ten men. Queensland had many stars that evening but they needed a hero to lead them beyond reach of a tragic loss. Who else? With 20 minutes left Wally

Lewis, as he so often had before, rose above even the most excellent, to produce the superlative.

"It came about through having Gillie on the field," he told me. I offered to re-run it on video, but there was no need. He knew this try in his mind, saw its form, was intimate with its shape and movement. "Bradley Clyde ran on to the ball and Gillie set out to either self-destruct or rearrange Clyde's ribs," he said. "As soon as he hit Bradley the ball popped out. Michael Hagan threw it to me." Because NSW expected to have possession, their backline was in attacking mode. For once Wally was detached from his evening's shadow, Chris "Louie" Mortimer.

"I ran to Louie's outside and gave a half-dummy inside," he said. "When I looked, nobody was there; I dummied to thin air. But Louie hung off a bit, a gap opened and I ran into it." In fact Wally ran up to and around Mortimer with surprising ease and then accelerated with that quick-stepping speed he liked the gullible to believe he'd lost, over the 22 metre line. Daley, on Wally's outside, back-pedalled, and seeing danger, turned frantically, chased and dived at Wally's legs. Feeling Daley's grasp, Wally half-turned once more looking for support — still none. Ten metres out it was Wally or nobody.

"Once I saw the line I got that bloody determined," he said. "Garry Jack got to me about five metres from the line and I suddenly knew, 'Gees, he's not going to stop me!' The thing that ran through my head was that he'd come back from a broken arm and that if he dived at my legs his bad arm would land underneath me. He went high and stayed high. I held him there and looked for another two steps before I went to ground and I thought 'I'm half a chance of bouncing over here.'"

Alan Thomas on Channel 9 called it in a clear crescendo for a million viewers: "Lewis ... Wally Lewis ... Lewis-Is-Going-To-Get-Theeeeere ... HE'S IN! OH YEEES! The Emperor of Lang Park, King Wally, call him what you want, he's taken them on, he's beaten them and he's scored!"

Wally stood up and with the ball under one arm did a Jimmy Connors war-dance, upper-cutting the air, defying the Wally Golly Guards, the jokers holding the Elton John signs, the whole stadium. At 16-6 Wally thought, "We've got breathing space." But he had none himself. He bent double, hands on knees, as his adrenalin rush gave way to the nausea of exhaustion.

A Chris Johns try brought NSW to 12-16 and then, with five minutes to go, Bob Lindner finally succumbed, stretchered off, having played 18 minutes with a fractured fibula, the lesser bone in the lower leg. If Hancock was worthy of mention in despatches for remaining in line under great duress, Lindner deserved a rugby league medal for his amazing valour. Queensland were down to twelve men. Wally yelled his orders. "One marker in the ruck, slow down their play, make it borderline, no penalties! Don't try and smash them in tackles, just put them down, don't risk injury." He told me later, "That was one of the gutsiest efforts I've ever seen from a football team. With five minutes left, if we got down to 11 men, unless you're playing a team full of morons — and we weren't — it'd be near impossible to hold them. Commonsense says that."

The clock finally did wind down. For the cameras Sam Backo and Martin Bella lifted Wally shoulder high — he didn't ask for it — and he spoke into media microphones as though in a daze. Once inside the dressing room he vomited from pent-up tension and relief. Around the room he saw the rest, some dry retching, some slumped over or rocked back. "We did it," was the word. But they'd hit the wall.

The post-match praise deservedly belonged to the entire Queensland performance, because as Wally said then — and it has been since proved true — away Origin wins would become rare. What I record here is only Wally's segment of accolades. It was substantial. He was both the media and the players' man-of-the-match. Arthur Beetson crushed what little breath Wally had left with a bearhug and said, "He's a champion, the greatest player I've ever seen. I just hope the public recognise that, in NSW as well as Queensland."

Peter Frilingos wrote in the *Daily Mirror*: "The genius and power of the man know no bounds — he must be the greatest player the game has known." Johnny Raper, himself a 1960s legend, wrote in the *Sunday Telegraph*, "He is the greatest player of his era and no one can do better than that." There was more, but Jack Gibson encapsulated it best with his idiosyncratic lateral thinking. "The problem with him is, if he has a good game everyone thinks he has played ordinarily." It was a memorable quote. Wally was so good he couldn't be judged by ordinary standards.

They played the third Origin, though inevitably it was an anticlimax. Queensland won 36-16 to make it the state's second successive series clean sweep. Wally rebuffed Beetson's attempts to replace him until eight minutes from the end, despite a bruised arm and a black eye. "I wanted to be on the field at full-time when we walked off and we'd won 3-0," said Wally. Paul Vautin's memory is that despite his arm injury Wally had no trouble holding the heavyweight Origin shield above his head.

From that series a record twelve Queenslanders, with Wally as captain, made the Australian squad to tour New Zealand. Sadly Gene Miles broke his hand on the eve of the tour but with his other good friend, Paul Vautin, as vice-captain, Wally looked forward once more to the honour of leading the world's best rugby league nation on tour.

The morning after the third Origin Wally rang up his surgeon Dr Peter Myers, concerned about a sore eye. "His vision was OK but he had pain moving his eye to the side," said Dr Myers. He ordered an X-ray scan and found a fracture to the inner wall of the eye socket. "I was quite concerned because it was potentially a serious injury," said Dr Myers. "The area that fractures is your sinus and since that is open to the outside air there is the risk of infection behind your eye." The question of the tour arose. Dr Myers told Wally if the site didn't blow up it would heal within a week or two. After that it need not interfere with his playing. "We had a serious heart-to-heart about it and I put him on high dose antibiotics," said Dr Myers. Reassured by that prognosis Wally couldn't see the point of declaring the injury before he left for New Zealand.

3
The Big Leap

The New Zealand media waited for Wally Lewis to arrive with the 1989 Australians like tow-truck drivers anticipating an accident. As captain he would be dealing with the sports media daily and since he never put up with fools and wouldn't let a jibe go by, he was a guaranteed news story on tour. His relationship with the New Zealand media had been uneasy since the World Cup final in 1988 when an Auckland radio station's morning program ran a tediously unamusing campaign ridiculing his name. Conscious of this, Peter "Bullfrog" Moore, manager of the 1989 Australian tour to New Zealand, suggested from the outset that vice-captain Paul Vautin handle all media interviews. The request put Wally in a quandary. He was glad to drop the media burden and yet he was justly proud of his public speaking skills, part of the captain's role.

The decision to agree to Moore's request was made easier by the choice of understudy, Wally's good mate Paul "Fatty" Vautin. "Having seen him miss out on two Kangaroo tours I felt nothing but pride for Fatty," said Wally. The team felt the same way. When Wally was rested from the opening game — his eye was still healing — and Vautin's name was read out as skipper, the squad burst into spontaneous applause.

Wally, Vautin and their coach Bobby "Bozo" Fulton comprised a triumvirate that made for a harmonious tour. Wally was close to Vautin, who had a long association with Fulton. Fatty had captained the Manly team which Fulton had coached to win the 1987 Sydney grand final. "Bozo knew Fatty's qualities as a leader better than anyone," said Wally. How Lewis and Fulton would get on was a different question. Both vied for the position of Australia's greatest postwar five-eighth. Wally possessed the confidence which came from captaining Australia since 1984 whereas Fulton, though he had played 20 Tests, was coaching Australia for the first time. The potential for power clashes or misunderstandings on the level of the infamous 1985 New Zealand tour was enormous. As personalities both were unpredictable. Both possessed charisma but were equally prickly characters, delightful for those on side with them, intimidating for those who were not. They shared the same birthday, 1 December, which made them both Sagittarians. People born under that star sign are said to share a common failing — a general lack of tact and a tendency to speak bluntly without thinking. The wonder is that Lewis and Fulton got on at all, yet they did, famously.

"He's a funny bloke," mused Wally. "People say we're alike. Maybe it's because we played a fairly similar game, were both captains, liked to run the show and yet be one of the boys." The first night of the tour Fulton had a big drink with the players. "He did it to get to know them, just like I would," said Wally. "Some coaches like to stay right away, give the players space to be themselves. But Bozo liked fun and games."

Two days before the first Test in Christchurch, Wally caught a cab to the studios of TVNZ to do a live cross to Brisbane. Manager Peter Moore had given him permission to talk to his Channel 10 employers in Brisbane. As Wally sat in the studio awaiting the link, local journalist-presenter Paul Holmes appeared on Wally's monitor and asked if he was ready. Wally replied that he was, and asked for the picture, expecting to see his colleague Terry Kennedy appear on the screen from Brisbane. Holmes asked Wally if he had Kennedy on the monitor. No, said Wally, he had Holmes. "Oh yes," said Holmes. "That's OK. We're just going to do a short piece for TVNZ while you're here." Holmes hosted an evening Derryn Hinch-type current affairs show for the network.

Wally told Holmes genially, "Fine, call the tour manager, Peter Moore, arrange it and I'll be glad to do it." After a short interval Holmes came back and assured Wally it was OK by Moore, they had just spoken to him. "Where?" asked Wally, his voice hardening. At the hotel, said Holmes. "Is that so?" said Wally. "Well, when I left him on the eleventh hole 20 minutes ago he was going to play the last seven holes. So you didn't speak to him at all, did you?" Holmes became agitated and asked if they could go ahead — after all, he said, they'd paid Wally's taxi fare there. Wally was astounded. The taxi fare cost just $1.80! "Jesus Christ, are you short of a quid?" Wally exclaimed. "Would you like me to lend you five bucks?" Holmes got angry but bulldozing Wally had no chance of success.

After several more sharp words Wally was finally switched through to Terry Kennedy in Brisbane. After the link ended, floor camera crew approached Wally, rolling their eyes. "*You* only have to put up with him once," they said, and recounted how America's Cup skipper, Dennis Connor, had stormed off the set earlier that year after similar treatment from Holmes. A station executive drove Lewis back to the hotel, apologising profusely all the way. Two hours later an excerpt of the Lewis-Holmes clash, principally about the $5 cash, was replayed on the "Paul Holmes Show" with an introduction about how they tried to get Lewis to air. Taken out of context, Wally looked abrupt and blasphemous. The media ban on Wally simply gave New Zealand reporters the incentive to bust it.

At the end of the first Test Wally told a Kiwi radio journalist, "You know the rules, mate. I can't say anything. Go and see Peter Moore." The next day a commentator on Christchurch radio station 3ZM-FM said that Wally looked 40, played like he was 20 and smoked like a train. He continued that he wouldn't want to talk to Lewis anyway and that the same went for the other Australians who might play well but were bad sportsmen. Wally couldn't help responding. "That must be very embarrassing to New Zealand rugby league," he said. "When a bloke can look 40, smoke like a train and still beat the home team in a Test."

Beat the Kiwis they did, 26-6, as Steve Roach, Paul Sironen and Sam Backo amply demonstrated Bobby Fulton's policy that in rugby league you can't beat a good big forward. Rookie Kiwi lock Brendon Tuuta sought to lop the Aussies with his own private head-hunting expedition. It was the old story; Australian players conditioned to clean games under the tight Sydney premiership refereeing, being battered in games under foreign control. Wally kept peppering English referee Ray Tennant; "Aren't you going to do something about him?" Tennant declined and Wally had his hands full damping his team's threats to get square. Said Wally, "I thought it was going to be a full scale war at one stage." As long as Wally kept demanding action from Tennant, the Australians kept their hands down, satisfied due process was being pursued even if justice was not forthcoming. Yet at the end of the series Tennant complained that Wally cried wolf. "After a while you ignore him, even when he probably deserves attention," said Tennant.

This echoed the remarks made by Jack Gibson before the Origin series that he didn't want the referee being bullied. Who was the bully? "Wally Lewis is certainly very inquisitive," Gibson had said pointedly. Retired NSW referee Mick Stone, who controlled the infamous beer can throwing Origin at Lang Park in 1988, defended Wally's captaincy. "When you come off the field people will often say to you Wally argued with you all game," said Stone, "when in fact he hardly said a word all match. At times I'm totally astounded by people who criticise the guy."

Wally was not innocent in this debate. He admits that at Valleys in Brisbane he was apprenticed to coach Ross Strudwick in the trade of manipulating referees. "I learned the different ways you can coax a referee into decisions," said Wally. "It wasn't whether it was right or wrong, it was that every referee is human. If a team is getting beaten 40-nil a few penalties will always go the way of the side losing." The corollary is that even in a close match a referee can be tempted to show pity for one side or the other. "Nine times out of ten the 'Rat' [Strudwick] earned favourable decisions," said Wally. "I thought, 'Well if he can get away with it, anyone can.' " Modern laws had made it more difficult, he said. "Once, when blokes were tired, I'd say to whoever had the ball, 'Drop, we need a spell.' They've countered that by giving the ball to another player. So I had to think of another way. The referee always has to be alongside play, so if you can take him out for 15 seconds with a question, that's one of the few ways left to slow the play down."

The Aussies wrapped up the series by grinding out an 8-0 second Test win, Tuuta kept his tackles low and relations between the teams relaxed. Walking off the Rotorua ground a passing lout punched Wally in the back. Wally, used to such abuse, ignored it. But big Kiwi second rower Sam Stewart, a policeman, grabbed the lad and clipped him over the ears. "Sorry about that, mate," he said to Wally. "You get dickheads in all countries, don't you," and the pair walked off together.

Niggling injuries meant Wally played the three Tests but missed the three midweek matches. In the last midweek game, against

Wellington, Fulton needed a five-eighth. "At training Fatty was forever chip-kicking and throwing cut-out passes," said Wally. "Bozo would stand behind me on the sideline and say, 'Check out Fatty, he thinks he's this, he thinks he's that.' And we'd both laugh. Then at Wellington he said, 'That's it, I'm putting Fatty at five-eighth.'

"We were right up high in a box watching the game and thank goodness we were because we couldn't stop laughing. I didn't know whether Fatty'd have time to muck around in the match but everything he tried worked. He dummied, pretended to chip-kick and after he'd done something he'd jump in the air and click his heels. We'd roar laughing. Then when he did put on a try he turned and looked straight up at us in the box as though to say, 'What about my style, coach?' At half-time Bozo basically ignored Fatty until they were about to run out and he said, 'Blue, you've got to be kidding!'"

After Australia's 22-14 third Test win in Auckland Vautin was voted player-of-the-tour which to Wally added weight to criticism of Vautin's omission from successive Kangaroo tours. From this Test emerged the hit-of-the-tour, Wally on hapless Kiwi fullback Darrell Williams. From a New Zealand penalty near half-time, the ball swung through five passes to Williams who chimed in at full speed. In the Australian backs Wally was standing wide and counting heads. "They had one over," he said. "Williams was coming pretty quick and I thought he would try to use the overlap by hitting the gap. So I stood wide as if I was going to cover the bloke outside him and he probably bought that. I don't think he really saw me."

Williams ran two strides with the ball and in that time Wally planted both feet wide apart and launched himself back in towards Williams. Although he actually hit Williams with his left shoulder it was almost a chest-to-chest collision. Wally's feet left the ground, Williams' head snapped backwards, his knees collapsed and his feet flew from under him. At one stage they were both airborne but Wally landed upright on his feet and Williams on his back. It was incredible that the runner with the impetus should be so abruptly stopped by the defender, standing still.

"All sorts of noises came out of him," said Wally. "I remember thinking, 'Oh gees!'" What offended the crowd was that although Williams was plainly winded, Wally then leapt upon him like a professional wrestler pinning his opponent. Wally told me that as

Williams landed, the ball was jolted half-loose and he went after it. A frame-by-frame video replay confirmed this, but only Wally would have seen it at the time. To the crowd it seemed Wally, not content with flattening Williams, was needlessly harrassing him. Williams rolled onto his hands and knees like a boxer recovering from a knockdown, his face covered with field marking chalk. He had somehow retained possession but by the time a trainer had attended, 90 seconds elapsed before he could play the ball. "There's only one thing I felt a bit funny about," said Wally. "It was that Darrell's a good bloke. I even said to him then, 'Mate, sorry'. But it was a Test." Wally's mother June Lewis has always said she has never seen anyone match Wally's front-on body hits. Coach Fulton rated it the best tackle he had ever seen.

After the match Wally, from long experience as a touring captain, inquired whether there was any official presentation. Nothing on, he was told, but there were sandwiches and a beer on the other side of the ground. "We'll be over," he said. Just then, as they emerged from the dressing rooms, Peter Jackson said to Wally, "Did you see that bungie thing on top? Why don't we go for a jump?" Wally, Jackson and Bobby Fulton had talked about bungie jumping during the tour but the tour management declared against it until after the third Test. Bungie jumping was conducted every Sunday afternoon after football, from the roof of the Mt Smart Stadium to an air bag 25 metres below.

Fulton said incredulously, "You blokes are not going to do it, are you?" Jackson said, "Bugger it, I'm going up." Wally looked at him and decided to jump too. Australia's newest world boxing champion, Jeff "Hitman" Harding, over for the Test, joined them. As they climbed slowly up the stairs to the roof of the grandstand Jackson kept looking at Wally and laughing. He couldn't believe they were doing it. The pair egged each other on all the way up the stairs, laughing and joking nervously. "I don't know, I don't know," said Jackson. At the top they did a swap with the bungie organisers — Aussie shorts and socks for a jump each.

Jackson went first. By then the sight of their Australian tracksuits on the rooftop had drawn hundreds back into the ground as well as television camera crews. As Jackson was strapped up, Wally chatted nervously to a local girl. He asked if she was scared, and she replied no; she'd jumped 40 times. Jacko was psyching himself up to do it.

Wally encouraged him. Jacko moved towards the roof edge. "Gator, am I doing the right thing?" he asked doubtfully. "Mate, if you want to do it, do it!" said Wally, though standing well back himself. From down below, where the rest of the Australians were gathered, came their faint cries of, "Jump, Jacko, jump!" Jacko looked back once at Wally, said, "Well, here goes," leant forward and fell screaming over the edge.

Then it was Wally's turn. He was weighed and his ankles strapped to the line. "I went to the edge and looked over and it looked eight times as high as it was," said Wally. "I'm scared of heights, absolutely petrified. I've only got to get up on top of my house roof and I feel like my feet are slipping towards the edge." The owner told him he was going to count Wally down from three. "You can't count down from ten, can you?" joked Wally. The owner laughed and assured Wally it wasn't that bad. The first time was always worst. All he had to do was lean forward, not jump. Wally shook his head. "I won't be jumping, mate."

He moved to the edge. "Are you ready? Go for it any time you like," said the owner. Wally hesitated. "What's wrong?" asked the owner. "Oooooh, mate," exclaimed Wally, shaking his head, heart pounding, stomach knotted. The crowd took up the count. "Ten, nine, eight ..." Just then Wally heard Jacko call him; he'd climbed back up. "Gator!" Wally looked back. "Mate, bloody scary!" Wally's nerve almost failed. "But fun," added Jacko.

Four, three, two, one .... "I leaned forward and this bag came up real quick," said Wally. "I had my hands stretched out in front of me and my fingers just touched the air bag. The first part is the quickest and you slow as the line stretches. The last part is actually the slowest. Grouse feeling." Wally bounced upside down, spinning crazily on his line. He called to be let up, but meant "let me down". He was lowered to the ground and watched Jacko take a second leap. No seconds for Wally. "I did it once for that adrenalin rush, and only once," he said. I told him that former Australian rugby union captain Mark Loane always wanted to parachute once, for the same reason. "Yeah, there's a couple of things I'd like to do just once in my life, like skydive. Not many more scary things you can do than leap out of a plane."

Wally climbed on board the tour bus. Fulton called out that the organisers were dirty on him for not going to the presentation. Wally swivelled, incredulous. "What presentation? Are they dirty on Jacko too?" he asked. Fulton said Jacko didn't have to accept the trophy. Wally got annoyed. "You knew where I was," but Fulton was smiling by then, and told him not to worry, it was a snap decision by the New Zealand organisers. He hadn't known anything about it either. Nothing ever came of this, which was surprising, because from just such misunderstandings were born the rumours which dogged Wally all the days of his career. Someone else's oversight usually became Lewis' slight to officialdom.

Three months later, Wally read a small newspaper item. A 21-year-old Auckland man suffered massive head injuries when his rope broke and he missed the air bag below, hitting the concrete floor of the Mt Smart stadium head first. Next time he saw Jackson, Wally asked him if he'd seen the news story. Jackson replied, "Gator, don't even talk about it!"

Back in the harsh world of the Sydney premiership, Vautin's performance on tour cut no ice with his Manly club directors. Ignoring his 11 years of staunch service, they virtually cut him from the club with a pathetic contract offer for 1990. A "Bring Back Fatty" appeal was opened, run by radio station FM104 in Brisbane. Wally even approached Broncos manager John Ribot offering to have $5000 deducted from each of the remaining two years of his contract, to help towards signing Vautin.

The appeal had barely begun when the Broncos were informed that such money would be included in the club's salary cap. That was the official reason the Broncos declined to buy Vautin. Wally sensed, however, that despite public statements to the contrary, the Broncos were not keen. Vautin was 30, his best football past. Although, in joining Gene Miles, Greg Dowling and Wally, he was another Origin Queenslander, he would also have been one more member of the Old Guard clique at the club. As we shall see, that was the antithesis of what Wayne Bennett intended for the Broncos.

With six Broncos away in New Zealand, Allan Langer out with a broken leg and Gene Miles with a broken hand, the club lost match after match. The Broncos had come to represent the spirit of Brisbane and everyone — not just the club directors, coach and fanatical fans — looked towards Wally returning to lead the team out of the doldrums. Their first game back was against their nemesis, Balmain — past record: three matches, three losses — at Leichhardt Oval. It was a calamity for Wally. Ray Price called it one of the worst games of Wally's career and for once Wally could scarcely refute his old antagonist. Balmain rolled them 24-6. "Balmain were a bogey side for us," said Greg Dowling. "It wasn't just Wally. It's unfair to just point the bone at him. There's 12 other team members as well. But he was the skipper and, like Allan Border, he had to wear the flak."

The following week Wayne Bennett called Wally in. "Listen, you never seem to fire well against Balmain," he said. "Is there any problem there? Have you got a problem playing Blocker, a mate, and you don't go as hard?" Bennett was searching for an answer. Wally couldn't help him. "I don't know. I approach the game better every time. I'm more and more determined to play well against them. It's just never worked out that way." Eventually Bennett grabbed Wally at training. "I've got something to ask you. Are you scared of them?" Wally was puzzled. "Scared of who?" Bennett replied, "I don't know — anyone in their team." Wally looked disgusted. "Turn it up! Why aren't I scared of Sirro and Roachie in State of Origin games then?" Bennett didn't know. "I'm like you," he told Wally. "I'm going through the reasons why you never seem to play well against them and I can't get an answer." Wally shook his head. He couldn't either.

Greg Dowling told me, "I know for a fact there was nobody in that Balmain team that would worry Wally. It might have looked like Wally didn't give it a dig but I know myself I've gone out and tried to go well some games but things haven't fallen my way." I asked Wally whether he felt flat after the New Zealand tour. "No. I could have offered that as an excuse but I'd been on tours before and come back and played OK," he said. "I wondered whether it was just me. Did I relax subconsciously after the tour? I felt I was trying in the game but I wasn't pulling anything out. You're always going to have one or two bad games a season. You don't plan them and you wish you didn't. They're the ones that get me shitty."

Mythology has it that it was at Leichhardt Oval that Wally lost the sympathy of the Broncos board of directors. It was not just Wally's off game. The owners believed that Wally, for whatever reason, did not try, turned his toes up, ran up the white flag. It was an extraordinary indictment, entirely based upon their disappointment rather than on reality. They had seen Wally captain Queensland to State of Origin victory with only 12 men, seen him blot out New Zealand 3-0, yet this was all he could produce for them.

Wally's form did not improve in the following weeks, largely due to a torn knee cartilage which he eventually had repaired when the season finished. Bennett transferred him to lock for two matches but midway through the second match Wally moved back to five-eighth and sparked a revival win over Newcastle. Wally's two most consistent Sydney critics, Ray Price and former Test hooker Ian Walsh, both wrote that if the Broncos were to make the semi-finals Lewis had to be five-eighth. There he played for the last two games, both wins, including one over Parramatta, before a club record crowd of 33,245 at Lang Park.

That earned the Broncos a play-off for fifth place against Cronulla, who they had walloped 42-10 earlier in the year without either Wally or Allan Langer. Yet once more the mysteries of Sydney football defied logic as the Sharks eclipsed the Broncos 38-14. Bennett left Langer, returning from his broken leg, on the bench early in the play-off, a decision Bobby Fulton later criticised as "red hot". By the time Langer came on the Broncos were behind. Wally was equivocal. "I might have thrown Alfie on first and said 'Run until you're rooted.' But Wayne probably thought he wasn't fit and Gary French had played super when we beat Cronulla before." Thus ended the Brisbane Broncos' second season in the big-time Sydney football.

Bennett blamed the New Zealand tour for the Broncos' untimely ejection from the semi-finals. Wally agreed and was so despondent in the aftermath of the Cronulla defeat he spoke of quitting representative football in the following season. Three days later, in a less emotional frame of mind, he re-committed himself to state and country.

The Broncos hadn't done badly. They'd finished sixth, one step higher in the ladder than in 1988. The reserve grade finished fifth and the club finished third in the club championship. The Broncos were the biggest crowd drawcards in the competition, second only to Parramatta in away game attendances and second only to Newcastle in home crowds. Yet the expectations were so high. Brisbane was shrouded in gloom about the Broncos who won 14 games and lost 8, while the Aussie Rules Brisbane Bears, who lost 14 and won 8, were praised for their success.

Wally personally had led the Broncos to win the Panasonic Cup, Queensland to win a clean sweep in the State of Origin, and Australia to a clean Test sweep over New Zealand. He was *TV Week*'s rugby league footballer of the year and Ray Price named his tackle on Darrell Williams the hit of the year.

Wally played 18 matches for the Broncos that year — only Chris Johns, with 20, played more. Despite his Test absences, of the Broncos 30 first graders, Wally ranked third, with Tony Currie, in minutes spent on the field for the club. On 2 September, club chairman Barry Maranta assured everyone there would be no blood-letting, no sackings at the Broncos such as occurred in American and European clubs, for their relative failure. But three weeks later, on Friday, 22 September, the Broncos executed a corporate decision which was to reverberate through Australian sport for years.

4
Sacked!

Wally had always wanted to take his family to visit Disneyland in America. He'd promised to take them at the end of the 1988 season but had broken his arm in the World Cup final in New Zealand. So they'd go at the end of the 1989 season, he told them. On 13 September, two weeks after the Broncos' last match, he visited Dr Peter Myers for a diagnosis on his damaged knee and shoulder. He needed an operation. He could not very well travel with two young children if he was on crutches, in slings and bandaged. He booked himself in for dual surgery on 28 October, a few days after he was due to return from America.

On Friday, 22 September, the Broncos held a media lunch at their Red Hill clubhouse. Wally, as part of the Channel 10 team, was to attend with colleague and friend David Fordham before both flew to Sydney that evening to cover Sunday's grand final. Fordham left his bags in Wally's car ready to drive to the airport after the lunch. Wayne Bennett had asked Wally to drop in that day for the usual end of season debriefing meeting. Wally, expecting a friendly critique of his season's performance, had no fears. Despite the Broncos' semi-final disappointment Wally was not unhappy with his own form. Indeed, on the representative front it had been a triumph.

Never a man to delay the truth — to spare his own feelings or others — Bennett's first words to Wally after they both sat down were, "I'm taking the captaincy off you." At first Wally didn't understand. Was Bennett serious? Was he joking? He wasn't a bloke who joked around. Wally got that sick feeling of galvanised apprehension — fight or flight. For 15 seconds of eerie silence Bennett gazed at him. Wally had not spoken. "I suppose you'd like to know why?" said Bennett. Wally recovered sufficiently to say yeah, yes he would, but he was still too stunned to comprehend as Bennett began listing his reasons — that Wally was away too much during the representative season and the club needed a full-time captain; that Wally did not talk to the younger players; that he didn't mix well; that he didn't arrive early enough at training to contribute to the young club's sense of unity; that he was preoccupied with his own work burden; that he was not approachable as a club leader; that some of the players were unhappy with his leadership. "One or two of the players believe you should have handled some things differently," he said.

Wally is an intelligent man, as quick in his mind as he is on his feet, but Bennett's barrage was like a blitzkrieg. Wally was at a disadvantage from the outset, too shocked to be angry, too amazed to mount a coherent defence. He sought conciliation. "If the blokes are unhappy with me, can I address them and ask them what they reckon I'm doing wrong?" he asked. No, he could not, said Bennett. Wally remembered that the ARL had just announced a representative program for 1990 that meant players like himself would only miss two club games during the year. "Does that make any difference to your major reasons?" Wally asked. Apparently it didn't.

Bennett finally asked if he was surprised. Wally looked at his coach, mystified. "Of course I'm bloody surprised," he replied. Surprised was an understatement. Wally was within minutes of descending into one of the deepest depressions of his life. Bennett, having delivered his salvo, sat back, silent. The scene reminded Wally of when the team watched match replays: how Bennett's psychological ploy would be to cross his legs and gaze at the player watching himself commit an error on the video. Bennett watched and awaited the dawning of enlightenment on the player's face.

Bennett said that a rep. player would not be captaining the team next year. Wally replied "You don't have to be Einstein to work out who it's going to be then. Because we've only got a couple of non-rep. players in our team. It's got to be GD [Greg Dowling]." It was bizarre; there was Wally, apparently calm, discussing his possible successor with the man who had just sacked him. Wally was operating on social skills alone. His real feelings were numb.

"So what do you think? Can you accept that?" Bennett asked

briskly. Wally computed the question and wondered: was Bennett asking him if he was going to say he would resign? Wally replied that he wasn't sure if he could, based on the reasons Bennett had given. Bennett concluded, "Well, that's the way it's going to be."

The meeting had lasted about 20 minutes. Bennett showed neither hostility nor sympathy; nor was he apologetic. What was he then? "His normal serious self," recalled Wally. "The person he is 99 per cent of his life."

Wally left Bennett's office, jumped in his car and drove straight home, a 30 minute trip to the suburb of Birkdale, on the south-eastern side of the city. He turned Bennett's words over and over; still rejecting full acceptance. The captaincy was more than a title to him, it was his role, it defined him, and much in his life flowed from it. He had captained Queensland since 1981, Australia since 1984 and all his club sides since 1982, except for his first season with Wynnum-Manly in 1984. To be captain meant he had a special place among his peers, especially Geno and GD. To lose it diminished him, upset the balance of relationships established over many years. It meant the last remaining challenge in his career — to lift the Winfield Cup above his head as had Fatty Vautin — was snatched from him. In his business life it meant he could no longer be introduced as captain of the Broncos, Brisbane's newest and most popular sporting phenomenon.

What did it mean for his future with them? If Valleys and Wynnum had been his youth and coming of age respectively, the Broncos were to be his last magnificent hurrah. He loved the Broncos and everything they represented, he loved leading them onto his favourite ground, Lang Park, week after week. He loved the friendships, the shared successes and failures, the masculine atmosphere, the drinks, the dependence. Yes, he was dependent on them. He even enjoyed the training. Although he would still be with the club, inevitably everything would change. What had Bennett done to him? The more he thought the more angry he grew. For days the media had been asking why the Broncos had missed the semis — again. "I'm being blamed here for something that's not my fault," Wally fumed to himself. Was his position the only change the Broncos were making?

Jacqui was surprised to see him walk in the door and then apprehensive when she saw his expression. "What's wrong?" she asked.

Nothing, said Wally. She followed him through the house to the back annexe where he sat down, out of sight of the world. "Something's wrong," Jacqui persisted. Wally shook his head, staring out at the eucalypts in the back yard. Jacqui retreated and Wally allowed the truth to settle upon him. As much as he was shattered to lose the captaincy there was another fear in the back of his mind. In those 20 minutes Wayne Bennett, with all the solemnity of a Solomon, had judged that Wally's career had peaked and had begun an inexorable slide. For 12 years Wally had ascended from one honour to the next and 1989 had been no different. He had imagined he would, some day soon, halt the curve at its highest point and retire. Now it was too late. Already Bennett had pencilled in a downturn and Wally was powerless to fight him.

Jacqui busied herself around the house. "He was strange," she said. "I'd never seen him like that before, so I waited." After an hour she finally coaxed him to talk and her growing dismay matched his. "I called Bennett all the hideous names I could think," said Jacqui. "How dare he?" Her anger gave Wally confidence in his own rage. Jacqui went to ring her mother. Wally warned her not to tell anyone. Jacqui rang the Broncos and told David Fordham that Wally would meet him at the airport with their bags. Fordham had noticed Wally did not attend the lunch. Bennett, he remembered later, had chatted away in a very relaxed manner.

Because of the long pilots' strike the television commentary crew and technicians flew by a chartered plane from the private terminal in Brisbane. Fordham arrived at 4.30 p.m. to find Wally, in maroon tracksuit pants and white T-shirt, sitting with his elbows on his knees, staring glumly ahead, holding a six-pack of beer. Fordham was taken aback. Wally always dressed neatly and the six-pack was totally out of character. Fordham said, "You're having a drink, what's your story?" Wally muttered he had problems. Fordham ventured quietly, "Trouble at home?" No, Wally said, he'd tell him about it later. But Wally looked so morose Fordham persisted. They found a private room and Wally said, "Say nothing about it, but Bennett's just sacked me as captain."

Fordham remembered the scene clearly. "He had tears in his eyes and an emotion I'd never seen on his face before," he said. "He was shattered. Wally is a pretty tough cookie but once you get through to him he's so vulnerable you can cut him like a knife through butter."

That evening Jacqui visited her parents and weathered her mother's observant eye. Nothing was wrong, she insisted. Grand final Sunday she attended a barbeque at friends of Wally's. "When Wally's not there I still go to all the functions so that he doesn't lose contact with them," said Jacqui. "They know he can't be there but I pick up all the news and gossip and when he comes back he slots in easily." One guest had recently been to a coaching seminar at which Wayne Bennett spoke. "I'm not sure I like that bloke," the fellow speculated. Jacqui sat there thinking, "If only you knew, mate, he's just cut Wally's heart out."

After the grand final weekend a close friend, Peter "Cal" O'Callaghan, who owned a hotel at Stanthorpe, rang Wally and invited him to play in the town's golf tournament. Cal was a front rower with Valleys in 1978, Wally's first year in first grade. "He used to have long hair then, had to brush it out of his eyes," joked O'Callaghan. Wally drove up and during the round spilt it all to O'Callaghan. Then he told Geno as well. "His jaw hit the ground," said Wally. "After we'd spoken a bit he said, 'Oh well, GD's the captain. Gees, I'd hate to be in GD's shoes.'" Finally Wally rang Fatty Vautin in Sydney. Vautin, who had only recently been dumped by Manly, fell silent on the phone. "Benny's got to be kiddin'," he finally said, resorting to his favourite expression of disbelief. So then Jacqui and Wally's four best friends knew, and were all committed to secrecy.

Wally confronted Broncos general manager John Ribot. Did he agree with Bennett's decision? "It's not whether I agree or disagree," said Ribot. "Wayne's got full control of the team and the board will back his decisions." Ribot then suggested to Wally that he announce that it was his decision, and his decision alone, to step down from the captaincy through pressure of work commitments. "That would be the best way for all parties," said Ribot.

This was a bad mistake. With those words Ribot cast the sacking into a new light. It was an admission that the Broncos were acutely conscious of the public furore that would erupt when the news broke. They were embarrassed. Furthermore it confirmed in Wally's mind that he was being victimised and that the only way he could fight Bennett's decision was in the public arena, where he could make a righteous stand. Public sympathy would be with him and he was a great media performer, one of the best. He was not about to forfeit his sole weapon to Ribot.

"Get stuffed," he flared. "I'm not saying that. It would be the best way for you blokes, not for me. The one thing I've never been scared of is the truth. If you want it to come out, you announce I've been sacked because Bennett's not happy with my club captaincy." Ribot again pressed Wally to release the news in a smooth fashion. No way in the world, Wally responded. Ribot asked him to think about it. Wally said he would be making no announcements. On that discordant note they parted.

In that moment the die was cast for all the rancour to come. Wally might have saved some future for himself with the Broncos had he gone gently from the leadership, but it was an impossible ask. "He couldn't have done it," Greg Dowling told me. "And I probably wouldn't have expected him to. Here's the man who captain-coached the local team to the premiership five years before, captained mighty Queensland and Australia and suddenly he says, 'Hang on, I don't want this any more.' People wouldn't have believed him."

On Friday, 29 September, seven days after Bennett employed the guillotine, Broncos centre Chris Johns held his wedding reception at Indooroopilly golf club in Brisbane. At a round table sat Wally and Jacqui, Wayne and Trish Bennett, Greg and Rhonda Dowling and Gene and Debbie Miles. Said Jacqui, "We all had to sit there and be nice to each other and not say anything about what we all knew by then. I was so tense I gritted my teeth but Wally just kept talking to Wayne. I was uptight but he copped it without a show. I presumed Wally accepted it as the politics of the game because I remember when Colin Scott was dumped as Australian fullback his wife was really upset but he just took it quietly. I thought. 'Well, that must be the way rugby league goes'."

However Wally had not accepted it. Another week passed and each night he sat with Jacqui, dwelling upon the injustice of it. He had no reason to make waves. He was waiting to be sacked publicly. Such sensational news could never be contained. On Saturday, 7 October, he went to Peter Jackson's bucks party at the Pinkenbah Hotel. He was astonished when several players sidled up to him and said, "Mate, we're sorry about the decision." Wally feigned ignorance. What decision? "The captaincy," they said. "Just put it this way, we don't agree with it." The next morning Mike Colman, in his *Sunday Telegraph* sports column in Sydney, reported that, according to a "loose-lipped Broncos heavy", Wally could be sacked unless the club received an assurance of a better showing in 1990. If only it was so.

Wally had long planned his American holiday but now he couldn't wait to escape. The day before he left he saw Ribot once more. They were old team-mates, football friends with soldiers' camaraderie. Wally and Mal Meninga had carried Ribot shoulder high from the field after Ribot's last Origin in 1985. They were close enough for Wally to expect frank answers. "Reebs, I can't cop this," he began. "It's absolute bullshit the reasons that have been given to me. Do you want me at the club next year or not?" Ribot assured him the club did, but Ribot's old team-mates knew he was no longer the easy going Reebs they had once known. Of course Ribot had changed. As general manager he had become a professional club executive owing his livelihood, and therefore his allegiances, to his employers. Peter Jackson joked that Ribot had a better sidestep now than when he was a player and he had a pretty good one then. Like all middle managers dealing with shop floor employees, Ribot could be placed in invidious positions. Wally put him in one. "Hang on," said Wally. "You're not the club boss any more. You're my friend John Ribot, the bloke I used to play football with. I'm asking you as a friend. Do you still want me?" Ribot hesitated a moment and said quietly that he did. So that's how it would be, Wally thought, 1990 Broncos playing non-captain.

Before leaving for Los Angeles, Jacqui told her parents of Wally's sacking. She sensed the news would leak out anyway, as it did. Off they flew, Wally, Jacqui and their two boys, Mitchell, three, and Lincoln, two, winging thousands of kilometres from care, away from the cursed Broncos and the heartbreak the club had suddenly inflicted upon them. They walked into their Los Angeles hotel foyer and suddenly heard four New Zealanders yell Wally's name at the top of their voices. From then on not a day passed in public without a friendly hooroo. A group of Sydney pensioners at Disneyland, a pair of Aussie rules lads and their wives at Alcatraz, even a Scot who'd spent a few months in Adelaide — they all recognised him. Photographs with Wally, videos of Wally, probably about fifty autographs in a week, in Los Angeles! Wally didn't mind. There's something endearing about Aussies overseas.

He and Jacqui took one look at Disneyland's hour-long queues for the main shows and took the boys through "It's A Small World" and "Little Story Book Land". "That took my mind off my own troubles for a little while," said Wally. "Just watching the kids enjoy it. We spent a couple of days there — it takes you that long to get around everything." They set off to drive to San Francisco, Wally making up word games with Jacqui. The Broncos were a distant memory.

Back in Brisbane Peter Jackson married his girlfriend Siobhan on 14 October and woke up the next morning to find that his wedding photo in the Sunday newspaper had been upstaged by front page headlines on Wally's sacking. Wally pulled in for the night at a motel in a small country town halfway to San Francisco. At 10.30 p.m. the phone rang. It was an international call. "No, it's a mistake, wrong room, no one knows I'm here," said Wally. Bob Fulton had organised their trip but this motel was a chance stopover. However, it was Peter Kelly, a workmate from Channel 10 in Brisbane, successful with a fine piece of telephone sleuthing. Could he talk about the captaincy sacking? Wally's heart sunk. He immediately thought, "Fordo, you low bastard!"

He asked Kelly to call back, and then he tracked Fordham down to a hotel in London where he was on a rugby union assignment. "Mate, I would like to have broken it, but it wasn't me," protested Fordham, who eventually got a rocket from his station for sitting on the story for three weeks. Kelly rang Wally back. They had a helicopter flying a news crew down. "Like hell you have!" exclaimed Wally, but agreed to do a live cross from a San Francisco studio the following night.

The next morning they arrived at the Vagabond motel in San Francisco. A harrassed receptionist checked Wally in and studied him in awe. "Who…the…hell…ARE…you?" she said, handing him about sixty phone messages from nearly every news media outlet on the east coast of Australia. "Don't worry about it," said Wally enigmatically, a rare light-hearted moment amid growing gloom. One message was from John Ribot in Brisbane. Wally rang and asked what the club had said about the captaincy. Near the phone Jacqui snarled loudly enough for Ribot to hear, "Ron McAuliffe told me to watch out for you Broncos and he was damn well right!" Jacqui later told me, "Wally couldn't have cared less. He didn't tell me to shut up or anything. I think it was what he felt like saying but I was saying it for him."

As messages mounted up, the Lewis family fled to a Chinese restaurant in a marina food complex about 200 metres from their hotel. The whole family was tired of American food. "It's just a hamburgathon," said Wally. In a video slot machine Jacqui watched old film of a great San Franciscan earthquake. She remarked casually to Wally that earthquakes must be horrible. Next day they escaped to Alcatraz but as Wally bought entrance tickets a radio reporter approached, microphone in hand. Wally warned him with quiet anger, "Mate, I'm telling you right now, put it away or the last time you'll see it is when it hits the bloody water over there." He was only doing his job, said the reporter. "Get the hell out of here!" said Wally.

Their holiday was over, sabotaged by the electronic global village. They drove over the Golden Gate bridge; the boys had picked up the tension and were crying. "Let's go," said Jacqui. "We'll clean up and go and eat at the marina again." At the hotel counter Wally tore up a dozen media messages and they retreated into the safety of their room. One hour later an earthquake, measuring 6.9 on the Richter scale, convulsed the city, killing 67 people.

Wally knew the time it struck was 5.05 p.m., because the clock stopped at that point. Jacqui had put the boys in the shower bath but the water kept running hot and cold. "Stupid hotel," she thought and then for fifteen or twenty seconds the building shook, tumbling the boys off their feet. They screamed, Jacqui screamed, the lights failed, the television flicked off. Wally had been sitting by the window, watching San Franciscans toil up the city's steep hills when suddenly they dived face down, flat to the ground. "What's happening?" Jacqui screamed. As the building swayed sideways Wally clung to the window and saw the picture postcard scene outside go haywire as shop display windows cracked and smashed, power lines snaked and sparked, fires broke out and alarms rang. He heard two bumps as the boys fell on their heads, raced in, wrapped them in towels and hugged and protected them and Jacqui in a bathroom corner. The quake subsided but not Jacqui's fright. "I was in tears, I'd never been so scared in all my life," she said. "I just wanted mum and dad."

Back at the window, Wally saw people racing from buildings and heard their shouts, "Hey man, wasn't that a shake and half!" The hotel backed onto a hill and though he was on the sixth floor, Wally's window balcony was only three metres above the street. "Excuse me," he called. People were laughing and shouting with the relief of survivors. Someone down below answered. Wally realised the naivety of his words but he continued. "Ah … I'm from Australia, I've never been in one before, but was that an earthquake?" About thirty people in the street burst into laughter. "Oh man, yeah that was a big one, there'll be big damage everywhere," they said.

Wally told me, "What I remember most were the sirens, hundreds of them, police, fire, ambulance going everywhere." Jacqui gasped and pointed down the road. The marina where they were going to eat was a fireball. The phone was out, power out, they had no food, and they were worried. Wally ventured downstairs but retreated from the crush of panicking tourists. "Stay in the building, don't even move out of your room," a local told Wally. "Stick your wallet in your pocket and your hand on your wallet because there's going to be enormous crime."

Wally told Jacqui, "I don't feel like sleeping, we'll take it in shifts." But neither slept much and small after-tremors kept them on edge. "We'd look at each other and hit the panic button," said Wally. They could smell gas and heard police patrolling the streets advising motorists to leave their cars and walk. At 3 a.m. the hotel brought emergency water to their room and Wally declared, "Let's get out of here." Their plane to Hawaii was due to take off at 6.30 a.m. They packed, woke the boys and walked downstairs into the foyer, which was lit by torchlight. Outside, a queue of over 100 people had lined up to use a public telephone which still worked.

Wally drove slowly through blacked-out streets of abandoned cars and stranded cable cars. Small fires smouldered, police car lights flashed red and blue and people swept up debris. It was a like a scene from *Blade Runner*. Wally headed for the airport freeway. Police with torches stopped him, telling him to detour. The double-decker freeway had collapsed, crushing motorists underneath. Wally nosed his hire car over roads split by massive cracks. The boys were wide-eyed, silent.

The airport was chaos as 25,000 people jammed the terminal, lying on seats, on the floor, making beds from baggage, and everywhere was the buzz of fear. Wally picked up conversations. "That's it man, stuff this, I'm outta here! They can have ma clothes, ma TV, everything, I'm gone, makin' a new start some place else." People had just grabbed their wallets, upped and left, homes, car and everything. As Wally told me, they were spooked.

The flight to Hawaii had been put back to 8 p.m. The nightmare continued. Wally hailed a cab to the Airport Hilton but it was booked out. "Two nice air hostesses took pity on us," said Jacqui. "They had a room each but they let us have one and shared the other." By 11 a.m. food and television had distracted the boys while Wally and Jacqui rang their parents. That evening at the airport Wally bought a T-shirt printed with, "I Survived The Earthquake". Said Jacqui, "They had them out already. Never miss a dollar the Americans."

Finally their aircraft sat on the runway in a long queue for an hour awaiting clearance, to the dismay of the agitated passengers. "When we finally took off I've never heard people cheer like they did," said Wally. They stayed several days in Hawaii calming their frayed nerves. Wally enjoys travel, but Jacqui would be just as happy if she never left Australia, or preferably Queensland. The whole trip had been an ordeal. She relaxed on the beach until she heard an American woman announce, "My husband says a tidal wave from that earthquake will reach here soon." Jacqui said to Wally, "Get me out of here! I want to go home, no matter what's waiting for us."

In Wally's absence David Fordham had gone to John Ribot and acted as an unofficial advocate, stating what Wally could not say himself. He pointed out how, by signing Wally, the Broncos had bankrolled the club, attracting players and sponsorship. "Surely if you're unhappy with him you can give him until February to change his ways — tell him if he doesn't, no second chances, he's out," Fordham said, but Ribot said the decison was irreversible.

Bennett was already casting about for Wally's successor but the problem was Wally had been captain for so long none of his contemporaries felt comfortable about leading him. The directors sounded out Tony Currie but he told them he was not that type of player; besides, he was still playing representative football. The obvious choice was Greg Dowling, who retired from representative football in 1988, the Broncos' first year, so he could devote his time to winning a premiership with the novice club. Dowling was shocked when

Bennett told him he was replacing Wally. "Why, what's wrong?" he asked. Bennett repeated his litany of reasons.

Dowling thought long and hard. He and Lewis had enjoyed a good association over the years; Greg ran the forwards and Wally was overall boss. He told Bennett that there would be friction, that no matter who got it, Wally would hate them for it. Possibly Wally would accept him better than anyone else but it would not be an enviable post. Eventually he declined. Dowling wanted to keep Wally. "I reckon he should have stayed captain for the simple reason of because who he was," Dowling told me.

Wally flew in to Brisbane and the next day, 24 October, held a press conference at the Parkroyal hotel. He answered questions for 45 minutes and the longer he spoke the more dejected and confused he sounded. At best he was resigned to playing for the Broncos. "I know that if I'm playing and I'm not captain, I won't be happy," he said. "But that's the way it's going to be I suppose, if I'm to play here." And play there he must, or nowhere. Within days Manly, Norths and Canterbury all spoke to him about transferring but Ribot warned them the Broncos would not release him from the last year of his contract.

Towards the end of the season Wally and Jacqui had decided to have another baby, their third. When Wally was sacked Jacqui cast her mind forward to the miserable year in prospect and dreaded being pregnant amid such unhappiness. She suggested they wait, but Wally would not have it. "They're not going to run my family life as well," he said. On 26 October Jacqui discovered, to her joy, she was pregnant.

The next evening she and Wally attended the Broncos' end of season presentation dinner. Said Jacqui, "I remember thinking, 'I don't like Wayne Bennett now, I don't know who's going to stab us in the back. How can we walk in that place and face them all?'" Test selector Johnny Raper had rung Wally and Jacqui that week and assured them that they were not in the wrong, and to try to grin and bear it. That they did, seated at a Channel 10 table with Wally's manager Billy J. Smith and David Fordham. Scott Tronc, Brett Le Man, Greg Dowling, Alfie Langer and various others wandered over to chat. Wally and Jacqui were coping well until Premier Russell Cooper made a terrible gaffe. Addressing the dinner he said cheerfully, "I've just been up in North Queensland and a bloke up there said, 'If you can get Wally Lewis back as captain you'll get 10,000 more votes up here.' " The whole dinner hall cringed, eyes swivelled to Wally. Said Jacqui, "I looked at Wally and we both had the same thought — let's get out of here. But Fordo gave a tiny shake of his head like, better to stay, and we did, grinning and bearing it."

The next day Wally entered hospital for extensive surgery. He had dislocated his right acromioclavicular joint — collarbone — years before and now it was irritating him, sticking up underneath his skin. Dr Peter Myers excised the outer end of the bone and transferred a ligament around the shoulder to stabilise the AC joint. While under general anaesthetic Myers did an arthroscopy of Wally's bad left knee which already was lax from an old posterior cruciate ligament injury. Myers stitched a tear in the knee's lateral meniscus. Wally was photographed leaving hospital, on crutches and with an arm sling, looking like a war veteran. His injuries would soon heal, the deeper wounds lasted until he retired.

5
Whispers and Rumours

When you sack the Australian captain you go down in history, it's as simple as that. The day after the world's share markets crashed, the *Sunday Mail* newspaper in Brisbane splashed with Lewis' dismissal, relegating the world's financial catastrophe to downpage news. Later the Broncos wished they'd made fewer headlines. It's difficult to know how they could have released the sacking satisfactorily. It probably deserved a press conference, not a loose tongue at a Brisbane nightclub, which is said to be how the news leaked.

Wally was much more than a football captain. Over the decade of his fame he had come to be identified with Queensland's ascent from country bumpkin state to sunny, sophisticated host of the 1982 Commonwealth Games, the international 1988 Expo, a tourism mecca and an economic performer. Though Wally's game was rugby league, he transcended sport.

The sacking sensation lasted for weeks and club morale sagged. Every day, in "Letters to the Editor", the public condemned the Bronco rascals. Any Wally drama sold newspapers and led television news and talkback radio, but this was a once-in-a-lifetime rugby league phenomenon. Reporters latched onto any comment by the club and phoned Wally for a reply. A radio poll of callers produced a 93-7 result in favour of Wally's reinstatement. The Brisbane *Sun* compiled a two-page analysis of the debate. The Broncos staff were driven crazy by phone calls from outraged citizens. Most conceded they weren't members of the club and had never attended a Broncos match, but they watched Wally on television, in the footie replays and at night when he read the sports news. He was the nice man who came into their living rooms every evening.

Television news can have that effect. Images blur, fact and fiction become indistinguishable. Wally, Kylie, "Days Of Our Lives" — the Broncos had shot the hero in the white hat! Viewers loved and trusted Wally. Broncos chairman of directors, Barry Maranta, was still receiving abusive phone calls about it a year later.

Wayne Bennett has never released the reasons he sacked Lewis. The explanations have come from Wally with sporadic comments from John Ribot. Bennett's motivations therefore are open to conjecture. First the red herrings should go — for instance, Wally's bungie jump in New Zealand was of no account. The club was less enamoured of the spitting incident against the Gold Coast, but remember, the directors were all ex-footballers who understood on-field misdeeds.

In 1988 the Broncos, had they beaten Balmain in their last match, would have made the final five. In 1989 they had improved to a play-off for fifth. Those results would have been fair if not for the quality of the Broncos squad, which verged on State of Origin strength. Few Broncos, from the chairman down, doubted they had the team to win in 1989. Tony Currie, who knew what it took from his 1988 grand final win with Canterbury, said "I can't work out how we missed actually." Broncos lock Brett Le Man believed if they had made the semis in 1989, the Broncos would have won the premiership then or in 1990. "We just needed to get used to playing in the finals," he said.

Bennett had hand-picked Peter Jackson and Sam Backo, both of whom had starred in Origins for him, but injuries made both these Canberra recruits poor value in 1989. Yet for the same money Bennett could have tempted Bradley Clyde or Laurie Daley, young players with long futures. For the expediency of a quick result, Bennett paid for being momentarily distracted from his declared philosophy of building a premiership win on his own nurtured juniors.

He needed a plan for 1990, the third year in his original five year drive to the premiership. He wanted bigger, stronger Broncos and he wanted consistency. He stepped up the "Bennettisation" of the Broncos, the moulding of a team in his image — dedicated trainers, no-nonsense lifestyle, an unquestioned club priority, club fraternity and equality (no big heads), personal honesty, a pristine public image and a single purpose. The team was to be greater than the individual and the club greater than the team. Peter Jackson, from Bennett's Brisbane Souths and Canberra days, cheerfully confessed, "I was already Bennettised." As Tony Currie put it, "The Broncos wanted 21 guys in a squad who got in the boat and rowed the same way, no questions asked."

Wally and Wayne Bennett were contrasting, powerful personalities, different personifications of an ideal Australian — Wally the larrikin, brave, a gifted opportunist; Bennett, stoic, selfless, contemplative. If Wally was worthy of Gallipoli, Bennett belonged on the Kokoda Trail. When their paths crossed and it worked to their mutual advantage, they were a formidable combination, for at their best they complemented each other. Bennett saw in Lewis a freedom that lay fettered within himself, Lewis saw in Bennett a conscience he couldn't bury. "They were as thick as thieves, a mutual admiration society," recalled Peter Jackson. But when their paths diverged they brought out the worst in each other.

The former Wynnum threesome, Wally, Geno and GD, all Test skilled, were the backbone of the Broncos. Occasionally, if the Broncos struggled with Bennett's match plan, Wally would discard it and revert to old Wynnum strategies. "We even had moves called 'Wynnum'," said Tony Currie. "Wynnum's on! And the Big Three would do something, which was good. But if I'd been the coach I'd have been slightly intimidated by it."

Greg Dowling confirmed this on-field independence. "We'd improvise," he said. "I ran the forwards and Wally and Gene ran the backs and everything revolved around us. All I had to do was get our guys to make the yards. I'd get the position off Wally, where he wanted us to go and I'd get us there. We'd succeed with that five times out of six, but when we lost, Benny wasn't pleased. He'd crack up at us for making mistakes."

Wally could see the problems. "Wayne liked to plan a game, whereas I've always done pretty well whatever I liked," he said. "It's what made me successful. Plenty of players have defended well against me, but they can't plan it. It's just spur of the moment stuff they have to react to." Wally was a match for Bennett in talent, exploits and experience. Rumours began that Bennett could not handle Wally's high media profile. Wally discounted that. "I'm quite sure that Bennett didn't sack me because of jealousy," he said.

Bennett's principal complaint appeared to be Lewis' lack of involvement with the club and the players. Wally conceded he arrived 15 minutes before training rather than 45 minutes. He was working full-time at Channel 10, visiting sick children and the elderly in hospitals, holding school workshops, speaking at charity functions like the Sporting Wheelies and making a host of other personal appearances. He had little time for Broncos promotions — one of the strikes against him.

Anyone around Lewis in those days knew they had his attention for a very limited time span. His phone rang every few minutes and his crowded diary of appointments tested even a driver of his skills. Family demands descended upon him. "In the end it probably did get me down to the point where I was flat, had no energy," he said. "Bennett used to say, 'I know you've got a million things to do but try to get home and lie down for ten minutes before you head off to train. Put everything else out of your mind.' I used to like to do that but I rarely got the chance."

Broncos trainer Brian Canavan, a friend from Valleys days, noticed Wally arrive at training with a frown on his forehead. "Not brought on by football, but from where he'd come," he said. "He had a hell of a lot on his plate. It was good in a way because he was learning about the commitments that we all have in life. But he was bringing that luggage to training. He was still thinking about where he'd been."

His manager, sports commentator, Billy J. Smith, also recalled that around this time Wally seemed preoccupied. "I'd introduce him to some VIPs, who could help him, and Wally would listen for a while and then get this vacant look and gaze over their shoulder as if he didn't give a damn. It used to annoy me. But I suppose over the years Wally had to put up with so many yobbos he had this inbuilt turn-off, take-no-notice defence."

The upshot was that when Wally arrived for training he didn't switch on until the session started. "I'd head straight for Geno and GD and start chatting," he said. "They'd been my friends for ten years, surely I had that right?" Indeed, but it left him no time to fraternise with other younger team members. He'd cruise up in his low-slung, sporty red Nissan ZX and park beside the younger players' utes or kombie vans. They watched him as foot soldiers might have regarded Napoleon, hoping his gaze might light upon them. Said Greg Dowling, "I'd been a young fellow come down from the bush to make it in the city and I understood how they felt. So yeah, I went out of my way to speak to them. Wally was hard to approach because of the aura that surrounds him. So he never went over to chat and these young blokes would be too scared to talk to him. But he was the club skipper, we were a new club fighting for survival and they needed all the help they could get."

Gene Miles had similar memories. He suggested I read the profiles of young blokes now playing for Australia. Steve Renouf, Willie Carne, Michael Hancock — somewhere they would have listed Wally Lewis as their favourite player, five-eighth or captain. "Suddenly they found themselves playing alongside the guy they used to watch on television in Roma or Stanthorpe," said Gene. "They held him in awe. Maybe a bit of effort from Wally would have broken it down."

At a team meeting from which Wally was absent, one of the young players commented that they really didn't know Wally that well. Gene Miles chimed in, "Listen, I've known him for ten years and I still don't know him. No one can get that close to him. That's the way with Wally."

Trainer Brian Canavan agreed. "Some players only saw him as a person who could be obnoxious, who had his failings and seemed distant," he said. "It was the enigmatic nature of the man. He was carrying so much baggage in his life by then it was hard to get close to him. You had to know him for a long time to get through all that, to see his good points, to know that when he's himself, there's no nicer guy."

Wally's explanation is that he deliberately did not approach younger players because he didn't believe they appreciated unsolicited advice, especially being told what they were doing wrong. "If they're told by a coach it's completely different," he said. But surely they would listen to someone of his stature, who had been a coach? "They half-accept it but they half-think, 'What's this bastard on about, telling me what to do.' They'd automatically turn off. If a bloke was having trouble and came and asked me, I'd help him any amount. I thought that was the way to do it."

The gulf may be further explained by a peculiarity of Wally's personality. Except with his very closest friends, he does not initiate conversations. I've noticed it, his manager Peter Hickey has, so has

Broncos coaching adviser Bob Bax. "He's not an easy man to know," said Bax. "I said to my wife, who is a firm Lewis fan, 'He never speaks to you first.' You say 'Hello Wally' and he'll say 'Goodday Bob', but he doesn't volunteer it. Get him into conversation and he's fine." Manager Hickey, when he first met Wally, played a game with himself on a plane flight. He waited to see if Wally would start up a conversation. "Sure enough after ten minutes, fifteen, twenty ... nothing," said Hickey. "I thought, 'Well bugger me, I've got my answer.' But then you comment on the flight or the food and he'll respond fine."

Jacqui confirms it for us all. "It doesn't worry me because I just keep talking to him and eventually he has to say something," she said jovially. "I just don't shut up." Jacqui's parents confided in her they didn't know how to begin a conversation with him. Jacqui's advice: "You've got to start on a topic he's interested in — not football, he doesn't need that. Just say something about his children and you'll as likely get the three births right through." Lewis attended them all, bawled his eyes out at every one.

Wally's reserve could be caused by natural shyness, or result from the admiration his family gave him as a boy, so that he needed to speak only when spoken to. Maybe his mind is crowded with responsibilities, or perhaps he has been barked at, interrogated and doorstopped by the media for so many years he has become conditioned to respond rather than to initiate. More probably, Wally just gets tired of talking; silence is golden to many people in the public eye. The corollary is that Wally's reticence was mistaken for aloofness or even arrogance when he didn't approach younger Bronco players.

Bennett also listed player dissatisfaction with Wally as being among the reasons for the sacking. Player jealousy of his status certainly existed, of his constant publicity and of his rumoured contract. Never mind Lewis' genius, players who ran four laps more than he did at training and made ten more tackles in matches, were disgruntled. As the leading pack of runners jogged half a lap ahead of him, Wally was an easy target for snide comments. "Where's the King? Has he done a hammy?" In matches, as captain, when Wally blew up whoever missed a tackle, that player would check the stats sheet afterwards to see how many tackles Wally missed.

Greg Dowling admitted that he himself was never the world's

greatest trainer. "I'm not a speedster but I'll put in and do my best, as did Wally," he said. "We'd go neck and neck in a race and then have a chat during the jog. But if they wanted us super fit we couldn't do it, because our bodies were too old by then. All we tried to do was give ourselves enough fitness so we could perform in a game." Brett Le Man confirmed Dowling's analysis, saying Wally wasn't as fit as the younger men, but he trained just as hard.

The Broncos decided Wally's occasional poor game could be attributed to his comparative unfitness. No matter what a player's natural abilities were, the standard of Sydney football was so high that nobody, not even Wally Lewis, could turn in optimum games without matching up in training, they said. After 1989 the Broncos decided that everyone had to train ten months of the year, flat out, with no corners cut. Therefore a major criticism was that Wally never completed an off-season training with the Broncos. Said Bob Bax, "I remember that year, 1989, they asked him to get his injuries fixed up at the end of the season and he waited until he got back from America. They weren't real happy about that."

The suggestion was that somehow Wally orchestrated his life to avoid off-season training. It made Wally seethe. "I can't believe some people," he said. "Do they really think I'd undergo a bloody operation just to get out of a couple of training sessions?" His medical record shows that on 1 December, 1987 the Broncos doctor had ordered rehabilitation on his right knee. When it did not respond Wally had an arthroscopy on 18 January, 1988 to repair a torn cartilage. That cost him his first off season. On 11 October, 1988 he had had a 20 cm steel nail inserted through the marrow of the bone to help mend his right arm, fractured in the World Cup final against New Zealand. That ended his second off season. Then on 28 October 1989, he had dual surgery to his right shoulder and left knee and two months later had a further arthroscopy on the same knee. That wiped out his third off season. Perhaps he could have cancelled his Disneyland trip again, but the truth was that Wally — aged 30 at the end of 1989 — was starting to show the effects of the punishment he had taken for over a decade on behalf of his clubs, Queensland and Australia.

Both Greg Dowling and Gene Miles were aware of the insidious undercurrents eddying around Wally. To tease him they often called him "King" as a mocking reminder he was not. Wally refused to answer to the title, which reassured the pair they were reaching him. The pecking order at the Broncos during his captaincy was Wally, Geno, GD, Tony Currie, Peter Jackson, Chris Johns and Sam Backo, followed by the young ones of whom Langer was leader. The big three were Wally, GD and Geno and the rest were go-betweens, least among equals. Geno and GD would regularly grab Wally and tell him, "Mate, you've got to spend more time with the blokes, you've just got to find the time." They did it discreetly because they had known Wally so long, but even for them it was no easy task, sitting the captain of Australia and the triumphant Queensland side down and telling him to pick up his act as club skipper. Wally did have the gift of the gab; he could talk his way around them.

Sam Backo was not so discreet. "You're not the King, you're just one of us," he would say. "You too big-headed to drink with us?" After a few beers, being Big Sam, he rode Wally even more. GD and Geno would step in, "Sam, what are you going on about, leave him alone." Dowling felt Wally was in a no-win situation. No other player had to bow to the demands of team, media, work, publicity and family. Dowling himself rarely hung around the club after matches.

On one celebrated occasion, 24 October 1989, a group of Broncos watched Jeff Harding defend his World Boxing Council light-heavyweight crown in Brisbane. Wally had held his press conference that morning after returning from America. That evening was the first occasion he had socialised with the team since the captaincy news broke. Wally was still despondent and the players were solicitous, including Sam Backo who invited Wally to join them for a drink after the fight. Wally was not in the mood. "No thanks mate, I'm heading back home," he said. Backo asked him why not. "I just don't want to," said Wally. "My spare time's my own and I want to spend it with the kids." Backo insisted he too had children but he was still having a drink. If Wally had come back to the boys he wouldn't be where he was, argued Sam. And so it went.

Wally understood the need for team camaraderie but his own priorities were changing. "Sunday night after a game I was more interested in going back to the club and having dinner in the restaurant with my missus," he said. He was usually joined by a couple of other players and their friends. "I'd go in for the game awards, have a few beers at the bar, then we'd pick up the kids from Jacqui's

1989. Wally holds the Panasonic Cup, the Broncos' first triumph. (Unless otherwise acknowledged, all black and white photos are courtesy the *Courier-Mail*)

1989. Wally in typical attacking mode against Wests for the Broncos

1989. Old friends prepare for Origin battle; from left, Paul "Fatty" Vautin, Wally and Mal Meninga

1989. Second Origin — the first disaster, as Allan Langer is carried off

1989. Third Origin. Two on one — Wally shows his strength

1989. Wally and Big Artie Beetson celebrate

1989. Third Test against New Zealand in Auckland. Wally gives Steve "Blocker" Roach a high five after Roach set up an Australian try

1989. Wally takes the big leap

1989. The operations which angered the Broncos directors

1990. War games at Mudgeeraba

1990. The start of Wally's troubles. He hobbles off after tearing his hamstring against Balmain

1990. Wally goal-kicking for the Broncos — not a regular duty

1990. First Origin. Wally rules himself out with a corridor sprint

1990. Third Origin. NSW five-eighth Brad Mackay going the way of previous Blue five-eighths who opposed Wally

1990. Wally leaves hospital after breaking his arm in the Broncos' match against St George

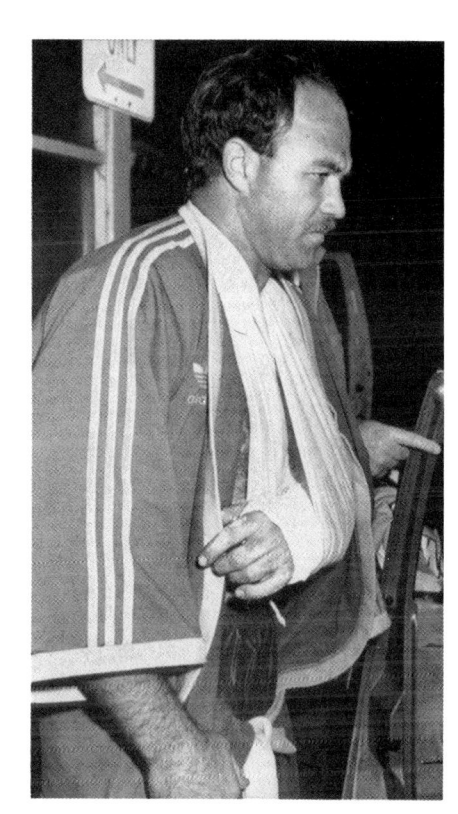

1990. The arm fracture is clearly evident

1990. Broncos trainer Kelvin Giles pushes Wally hard in training, preparing for a fitness test after he recovered from his arm fracture

1990. With good friend Greg Dowling the day before Wally was cut from the Broncos

1990. ARL doctor Nathan Gibbs (left) directs Wally during the fitness test which ruled him out of the 1990 Kangaroos tour; a trainer looks on

1991. Welcome to the Gold Coast. Wally cops a can on his head during his first match for the Seagulls

1991. First Origin. Training with Kevin Walters, who displaced Wally as Broncos five-eighth the previous year

1991. First Origin. Captain Lewis and coach Graham Lowe as Queensland goes one up in the series

1991. First Origin. Mal Meninga after the try Wally set up for him in Queensland's win at Lang Park. Allan Langer is well pleased

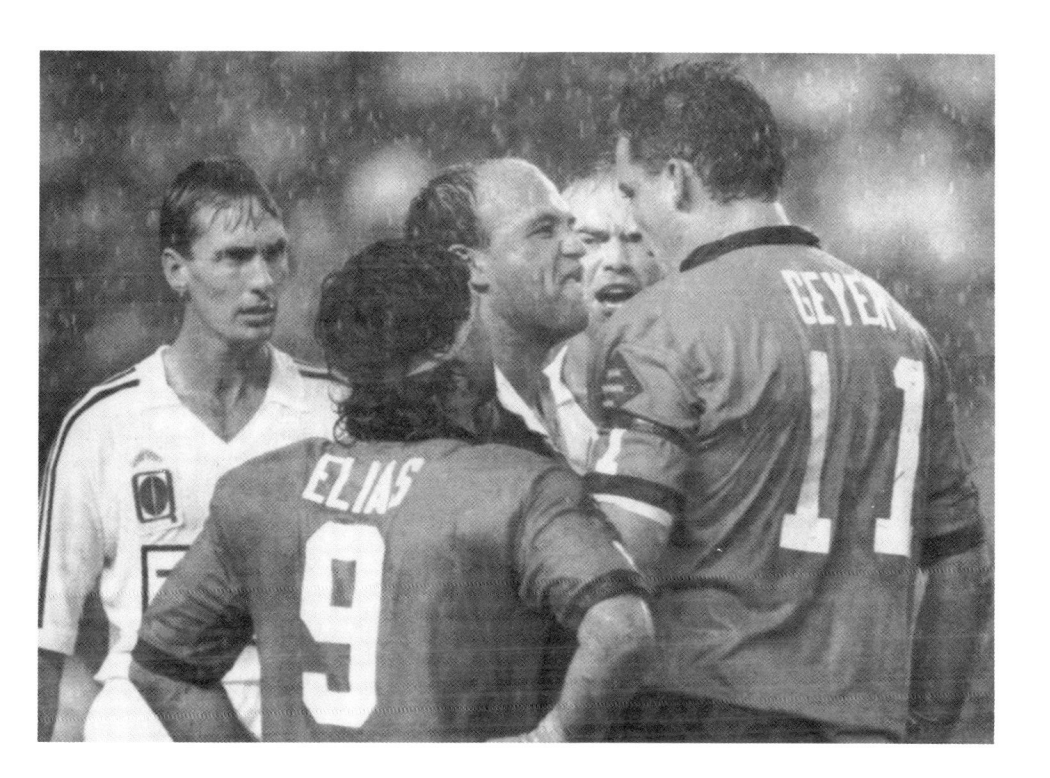

1991. Second Origin. The snarling scene with Mark Geyer in Sydney which ended Wally's hopes for the Australian captaincy

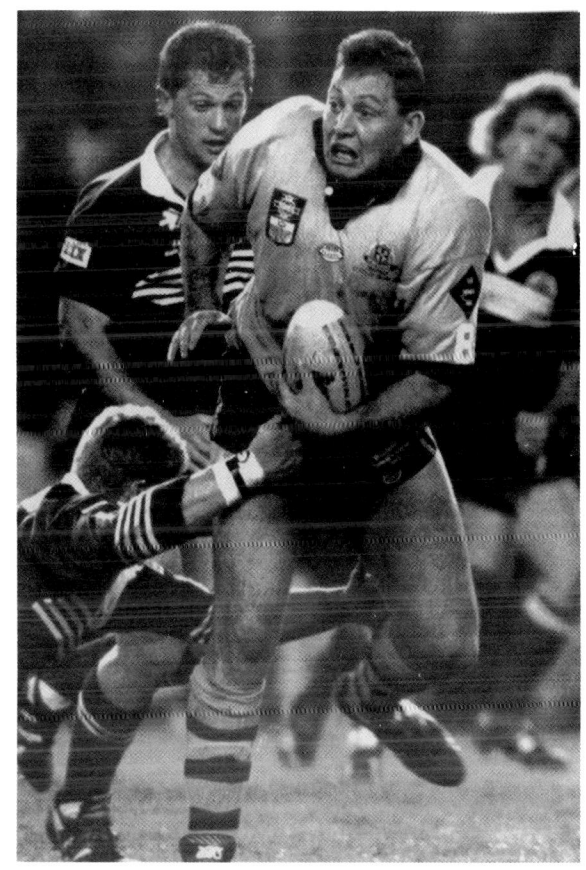

1991. Second Origin in Sydney. Steve "Blocker" Roach, always making ground for NSW

1991. Third Origin. Paul Hauff in full stride for the try line evades pursuing Ricky Stuart and a despairing Greg Alexander

1991. Third Origin. Farewell time for Wally, carrying Lincoln and leading Mitchell

parents and go home," he said. "I thought, 'Stuff it. Football's finished, family man takes over.' " Wally estimated that in 1988 he stayed at the club until 11 p.m. whereas by the second year, 1989, he began leaving at 9.30 p.m.. He said, "The only real difference was that I wasn't having my ear chewed by my missus saying, 'Come on, you've had enough.'" Wally is not a drinker. He drank nothing but light beer his entire three years with the Broncos.

As the 1989 season drew to an end, before Wally was deposed, Wayne Bennett held several team meetings to discuss the new year. Wally's busy schedule meant he missed one team dinner of senior players at the Parkroyal hotel attended by Ribot, Dowling, Miles, Currie, Jackson, Backo, Johns and Langer. Bennett quietly sounded players out about Lewis' leadership, gathering intelligence for his imminent decision. The next meeting was held in the Broncos board room and high on the unspoken agenda was the subject of some players' rumoured unhappiness with Wally. The meeting was scheduled for 6.30 p.m. and as the players filed in they spied Wally on the board room's television screen reading the last of the sports news for Channel 10. The players were somewhat tense at the prospect of Bennett's open therapy session until big forward James Donnelly broke them up. Looking up at the screen, he exclaimed, "What's going on here, we doing a live link-up with the King, are we?"

Wally raced down from Mt Coot-tha and with Bennett in the chair the meeting began. Peter Jackson stood up and said he had no problem with Wally. Jackson told me, "If there was a plot to ditch Wal, I didn't know about it. We've always been pretty good mates. I invited him to my wedding but he was in LA. It's always been sweet between us."

Wally took his turn. He had heard that players were continually bagging him and asked Tony Currie to explain the infamous Gympie incident where Currie had allegedly publicly criticised Lewis. The room grew quiet. All knew animosity existed between them. Currie explained that he had an evening engagement in Gympie where he spoke to about 200 people. "Despite all the probing questions, anyone there would tell you I answered them diplomatically and had nothing but praise for you, Wally," Currie said. Later in the evening he went to a nightclub and at 3 a.m. the evening's organiser asked Currie what he really thought of Wally. Currie, pissed — on his own admission — bagged Wally then, at the bar — not as a player, but along the big-headed lines favoured by Sam Backo. Currie said the organiser subsequently wrote to Lewis dobbing him in, omitting to mention the criticism had come privately at the bar, not publicly to an audience. Currie came clean to the players' meeting. "So yes, I did do that, Wally, but it was nothing I've never ever heard you not do at the bar when you're pissed, when you've said, 'Oh he can't play,' and thought nothing of it. And that's a fact. So before you leave here tonight I want you to know that's what it was." But open therapy doesn't always work. They have not spoken since.

Next up came big, friendly James Donnelly, a man with a comic touch. "Listen Wally," he said, "when I first joined the club I've walked in and you've shook my hand and said 'Welcome to the club James'. You know you've always been my hero and I was over the moon. I trained well that day and went home and told everyone you shook my hand and all that and the next minute I'm playing first grade with you. And the first three weeks of first grade you called me John!" (John Donnelly, a Test prop, was a well known Sydney Wests player of the early 1980s.)

Wally began to deny the oversight but Greg Dowling interceded with, "Ah well, yeah, I'd have to back James up on that Wally, you were calling him John." So it continued, Michael Hancock and Kerrod Walters both agreeing they would have liked Wally to talk to them more as youngsters. It was like a Hollywood roast, except these stories all contained barbs. Turn any football team's attention to one player and most could find some fault with the subject. It smacked of a mini-kangaroo court.

Thus, however small and trivial the complaints seemed, their total amounted to a body of criticism. Whether valid or not, their reproaches represented how the team felt and Wally had to recognise that, but he was on the defensive and even if he was so inclined, he would have had difficulty overcoming his pride to apologise. The meeting broke up with Wally justifying himself and, unbeknown to him, inexorably set on a course of destruction.

Football teams are nests of personal interactions overlaid with a professional unity of purpose. Players team with players they might otherwise shun because if a winger scores tries, the winning bonus outweighs his dodgy personality. Wally was in that top echelon of individuals universally respected for their enormous ability. Players were more likely to persevere with him than give him up. Peter

Jackson dismissed the idea that a players' revolt ousted Wally. "Some may not have liked him or may have disagreed with things he did," said Jackson. "But in Wally's position you're never going to please everyone all the time. How could you conspire against a bloke who you've seen do so many amazing things?"

Wally believes that nothing would have altered Bennett's captaincy decision. "The only way Bennett's mind could be changed would be if Bennett was arguing with Bennett and then there would be a stalemate," he said. Several players said that meeting was a last lifeline thrown to him. If Wally had told that meeting, "Fellas, sorry, sorry, sorry, I'll be your leader, I'll work hard for you," the feeling was that the room would have risen as one and said, "Captain, my captain." What they really wanted was a harmonious team lead by Wally. The players didn't sack Wally, but perhaps they might have saved him. When I put that to Wally he shook his head. Even such a team uprising would not have swayed Bennett, he said. "I would have had to have won the lottery and bought the club to have saved myself," he said, "or been on the board, like him, and been given the chance to defend myself to the directors."

Because Bennett himself declined to explain publicly Wally's sacking the Broncos singularly failed to sell their story to the public. They did Lewis no favours, however, because the more insubstantial the reasons looked, the more the public cast about for more definite ones. The mills of gossip powered up and spun their tales.

Lindy Chamberlain once said a rumour will circle the earth while the truth is still pulling on its boots. The rumours about alleged womanising which pursued Wally after his sacking escalated into the most sustained destruction of a person's character by innuendo since the rumours generated about Lindy herself. The most consistent was that he was having an affair with a Brisbane television personality. Close friends and colleagues of both knew this rumour to be nonsense. Wally and a friend jumped in a cab once, Wally in the back, to be regaled with the driver's assertion that the rumours about Wally and the television sheila were dead right. The friend mischievously encouraged the driver to recount a detailed description of how he had driven Lewis to a hotel assignation with her. The friend asked, "And you'd know Wally Lewis if you saw him, eh?" Of course, said the cabbie.

Wally leaned over from the back seat. "How does this head look mate? Does this look like him?" The driver was speechless. Wally hissed at him, "Hans Christian Andersen had nothing on you fella, that's one of the best stories I've ever heard, that's a classic." The shamed driver looked straight ahead and turned up his two-way radio.

Wally was acquainted with the television personality and occasionally exchanged stories with her and laughed about the fantastic rumours. Wally asked her had she heard the story about them supposedly having been seen boarding a plane for Sydney together? No, that was a new one, she said. Another nasty rumour spread around was that Jacqui Lewis arrived home, surprising the woman who fled the house in a bath towel. Jacqui even heard this incredible story from her own friends. Knowing the rumours to be patently untrue, the TV personality brushed them aside and told friends that to survive in the fishbowl world of television required a hide as thick as a crocodile's.

Occasionally Wally and Jacqui came face to face with snoops. Out shopping once, Jacqui, who at 30 is pretty and youthful looking, left Wally for a moment. A woman approached Wally and asked him sneeringly what his wife would say about him being here with "that girl". Wally, sick of such intrusions, pointed at Jacqui and whipped back, "Why don't you go and ask my wife, you nosey bitch!"

Another time Jacqui was farewelling Wally and the Queensland team at the airport when Jacqui's brother overheard a woman at a shop counter say, "Look at Lewis over there cuddling that young girl, he ought to be ashamed." After the plane departed Jacqui confronted the woman. "I'm Wally's wife, he has the right to cuddle me, so get your facts right before you open your mouth and others overhear you."

Rumours were not new to Wally. Even in his Brisbane club days locals spread talk of him. Said Greg Dowling, "I've seen it over the years and I feel sorry for the guy. I've been with him in State of Origin and a guy's reckoned Wally's decked him and Wally hadn't gone three feet near him."

The longer Wayne Bennett remained silent the more fantastic the rumours became. "It got worse and worse," said Wally. "It really started to annoy me. It was this bloke's missus, then that bloke's. I mean if you weren't named you'd feel left out!"

Jacqui went to netball and her friends said they had heard it was with a former player's wife. "Oh, in that case I don't mind, she's quite nice," joked Jacqui. She had to laugh the stories off because as she told me, "Otherwise I would have gone cactus." Fortunately she had her own experience. She was dancing at a party when a girl passed a remark — enjoying herself, was she, while Wally was away? Her dance partners were two of Wally's brothers, neither of whom look like him. Rumours also reversed direction and reached Wally. Jacqui was supposedly seen drunk in the back of a car, all over some bloke. "Jacqui doesn't touch alcohol," said Wally. "Never had a drink in her life."

Jacqui's girlfriends supported her by discrediting the very nature of rumours. Never jump to conclusions, they said. They themselves had innocently walked from functions with strangers and separated, caught cabs together and separated. Unless someone was there, they wouldn't know. Friendships did suffer, however; old friends returning from living in another city didn't contact the Lewises because they didn't want to become involved in any imminent marital separation. At the time, Jacqui told *Sunday Mail* journalist Kate Collins, "If the rumours were true, I wouldn't be being interviewed as Mrs Lewis right now. Believe me, I wouldn't hesitate a second. We'd have been divorced on the spot." Jacqui told me, "Honestly, people don't credit me with any brains."

The Broncos under Bennett were heavy on football discipline, light on interference with private lives. For all his teetotalling, Bennett was no wowser. He is on record as objecting to the ARL testing players for the use of non-performance-enhancing social drugs such as marijuana, which was just as well, because footballers are no different to any other cross-section of young Australian males in regard to its usage. If Bennett felt uncomfortable in the presence of wild young bloods he would never have remained friendly with Peter Jackson in Jacko's single days. As evidenced by Bob Hawke, Australians do not judge their captains on their private lives.

Over the course of the years one Broncos director told me it was Lewis' alleged womanising that brought him down, while another said that if such rumours were true the club would have been more likely to close ranks behind him rather than to crucify him. The directors' combined beliefs remain a puzzle. David Fordham simply asked, "Who were the Broncos to sit in judgment on Lewis' private life? Many champions have a bit of villain in them, arrogance and abrasiveness. I'm not saying Wally's a saint, but there has been nothing in the 12 years I've known him very closely that would suggest to me it should cost him the captaincy."

Australian coach Bob Fulton and Queensland coach Arthur Beetson both agreed. Fulton rang Wally within days of his return from America and asked if Bennett had criticised Wally's captaincy on the field at all. No, said Wally. Beetson took the same line. "Did he say to you that your field decisions were costing the team matches?" No, said Wally. "Did he say that the team's performance was being adversely affected by your leadership?" No. "Well mate, you've answered the important questions, haven't you." Jacqui Lewis found solace in Beetson's logic. On the field his captaincy was unquestioned. She said, "As far as I'm concerned, if they believe he's not a nice bloke off the field, so what?"

Then, unaccountably, John Ribot dashed fuel on the dying embers of controversy when, in May 1990 — eight months after Wally was sacked — he told an ABC investigation on the "7.30 Report" that among the reasons for deposing Wally were "misdemeanours in relation to the captaincy role". What constituted a misdemeanour? Was Wally's behaviour unacceptable in a captain but acceptable in an ordinary player? Ribot did not elaborate.

The final straw came on the eve of the Broncos' 1992 grand final when Ribot was reported as saying the Broncos would never disclose the real reasons for Wally's departure. Said Wally's friend Peter O'Callaghan, "To bring up something that happened three years ago was pretty cheap." It was more than that. It led to public speculation that Wally might have committed some unspeakable crime. To keep harping on this theme so long after the event only confirmed how traumatised the Broncos were by the episode. They built the club around Lewis and, as one director told me, "He nearly brought it down." Closer to the truth, they nearly brought themselves down.

There was no single reason for Wally's overthrow. Nor were there any mysterious "other" reasons as hinted at by John Ribot — nothing, anyway, that constituted a single overriding justification for Bennett's action. To dwell upon Wally's on-field captaincy misses the point. Why would a player of his vast experience suddenly lose his touch? Brian Canavan, who ran messages on-field, told me, "I can't recall anyone ever saying to me, 'Oh Wally's in poor leadership mode tonight.'"

At the end of 1989 Bennett was under extreme pressure, not from poor results but because, being a one team town, Brisbane expected too much too soon. The Broncos directors were not immune to the burden of public opinion, to the pub and board room talk. Though rational businessmen all, they panicked when the Broncos stumbled once more at the final five hurdle. What went wrong? How would it be different next season? They began staring hard at Bennett. Talk began that Bennett himself was for the chop, to be replaced by Wally as captain-coach. That was never on but the rumour had its genesis in the directors' growing uneasiness with the alternative leadership Lewis seemed to be presenting within the club. The board felt that by Lewis' own marvellous standards — demonstrated in every representative game that year — he had failed the Broncos. He hadn't led them into the promised five. Yet his star still waxed while the Broncos waned. He was of the club yet his reputation did not suffer with the club. He had become bigger than the club. He was a law unto himself. He was not out of control but uncontrollable.

Further, he represented a past culture in rugby league, the star player system, and for revenue purposes as well as their personal egos, the directors needed the club to be the star, not Wally. If the club's fortunes were too closely identified with him they risked crowds diminishing when he was absent, or that club sponsorships might become somehow allied to him remaining with them.

Once Wally was perceived to be a danger to the Broncos' corporate health his fate was sealed. Institutions are depersonalised, lack compassion and subjugate the individual to the greater corporate need. Institutions have no conscience. As chairman Barry Maranta told me at the time, "It's like the Copernican revolution. Everyone thought the sun revolved around the earth. The Broncos do not revolve around Wally Lewis."

The directors required a gesture from Bennett that he recognised that the club took priority over the player — any player. They watched and waited because this had now become a test of Bennett. If he didn't see the way and the light then maybe they had the wrong coach. As it happened they had not mistaken their man. Bennett would have had to fight the directors to retain Wally as captain. Lewis was sacrificed but he was not a scapegoat. It was far more serious than that. He was a threat. He was different and institutions, like armies, demand conformity. When Bennett met the directors in the board room and told them he was sacking Lewis as captain, they solemnly nodded their heads. No discussion was necessary. Policy was understood.

Wally maintained a professional relationship with Bennett thereafter, but Jacqui did not. "For a while there he kept saying hello when he saw me and I would just ignore him," she said. "Now he doesn't bother and that's fine by me. I don't think I should be a hypocrite. I had to get rid of the anger inside me. Wally seemed to get on with business but obviously deep down he was still angry. He was for years. It was there eating at him. Wally talks to Wayne. That's men. They're like that. Not me."

6
Losing Geno

Wally and Gene Miles weren't just good mates, they were great mates. They were like Strop and Hoges, Lillee and Marsh, near equals and top of their turf. They were trusting partners, each aware of the gentle side to the other's character and delighted by that most precious bond of all, a shared sense of humour. They moulded a close friendship on the 1982 UK tour and Gene influenced Wally to join him at Wynnum in 1984. They met at training twice a week, at the match every weekend and relaxed with golf at least once a week. Sometimes Wally would come home from training and immediately ring Gene for another chat. They'd talk about anything. They roomed together in Origin camps even though Wally, as captain, was entitled to a room by himself. When Wally's media controversies became too hectic he'd escape to Gene's. They negotiated QRL contracts in tandem, to the point where QRL secretary Ross Livermore described them as the "Beagle Boys". Kerry Packer nearly bought the pair of them for Manly in 1986.

When Jacqui Green first started going out with Wally she used to joke with Miles' then girlfriend, Beverly, about how people were suspicious of the friendship. "Yeah, makes you wonder sometimes," said Beverly doubtfully. Young Jacqui's eyes widened, until she saw Beverly laughing. Wally, by virtue of his fame, appeared the dominant one. Gene was easygoing and unambitious. He watched daytime television and knew all the soapie plots. He'd slope up to where the wives and girlfriends were sitting at Wynnum matches and say, "Hello girls, any gossip this week?" Oh, sit down Gene, they'd chorus, listen up.

Miles broke up with his girlfriend and a year later Wayne Bennett introduced him to Debbie, a close friend of his. They made a match and married. No friend of Bennett's is a friend of indolence and Debbie slapped some order into Gene's life. Over the years many of Queensland's Origin players escaped the long shadow Wally cast. Fatty Vautin led Manly to a Sydney premiership, Mal Meninga was to do the same for Canberra, Mark Murray became a Sydney coach, Dave Brown coached in Perth, Colin Scott in north Queensland. The Maroons spread all over Australia, but Geno stayed. He'd spent eight years under Wally's leadership at Origin level, five years with clubs.

Wayne Bennett, having been rejected by Greg Dowling, had lost the most obvious replacement for Wally as captain. There were not many more suitable candidates. While Wally was in America, Bennett had held another meeting of players at which he revealed he was deposing Wally. "Why?" asked Gene Miles, who already knew. Bennett once more provided his pro forma explanation. Afterwards he drove Miles home and sprang the question — he wanted Gene to captain the side next year. Miles was astounded, as those who knew his gentle, quiet nature would expect him to be. Bennett didn't want an immediate answer, but he wanted Gene to think it over. Geno had before him a chance to fulfil a potential he had never explored. He was modest to the point of reticence but he knew he was as qualified to become a captain as Vautin or Meninga. He had never given it much thought before because, as long as he stayed in Brisbane, Wally would always be his skipper. Now Wally had been removed from the equation.

Only that season Gene had reversed his decision of the previous year to retire from representative football and had helped Queensland to the Origin clean sweep. But Miles could not lead the Broncos if he played rep. football, not if Bennett was to be consistent. Gene reassessed his future with the captaincy in mind. He was 31. He had married late, aged 30, and his first child was due to be born during the 1990 Origin weeks of May. Football had been good to him but he knew it could be cruel too. He didn't want others — the selectors — dictating to him when he should retire. "I'd enjoyed myself, been at the top for quite some time," he told me. "I thought this might be a good time to jump out."

Gene's friendship with Wally, though strong, was not inviolable.

It could not govern Gene's decision making for ever more. Yet, being such close friends, Gene was expected to share Wally's pain, not take advantage of it. His own personal fulfilment was probably sufficient justification to allow Gene to accept but he needed a further reason. He decided he could accept the leadership because Wally then wouldn't have to play under anyone else. "I thought maybe I would ease the pain a bit because of our association," said Gene. "I knew how upset he was. I think I was as close as anybody can get to him. And I thought it might help somehow. Because nothing else was. It was a shocking decision to make. One morning I'd wake up and want to do it, next morning I'd be against it. But it was my decision and mine alone. On my dying oath I was never pressured. In fact I avoided Bennett for weeks while I was making up my mind."

How to tell Wally? Jacqui had been planning a big birthday for Wally, his thirtieth, on 1 December 1989 and she had invited Gene and Debbie. At the last minute Gene had to go to Cairns. A week later Gene and Wally were undergoing physiotherapy at a Mt Gravatt clinic. Gene finished his session and entered Wally's curtained cubicle. He began, "Can I talk to you a minute?" Sure, said Wally. "No, in private," said Gene, nodding at the flimsy curtain walls. Wally looked puzzled. They'd never needed brick walls before. What was wrong with there? "No, in private," Gene insisted. They found a change room. Gene believes Wally already knew of Bennett's offer. Wally says no, he had no idea. Gene took a deep breath. "Do you think I should accept the captaincy?" Wally was dumbfounded.

"You can't," said Wally. "You're a rep. player." Gene said he was thinking about retiring again. He wanted Wally to be the first to know. Wally couldn't believe what he was hearing; that Gene could be talking about accepting it. "So you agree with Bennett's decision?" he said. Gene shook his head. No, but he wouldn't mind having a go at the job, he said.

Gene never got the chance to explain his motives. Wally got brisk. "Listen Gene, if you really want the job, you take it. It's your choice. Do what you want." Gene all but wrung his hands with the conflict of emotions. "Shit, I don't know," he murmured. Wally rose, left the room and resumed his physio. Miles walked out a back door. The next day, 8 December 1989, eleven weeks to the day since he was sacked, Wally read that Miles had accepted.

"It turned out exactly the opposite to what I hoped," said Gene. "If GD had taken it Wally'd have been dirty on him to a degree but he probably would have handled it a lot better than he did me. He wouldn't talk to me, Jacqui wouldn't talk to me, in the wash-up it was just what I didn't want."

Wally placed great importance upon Miles playing representative football. They'd been a team duo for so long, like Newcombe and Roche, or Simpson and Lawry, that Gene's presence was an integral part of Wally's enjoyment of, and success in, Origin and Test football. "I was nearly as disappointed in losing Gene from the rep. scene as I was at losing the captaincy," said Wally. "Suddenly he wasn't going to be there any more." He wouldn't be with him on the 1990 Kangaroo tour to England. Wally suspected Gene had caved in to pressure by Bennett, that he had sold himself cheap. All Gene knew was that, overnight, Wally stopped calling him. He'd supported Wally's leadership for years yet the moment he took some initiative himself Wally pulled the plug. Both were mightily offended. "I'm not saying he was disloyal, but I am saying I know what I would have done," said Wally. "Just the way I was brought up."

When I put to Wally the argument that though the timing was unfortunate, Gene had as much right to reach for the stars as Vautin and Meninga, he said, "Well mate, you may be right. I'd like to be there when you put that to Gene. It was sad because he was my closest friend. I missed that. We used to laugh with each other a hell of a lot."

As time passed Wally asked himself, "Am I being too harsh with Gene?" In the end he blamed himself 70 per cent, and Gene 30 per cent, because Gene got angry with him and stepped back from the friendship as well. At training they spoke little, but each talked to Greg Dowling. Gene would scowl and ask Dowling if Gator was still bagging him. Dowling told Wally not to worry, it would fix itself up one day. Meanwhile he should just keep playing football. "The football was a little bit of a saviour," said Wally. "Because when we played we talked to each other on the field like normal footballers. But after the game it wasn't that close at all."

Dowling tried to mend the rift. "I told them if they let this come between them, they mustn't have been such good friends in the first place," he said. He told them both a story of how he had been unwillingly compelled to abdicate as captain of Brisbane Norths in

1987. "It hurt, it hurt, but life goes on," he told them. "I did it for the good of the team, so come on guys, bury the hatchet." But Dowling thought that Wally now bore a huge chip on his shoulder. "I know the captaincy meant a lot to Wal," he told me. "Maybe he thought Gene stabbed him in the back, which he definitely didn't. Gene was very reluctant to take the job on, just because of Wal. And that's where Wally lost out," he said. "In the end it needed more than a phone call to repair it. It needed a big talk, understanding and maybe an apology. Wal could have bent a lot more and when he did it was too little too late."

Gene was the sideline eye for Channel 9 during the telecast of Wally's last Origin in 1991. He shook Wally's hand but he says Wally scarcely responded. Wally doesn't remember Geno doing that but, as we shall see, much of that night passed in a blur of emotion for Wally. It was no night for examining old wounds. Too little too late came fully two years after their break, in February 1992, when Gene arrived in Sydney with Wigan for the World Sevens. Wally's Gold Coast Seagulls were drawn against Wigan first up. In a genuine, but belated, spirit of reconciliation Wally rang Gene at Wigan's Sydney hotel and left a message. "To be honest I didn't expect him to call me back," said Wally. "Thought he'd just be in shock." Gene got the note an hour later. Please ring Wally. Gene thought, "Who the hell is this? The only Wally I know is not talking to me." He rang the number and sure enough, heard "Gator here." Gene was amazed but cautious. He was civil but he was not going to be turned on and off at Wally's whim. They agreed to meet at the Sevens.

Gene was in the players' stand at the Sydney Football Stadium when Wally found him. They sat and chatted; Brett "Bert" Kenny joined them, and Alfie Langer too. After Wigan won the Sevens, Wally congratulated Gene, and said it had been good to talk again. Gene replied, "Yeah, it's been a long time." But he was still wary. "He acted as though nothing had ever happened," said Gene in wonder. "I found that hard. A guy doesn't talk to you for so long and suddenly a phone call, and never a word about the original cause." Yet the grandstand was hardly the time or place and Wally had swallowed his pride to make the approach.

A few months later, in May 1992, when Wigan made the English Cup final at Wembley, Wally faxed Gene a good luck message, then thought, that was a piker's way out, and rang on the eve of the match. "How he ever found me has got me stuffed," said Gene. "We were an hour's drive from London and no one knew our hotel except our families."

Wally got through. "Long Neck?" said Wally. Gene knew only Wally used that nickname. They talked briefly before Wally offered, "Well you've probably got a lot on your plate, I'll get out of your way." No, said Gene, he had a bit of time, just watching television. After half an hour, Wally said provocatively, "You're finally back playing in your right position, centres. If you'd have been playing there for the Broncos ..." Gene cut in, "Now don't start bringing that up again, I was doing it for the Broncos." Wally hastily assured Gene, "I didn't even mention Bennett's name. All I'm saying is centre is your best position." Gene laughed and agreed.

Miles now lives in Brisbane, Lewis on the Gold Coast and they see little of each other. They have never re-opened the reason for the rift — the captaincy. In retrospect Wally is angry with himself for letting the friendship slip away. "Perhaps Gene played a small part in it," he said. "But maybe it should have been me that just said OK and shut up."

Jacqui Lewis sat helplessly by as her husband lost his best friend on top of the captaincy. "They went from so close to nothing," she said. She remained friendly with Miles' family but not with Gene. "I was upset with Gene, but more sorry than angry," she said. "I'd never put him down in front of Wally," she said. "Nor have I ever heard Wally say anything bad about Gene. He was never in the mood to hate Gene. He was just hurt. Even to this day."

Predictably the Broncos' 1990 pre-season was rife with tension. A sports psychologist, having addressed the 20 first graders, concluded by inviting questions. Not a player spoke. Feet shifted uncomfortably, few met the speaker's gaze. "What's wrong with you blokes?" he asked, perplexed. No one wanted to expose themselves. The captaincy drama had shaken the team's confidence — a pillar of their foundations had been removed. At training Gene was supersensitive to Wally's presence. "I was insecure, Wayne always used to say that about me," said Gene.

Bennett contributed to the unease by advising players to burn their scrapbooks. He would not persevere with anyone who was on the skids, he warned. Bennett was so engrossed in sounding tough he did not realise that Wally's own confidence was in such tatters his one aim was to keep a low profile and train hard. Bennett had imported just the man for hard training. One evening at Red Hill a cocky Pom, his baseball cap back to front, addressed the squad, declaring like John Wayne in a macho role, "These are the rules and you'll play by them or else." Trainer Kelvin Giles had arrived from Canberra to stop teams like Penrith and Balmain bullying the Broncos.

Gene Miles confessed, "I was a whimp when I first went to the Broncos. We just weren't physically strong." When Giles began his strength programs the players thought him a maniac. Said Gene, "We thought, 'There's no need to put ourselves through this sort of pain.' He had us lifting unbelievable weights." Some players, like Alfie Langer, overdid it the first year and lost a little zip.

Wally began slowly after his knee surgery, running in the water at the Valley pool, wearing a flotation jacket. He asked Giles if it was hard. The trainer pointed at a large figure lying exhausted at the pool edge. "That's Brett Plowman," he said. "He finished five minutes ago; I had to help him climb the ladder to get out."

Wally's turn came, sprinting, his legs whirling like an egg-beater beneath him. "By the end I was bobbing around in a pool with 10 million litres of water and my throat was as dry as a dead dingo's bum," said Wally. "The first 20 seconds of my shower didn't touch my body, it went straight down my throat."

Weights had never been a big part of Wally's preparation but under Giles his natural strength improved dramatically. Though not as strong as some in the bench presses, Wally's bounding, jumping and hopping sequences approached Australian Olympic athlete standards. Giles regarded Lewis as the most naturally powerful footballer he had trained, challenged only by Glenn Lazarus when he arrived at the Broncos from Canberra the following season.

Brian Canavan watched Wally's dedication with growing admiration. "He knew he was behind the eight-ball with his lack of history in buckling down," said Canavan. "He wasn't just trundling around with GD like in the old days. He had to put in." Greg Dowling was impressed too, because Wally wasn't dropping his bundle or sulking. "He trained his backside off," he said.

Not all pre-season activity was meant to be agony. One day the squad dressed in jungle greens, helmets and goggles for a game of "Skirmish" at Mudgeeraba. The players were armed with paint guns which fired red paint bullets accurate to about 25 metres. "They sting like all hell when they hit, leave a bruise," said Wally, "The bullet splashed red paint on your uniform to show you're hit." The squad split into two opposing camps. Wally commanded one side and charged 20 metres for bush cover. "The very first shot fired hit me right in the nuts and dropped me like a stone," said Wally. As he lay there in excruciating pain, Alfie Langer, though on Wally's side, couldn't resist the easy target. He drilled a couple of shots at Wally. Dowling, seeing the rules of war were open slather, pumped a shot into Wally's backside as well. Wally, squirming on the ground like the bad guy in a western movie, dragged himself into some bushes for protection and blasted anyone who came near him. By the time his pain subsided Wally thought he might prefer Giles' pool agony to this team fun.

But Wally's pain for 1990 had only just begun. The next shot was fired by Bennett when he read out the Broncos team for the first match — Kevin Walters five-eighth, Wally lock. That's how it began and that's how it stayed. Bennett was good mates with the entire Walters clan and an admirer of the three footballing sons, the eldest Steve, and the twins Kerrod and Kevin. Of the three he thought Kevin was the best footballer. To some players it seemed that in Bennett's eyes, Kevie could do no wrong. Bennett had coached him in the Queensland under 18s, again at Canberra and had unsuccessfully sought Kevin's transfer from Canberra in June the previous year after Allan Langer broke his leg.

When Wally looks back now he sees the significance of Bennett's efforts to obtain Kevin Walters. At first the idea was to replace the injured Langer, but when Bennett persevered it was not to understudy Alfie. The Broncos had never succeeded in grooming a natural successor to Wally. Grant Rix, Craig Grauf — they'd come and gone. Champions have that effect; they make their territory exclusive.

Bennett told Wally he wanted him and Kevin in the team. "It's better than having one in the team and one on the bench," he said. His reasoning was that whichever of them was left on the bench would be wasted, because he would be better than whoever was on the field — in this case Terry Matterson at lock.

Wally felt a trifle embarrassed for Matterson, tipping him out of his position, and Kevin felt embarrassed for Wally. He told him he was sorry about the five-eighth thing. Wally stopped him. "Don't worry about it. You're picked to play now so don't apologise. You should go out and try and cement your spot. Give it your best shot and we'll just try and work in together. I'm just glad to be playing the game. Let's go and play footie."

In Sydney the reactions were scathing. Fatty Vautin, in his *Sunday Telegraph* column, labelled the Broncos the Bonkers, and said not even a knave would waste a king in the pack. Bobby Fulton found it strange, the world's best five-eighth playing lock. He said, "Five years ago I was saying he should be Test lock, but at this stage of his career he will find it pretty demanding." More shrewdly Fulton commented, "You get the idea they're trying to make things difficult for him." He told Wally this in no uncertain terms on the phone. "What's Bennett's story? Doesn't he want you?"

After that first match — a draw with Wests — former champion lock Johnny Raper echoed a call that was to hound the Broncos for months — reinstate Wally as captain and five-eighth or kiss goodbye to the premiership. "Lewis is definitely feeling out of place at lock," said Raper. "I know the feeling. A few times in my career I was switched to five-eighth and it wasn't an easy change to make."

As the season progressed Wally knew what Raper meant. "It was hard for me to play a different type of game," he said. "I hadn't played lock for eight years or so and I just wasn't enjoying it." Bennett told him Walters had to be in the team for his back-up play. Wally wondered why Kevie couldn't play lock, where he'd filled in before. He told me, "I mean, I could have blown up and said, 'I'm the bloody Test five-eighth, what's going on?' But I didn't say anything. Everyone kept saying 'Put Lewis back at five-eighth' and he refused, refused, refused. Then he came up and said, 'OK, you can play five-eighth this week.'"

Wally hadn't known, but at a selection meeting that week Bob Bax had gone in to bat for him. He made an eloquent speech, invoking quotes from Winston Churchill and ending with the bald advice, "Play him at five-eighth, surely to Christ that's where he's best suited." Bennett relented. But Wally by this stage of his persecution was shying at shadows. Walters had won man-of-the-match at five-eighth the previous week and Wally thought he was being set up. He told Bennett that he didn't really care where he played, and if Bennett wanted him at lock, he'd play there.

"And you know where he played, don't you?" said Bax. "Back at lock! It was his own fault. If he had just got the bit between his teeth.

He was a good lock. No one was going to run into him unless they had to, not by choice. But as five-eighth, he was the best."

Looking back, occasional Broncos lock Brett Le Man believes that playing lock sealed Wally's fate. "Forget about him once he got into the forwards because he got twice the amount of injuries as he did in the backs," he said. "It was the most disgusting thing that ever happened in rugby league. Bennett sacrificed Wally for his favourite Kevie Walters. Destroyed Wally's career. The Australian five-eighth, probably the best ever, at lock. What a joke! Wally intimidated the directors, he intimidated Bennett, he was bigger than them all. Jealousy played a big part in his fall."

Once paranoia set in it was difficult to displace. At training Wally tried to fit in with Bennett's style. "But there just seemed this tension in the air," he said. "Anything I did wrong, dropping a ball in a skill session, he'd get up me, give me a kick in the arse." And then there was the Ipswich connection, the twins and Alfie, throwing passes past him, cutting him out. He was never in the right place. "They'd been playing alongside each other since they were kids," said Wally. "I don't think they meant anything."

Third match up, at Leichhardt Oval, was against Balmain, the Broncos' nemesis, and they lost again. That was the least of Wally's worries. He saved a try with a superb cover defending tackle but felt a sickening pain rip deep in his thigh as he dived. "I'd never done a hamstring before, but I knew then," he said. As he hobbled down the sideline, taking tiny suffering steps, the crowd hissed and pelted rubbish at him. "Bloody Balmain, they hadn't forgotten my *Penthouse* interview, they let me know what they thought of me," he said.

As he iced the injury he was pleased, at last, to earn a civil word from Bennett, "You've had troubles with Balmain before, but you were fine today. You were having a go. Just bad luck this. I was happy with your efforts."

Worse than the hamstring was an allegation by Balmain's John Elias that Wally had gouged him in a tackle. When referee Graham Annesley called him over, Wally said, "I'm not the captain. You'll have to tell the captain," motioning to Miles. No, said Annesley, Elias is accusing you. Wally blew up. Only he knew how the media would run with this, the headlines, the hearing, the interviews, the mud that stuck. "You lying bastard!" he seethed.

Balmain captain Benny Elias intervened, "Yes he did sir, look at my player's eye." Wally whirled on Benny, "Turn it up Benny, I didn't do that shit!" Too late. Once made, the complaint had to be adjudged.

After the game, in the players' tunnel, Wally approached John Elias, a former Brisbane Souths player, and said, "Listen, it wasn't me. Whatever happened, it's not my go." Elias replied that someone had. Wally tried again: "I'll swear on my kids' lives, it wasn't me." Elias responded that if Wally admitted he'd done it Elias would drop it. Wally repeated, "It wasn't me." Elias then surprisingly asked, "Well who was it then?" Wally stared at him, shook his head and walked away. Disconsolate at the process he must now begin to clear his name, he once more appealed for help from his friend David Fordham at Channel 10.

Said Fordham, "Wal, if you've gouged him, I can't help you. Much as I'm a mate, I won't condone that." Fordham had new film coming up from Sydney. He said, "I want you to tell me now, is there anything damning in that vision? Because if I find out later ..." Wally gave his word. Fordham looked at the vision, nothing.

The Broncos engaged top Queensland QC, Ian Callinan, who sat down and studied the videos. "Good," he told Wally. "I wish all my cases would be as easy as this." In an almost farcical hearing by the NSWRL judiciary, the chairman Dick Conti QC did not even bother to retire before exonerating Lewis.

The Broncos were so incensed by the Elias allegation that they filed a counterclaim, that Mark Hohn had been gouged. Hohn told Wally he would have put up with it, but not when they laid the claim on Wally. The Broncos later withdrew the charge and Hohn was fined $1000 for bringing the game into disrepute. "He's a good bloke, Hohnie," said Wally. "I had nothing to do with his incident but somehow I felt I was responsible." Wally paid Hohn's fine.

After five matches the Broncos were on just five points. Public and expert sentiment — including Test prop Steve Roach, former Test half Barry Muir, former Test hooker Royce Simmons, Norths coach Steve Martin and Manly coach Graham Lowe — favoured Wally's return as captain and five-eighth. "As an outsider I get the impression they're trying to squeeze Wally out of the club," said Lowe, echoing Bobby Fulton's earlier suspicions. Even Wally's most persistent Sydney critics, Ian Walsh and Ray Price, urged Wally's return. Price suggested a compromise, Wally as team captain, Gene as club captain. It had some merit. Street polls called for Wally's reinstatement, talkback radio revived the topic, and Bennett once more was compelled to defend his decision. "The captaincy is not negotiable regardless of how much people carry on about it," he said irritably.

All the pressure had to be directed somewhere. Wally was working his hamstring on a gym bike and applying ice at night. He had missed two matches when Bennett and trainer Giles approached him at training. How was the hamstring, they wanted to know? Getting there, Wally responded cheerfully. "We want to talk about it," said Bennett. Giles told Wally the club physiotherapist had done all she could for him, but he had not continued to improve. Giles suggested the problem was in his head, not in his injury. Wally, speechless, looked at Bennett, who said Kelvin had told him all the facts and he tended to agree with him. Wally clenched his fists, furious. "What did you just say?" Giles repeated his opinion that they thought the injury had healed and there was nothing wrong with Wally. Even from 20 metres away the trio's body language and facial expressions told a story. Ubiquitous television lenses focused on the trio. Wally glared at Giles. "I'm going to be very honest with you," he said. "If those cameras weren't behind me I'd walk forward and knock you out right now."

Giles remained cool. "I can understand your reaction, but I've got to tell you my opinion." Wally walked away. He knew what was behind this approach. With some three weeks to the first State of Origin the Broncos suspected he was putting himself in cottonwool for the series. It was the same twisted bias which had caused him to be accused of entering hospital to avoid pre-season training. It says much about the deterioration of relations between Bennett and Wally that the coach could countenance such cynicism. All trust was gone. For Wally there was no way out. He warmed up and did some run-throughs at three-quarter pace. Giles commanded, "I want you to open up." Wally said he couldn't, he could feel the tendon twanging. "That's the pain barrier," said Giles. "You've got to beat it up there", he said, tapping his temple, "not down there," pointing to his leg. "Let's do it faster, tell yourself you can." OK, Wally resigned himself. He'd do it their way.

He told me, "I got to almost full pace and bang! I went down like a bag of spuds, landed on the ground and slid everywhere, my hammy torn again." Television crews raced over. Giles assured them

Wally was OK. Wally hissed to Giles, "Kelvin, I told you I wasn't right, I bloody well told you!" Giles apologised, saying he thought he made a correct judgment. Yeah, said Wally. It had just set him back another week. Wally got on well with Giles but he saw now how no one was immune to the tensions surfacing at the Broncos.

When Wally recounted the incident to Jacqui she too exploded. "Nothing wrong!" she yelled. "They haven't had to get up at two or four in the morning and change the ice bags on your leg, change the sheets from the melted ice, hear you moan when it locks up, watch you limping around the house. I'm going to ring that Bennett up!" Wally soothed her. That's how it worked in the Lewis house. Wally repressed his anger, Jacqui let rip; it worked the hostility out for both of them.

Wally missed another match and then the wheel turned full circle. He convinced Bennett and Giles, now against their better judgment, that he should play against Norths. He was keen for a hit out with the first Origin just ten days off but he also wanted to show his pair of accusers he was not malingering. "They made out I was wasting time, sulking about the captaincy, so I thought, 'Bugger them, I'll come back, I'll show them I can do it their way.'"

Wally came off the bench after Tony Currie snapped an Achilles tendon — out for the season. "I didn't know whether they were cheering me off or the King on," joked Currie. Wally dramatically lifted a listless performance by the Broncos. David Fordham recalled that Wally instantly inspired the players and led them. But after eight minutes Miles threw a poor pass and, in full stride, Wally bent to pluck it off his toes and felt his hamstring tear again. He got up and told Miles, "Great ball!" Gene apologised. As Wally trudged off Kelvin Giles told him he'd known it wasn't right. Wally replied, "Ah well, I was just proving to you two I wasn't sitting out. That I'd have a go."

When Gene Miles first assumed the leadership, still smarting from Wally's rejection, he declared his style would be different to Wally's. "Without wanting to bag Wally, I saw a few incidents I wouldn't want to be on the end of," he said. "A quiet word is better than to verbal someone."

Wally does not deny he occasionally revved players. "Sometimes you've got to give blokes a gobful to get them going," he said. He did not respond to Gene's remarks. He remained neutral. "If Gene asked me anything I'd try to help him," he said. "As disappointed as I was, as much as I shook my head over his decision, I'd always respected him and I wasn't about to suddenly turn 180 degrees against him."

After seven rounds for just seven points the pressure on Miles became immense. "I'd never ever had responsibility in my life," said Gene. "I used to go out and play footie and after that, who cared?" Now he led a failing side in a one team city with controversy raging around him and calls for his own head. He began to understand what Wally had copped, and coped with, for years. "The media rang every morning, that really got to me," he said. "Being quoted in the paper on the game coming up, the game yesterday, not just Brisbane but Sydney newspapers as well. Then there was radio and television and the league press. I'd never experienced pressure like it. I thought, 'What the hell is this?'" Gene had picked up a few tips about media work from being around Wally but it didn't help when the team lost a match. "The first person they look at is the captain. You know, 'What happened?' I was trying to please everyone, didn't want to have an enemy in the world but as captain it's hard not to."

After ten matches Miles went to Bennett. "This is not for me," he said. "I've never had responsibility and I don't want it now. You can shove this captaincy business." Bennett encouraged him, "No, hang in there. We'll ride this storm through together." Those words stuck in Gene's mind. Sure enough there came a turning point in the season. The Broncos strung together 11 wins on the trot and Gene enjoyed a respite, but to lead the Broncos from their slump he had to transform himself overnight from footie layabout to captain with a mission. He said, "It became the turning point in my life, not only on the field but off the field." Gene emerged a changed man.

He had one final taste of Wally's past trials. At the season's end, the Broncos played Manly in a knockout semi-final. Gene took the phrase literally and delivered the same upon Manly forward Ian Roberts. "I got away with it on the field but gees, I wish I never had, because I got crucified," recalled Gene. "Ian bounced me off and stupidly I got dirty and chased him. As he was going down I caught him headhigh in an illegal tackle. With hindsight it was the worse thing I could have done. Because they carted Roberts off on a stretcher, not because of the whack I gave him but because he did his groin in. They replayed it ten times on the scoreboard and each time it looked worse."

Then, midweek, irony of ironies, Miles was named Captain of the Year in the Dally M. awards. That year, for the first time, the gala evening was open to the public and as Gene rose to receive his award he was booed all the way to the podium. "I can tell you I was embarrassed walking up there," said Gene.

Wally allowed himself some sympathy for his old friend. "We weren't sort of talking much," said Wally. "But at training I said to him, 'They didn't miss you down in Sydney.' And Gene grinned and said, 'No, they gave it to me all right.'" Wally remembered how, during his own worst moments as captain, Gene used to say how glad he was not to be in Wally's shoes. Wally thought to himself, "Well you're in them now, big fella."

7
Cut From the Club

A rugby league fan knocked on the door of Wally's hotel room where the 1990 Queensland State of Origin team was in camp. He knew how to heal Wally's torn hamstring, he said. Wally watched, astonished, as he placed four coloured crystals in the corners of the hotel room and manoeuvred them until he was satisfied. "This will fix it," he assured Wally. "You'll feel it getting better, you'll feel the magnetic pulse coming through and getting stronger." Wally shook his head and smiled to himself. He thanked his New Age visitor for his care and consideration but continued with his physiotherapy, just in case.

Wally did not play in the first State of Origin because of his torn hamstring, but it was not for want of advice. Phone calls and letters poured in, from faith healers who would enter his aura, magicians who would extract toxins, Christians who were praying, natural therapists who knew of special linaments, even a blind man who worked miracles with his hands. He was offered lotions and potions, poultices and ointments. A farmer wanted to send some special soil down. "My crops have grown magnificently in this soil," he wrote to Wally. "So I thought if you packed it around your leg it might help too."

Such an outpouring of sympathy arose because the public recognised that after his raw deal at the Broncos, the Origins were where Wally could restore himself. Public criticism may not have moved Bennett but the Origins were Wally's patch. To captain a victorious Queensland side, from five-eighth, would be Wally's answer, if it were not for his blessed hamstring.

Rarely has a sportsman's injury commanded so much media attention. Broncos trainer Kelvin Giles, who worked with Olympic superstars Steve Ovett and Sebastian Coe, said he had never seen anything like it. The subject lasted for nearly two months. Newspapers ran stories with diagrams: "Hamstring muscles are situated at the back of the thigh and control knee flexion and hip extension. There are three muscles involved: bicep femoris, semi-tendinosus and semi-membranosus." Brisbane radio personality Jan Power declared she wanted to meet Wally's "hamster"; a returning Australian photographer said he had even read the news in the *Bangkok Post*. In the *Sunday Telegraph* in Sydney, Mike Colman wrote a humorous column interviewing Wally's hamstring.

> Q: I get the impression you're a trifle bitter?
> Hammy: Why shouldn't I be? I've been carrying him for years.
> Q: Surely there must be some sadness.
> Hammy: Sometimes, but just a twinge.

Wally's support within the Origin circle, from coach Arthur Beetson, manager Dick "Tosser" Turner and QRL chief Ross Livermore, was as strong as ever. From the beginning Turner told Wally, "No matter what the story is you're in the camp, you're part of the team, part of the build-up."

Having been given this unqualified affirmation Wally was amused to read NSW coach Jack Gibson ridiculing Queensland's fabled team spirit. "We smiled because no one who hadn't been in a Queensland Origin camp would understand," said Wally. "The funny thing was that Gibson used to say Parramatta were one big happy family because they were away from Sydney. When the boot was on the other foot he changed."

Turner gave Wally until the Sunday before the match to overcome his injury but by Thursday Wally knew he was gone. Media personnel were amazed when he appeared to rule himself out after a bizarre fitness test, a spontaneous sprint down the team's hotel corridor, but Wally told me, "At training all week it had felt good, felt good, felt good but then on my last run I sensed something. I told Tosser no, and then thought, well maybe, so I ran down the corridor, and I felt it again." Turner urged Wally to delay, but Wally insisted: prepare without him.

So he missed only the second Origin match of his career, the second of 27, and Queensland, led by stand-in captain Paul Vautin, lost 8-0 at the Sydney Football Stadium. Greg Dowling in a newspaper column wrote, "Let's be frank, Vautin just hasn't got it anymore." The pair, both good friends of Wally's, were forever sniping at each other in their columns.

In Sydney, Vautin was clashing with Easts coach Mark Murray as well. "I can't believe how Muppet's changed," Fatty told Wally. "He's become an apprentice Jack Gibson. He's got all the cryptic one-liners." The tensions which eventually emerged between all these Origin originals — Ribot and Wally, Wally and Currie, Vautin and Dowling, Vautin and Murray, was testimony to the powerful bonding that Origin football possessed for those special few weeks every year.

Ross Livermore rang Wally with the team for the second Origin, to be played in Melbourne. "They've dropped Fatty," said Livermore. He knew that apart from Wally, Vautin, with 20 Origins, represented the spirit of Queensland rugby league. Wally decided to reach his friend before the media did. The season was becoming a bad joke. Wally dialled Vautin in Sydney. "They've picked the team," Wally began. Vautin picked up the vibes. "Mate, you sound like you've got some bad news for me," he said. Yeah, said Wally. Vautin guessed the truth. "I'm not giving myself a pat on the back, you know, but I thought I was one of the best," he said. Wally said he hoped Fatty would make it back quickly. Vautin was crushed. He always believed Beetson didn't want him in the team.

It produced the one clash Wally had with Beetson in seven years of Origin collaboration. When Beetson had a go at Fatty's form after the first Origin Wally fired back, "Pig's arse, Arthur! He saved three tries for us." Beetson countered that Vautin was too slow. Wally replied, "I thought he was one of our best, there you are." It was quite a reprimand to his coach but Wally had been contemplating the philosophy of loyalty of late and he knew exactly where he stood. Beetson presumed it was merely Wally's mateship speaking.

Wally was happy to promote rugby league's expansion, even to such primitive outlands as Melbourne. He was suspicious, however, because after two straight Origin clean sweeps, for the very first time one of the states — Queensland — had to play two consecutive away games in a series. "To be fair, Melbourne should have been the third Origin," he said. It was just a small political point. He himself needed no promoting. A poll by *Courier-Mail* writer Robert Craddock at a

Melbourne suburban station revealed that 66 per cent of those approached recognised Wally's photograph or his name.

Olympic Park was sold out; there were 25,800 when the teams ran on, and Wally immediately noticed three differences to other Origins. The grass was longer, the lighting not as good and the crowd was totally unbiassed. "They cheered when we ran out and then went quiet, until there was a good tackle or a score," he said. "We were used to the crowd cheering or booing for the first 20 minutes no matter what happened."

Beetson got jittery in the first half and toyed with replacing Wally, and told Turner he was struggling. Tosser stared at him. "You're joking Arthur, he's going like a genius." Beetson worried about whether Lewis could keep it up. Turner said if Wally started missing tackles, to replace him then. Beetson didn't want to leave it too late. Turner assured him, "I think we both know Wally well enough that if he thinks he's letting the team down he'll put up the flag himself."

Wally soon showed Melbournians the true mettle of rugby league. He stopped Steve "Blocker" Roach with a headhigh tackle — nothing injurious. Blocker was offended and swung at Wally, who outclassed him in the ensuing shindig. Penalty to NSW, 2-0. After the game Blocker, who knows Wally well, jokingly chastised him, "What about you! Puttin' one straight on me beak and splittin' me eye!" Wally grinned and bought him a drink.

But the post-match talk was not about Blocker's beak, it was about a sensational penalty which referee Greg McCallum awarded NSW in the dying minutes with the scores locked 6-all. Close to the Queensland line, Wally back-slammed a rampant Glenn Lazarus who hit the ground, rolled, stood up and took two steps forward. Was he clearing the ruck to play the ball or was he taking off afresh for the try-line? Wally thought the latter, because he dived again to grasp Lazarus' ankle. Allan Langer thought so because he nipped in and ripped the ball off Lazzo. Channel 10's Queensland caller David Wright thought so too: "This is unbelievable! McCallum has found a penalty right in front, a gift two points for NSW!"

Langer protested to McCallum, "He was still running!" Wally, in his inimitable style, leaning forward, one hand on hip, the other holding his mouth-guard, his face a picture of sheer disbelief, furiously disputed with McCallum. The referee said he had called "Held" which made Langer's steal an offence. Several Queensland players said they thought they had heard a "Play on" call. "The only ones who didn't hear that were those out of earshot," said Wally. Langer, a dejected figure after the game, said, "I must be a deaf-mute if the ref claims he called 'Held'."

To the media Wally sought to keep a civil tongue in his head. "It was a very appropriate penalty, right in front of the posts," he managed. He added, "That was one of the bummest decisions from a referee of all time" — mild words compared to how the Queenslanders felt later. "If they could have found McCallum that night, they honestly felt like bashing him," said Wally.

All being strangers in Melbourne, the Queenslanders met the NSW players for drinks and were surprised to find them unhappy with McCallum as well. One NSW player told Wally, "That's the sort of thing that spoils a game. We were going to drop a field goal, that's what we were working for. We were going to beat you anyway. Now we're not going to get any credit for it because everyone's going to talk about that penalty."

But they didn't talk about the penalty, they talked about what Wally said about it. ARL chief Ken Arthurson, under pressure from NSW, called for transcripts of Lewis' comments. Yet when the ARL disciplinary committee read them, they found no breach of the league's code of behaviour, nothing punishable. Instead they heard a completely different issue, a complaint that Wally had sworn while disputing a linesman's decision. He was said not to have sworn at the linesman but to have used the magic four-letter word about the decision. A television sound effects microphone picked it up for NSW viewers, though not Queensland viewers. Hearing they had changed the grounds for the charge, Wally was disgusted and rang Arthurson, "If I'm being charged with swearing on the football field save yourself the plane fare, I'm guilty." After the ARL fined him $5000 Wally stated the obvious: "If they fine every footballer who swears in a match they'll make a hundred grand every weekend."

The ridiculous aspect was that QRL general manager Ross Livermore sat on the three-man committee which fined Lewis. When McCallum gave the penalty, Livermore, in the official box, gave McCallum such a burst that Arthurson, sitting nearby, felt compelled to reprimand him. Livermore rang Wally later. "Mate, I'm still furious," he said. "I can't believe they've fined you for swearing. We're going to pay the fine for you. The ARL can't stop us." Since the QRL is affiliated with the ARL, the ARL as good as fined itself, an example of how normal life went awry and events defied restraint whenever Wally was involved. He was like a criminal with a record. The Feds were watching him, ready to nab him on suspicion. Even normally rational Ken Arthurson said Lewis was putting a strain on their relationship.

In truth it was the media, not Wally, which was exerting the pressure. Still — same thing, Wally was losing support. One swear word was enough to generate the predictable headline, "Lewis May Lose His Australian Crown". When sanity returned, the *Daily Telegraph* actually ran a sympathetic editorial and the *Sydney Morning Herald* asked in a headline, "Why was Lewis singled out for his post-match comments?" Too late. Once more he was the villain and few would remember that at match's end Wally, despite his disappointment, gallantly held Benny Elias' arm in the air acknowledging NSW's series victory. He had called his dismayed team into a huddle and said, "We tried hard, we all agree about the penalty, but these people have come out to watch the game, let's put our allegiances to one side and thank them." He then led the crestfallen Maroons across to applaud the crowd. Few would have noticed that as he left the field Wally was introduced to a young handicapped boy in a wheelchair and that Wally spontaneously took off his boots and socks and gave them to the lad.

McCallum's penalty gave the series to NSW but Wally could not end his Origin career on such a bleak note. He pledged to Tosser Turner he would postpone retirement until Queensland won back the Origin shield. To cap a thoroughly unhappy week, Wayne Bennett commented that Wally should have been replaced 20 minutes into the second half: "When you're out of gas you're out of gas and Wally was running on empty."

Wally read it and shook his head. "He was the only one who thought so," he said. "It's true I hadn't played for six to eight weeks but Alan Jones said he regarded it as one of my best performances ever." When Jacqui read Bennett's comments she was ready to tear the doors off the wall. "What is it with this bloke?" she demanded. Wally told her, "Let it go. He hasn't finished yet."

Queensland recovered some lost pride with a 14-10 win in the third Origin but even this joy was dulled when Arthur Beetson was dumped as coach a few days later. For some reason Beetson had fallen from favour. Dropping Vautin? Doubting Wally? Wally disagreed with sacking Beetson. "Successful for four years, gave it away, came back in 1989 and won 3-0, next year loses 2-1 on a bum decision, dumped," he said. He shook his head. He was becoming inured to such news: first Fatty from Manly and Queensland; then himself as Broncos captain and five-eighth; now Artie. QRL chief Ross Livermore sounded out Wally for the job. Wally had heard a whisper that former New Zealand Test coach, Manly's Graham Lowe, was on a short list. After a wink and a nod from Livermore, Wally said, "I think I'll be content with the new coach." If Lowe had not accepted, Wally would have coached Queensland in 1991, the Origin's first ever captain-coach.

In the wake of the loss of the Origin shield, Wally was heartened by his selection as Australian captain and five-eighth for the Test against France on 27 June, 1990, two weeks away. It was another chance to show the Broncos the error of their ways. It was nine months since the sacking and Wayne Bennett quietly asked Wally if he was over the upset of the captaincy. Wally said he wasn't. He told me, "I wasn't as angry by then but time hadn't proved a healer. And if people ask me now I still can't accept it and never will be able to."

Was a vindictive God glaring down upon Lewis, a jealous God who thought him still too full of pride, unbowed by the blows dealt upon him? Four days before the Test, 24 June 1990, the Broncos played St George at Kogarah Oval. Eight minutes into the match Wally kicked downfield to fullback Mick Potter and followed through. He was second man in to tackle Potter and somehow jammed his left fist into the earth under Potter as he fell. The effect was the same as when you lean a stick against a step and kick it in the middle to snap it. Wally, and most players nearby, heard a sharp crack as his left forearm fractured. "I tried to move my hand and could feel the bone grating into the muscle," he said. He walked to the sideline and told Kelvin Giles to get Bennett on the phone. "Tell him I've broken my arm." With those words Wally was out of the Test against France and lost further ground in his year-long slide into deep personal depression.

He sat on the bench briefly, staring at the ground, a gown over his shoulders, before being driven to the local shire hospital. His arm was X-rayed and plastered but Wally declined their offer of an operation. "Peter Myers will do it," he told them. "He's done all the panel beating to the rest of this body, he can do this lot too." Jacqui had already heard the news on the radio and was in tears when he rang her.

He returned to the match and afterwards sat dolefully in a corner of the change rooms. Director Paul Morgan sympathised with him about his continuing bad luck. Dowling quipped, "You've had plenty of luck, unfortunately it's all bad."

In Brisbane Dr Myers compared the X-rays of the newly broken left arm with the right arm Wally broke in the World Cup final nearly two years before. "You're not going to believe this," he said. "They're almost carbon copies, same angle, just a quarter of an inch difference in the height up the bone." On 25 June 1990, Wally walked into the Holy Spirit Hospital in Brisbane for his sixth operation in two and a half years. He was on a first name basis with half the staff there by that stage. As he had with Lewis' right arm, Myers inserted a long stainless steel nail into the left forearm to hold it firm and help it to mend.

Myers warned Wally when he was discharged that it was going to be a race against time. Wally knew what he meant — the Kangaroo tour was three months away. Fulton rang, Arthurson too, each with the reassuring message — just get fit again and back on the track. A vote of confidence came from an unlikely source — Ray Price wrote in the *Daily Telegraph*, "Even if he comes back to football just prior to the tour, I'd still take him. His leadership skills are invaluable."

Wally needed every word of their encouragement. "I was at an all-time low," he said. "Probably the only time I felt worse in my life was when my brother nearly died in a car smash. I didn't feel like doing anything, going anywhere." At home Jacqui would suggest going out, but wherever they went people would talk to him about his arm, saying he must be upset at missing out on the tour. Wally would jump up: "Listen I haven't missed out on it yet!" Then he'd say to Jacqui it was time to go.

For the next two months the Lewis household relied heavily on good humour as Jacqui coped with the burden of her home. Her daughter Jamie-Lee had been born only a few weeks earlier and the boys were still only four and three. Wally couldn't dress himself, wash his hair or help with the boys. "It was just horrid because it was like I had four little children," said Jacqui. "I didn't know whether I was coming or going. He was pretty hard to live with those weeks."

From the moment Wally was overthrown as Broncos captain other clubs cranked up their fax machines with lucrative offers: Manly, Norths and Easts in Sydney; Featherstone Rovers; a $1 million five-year bid by Widnes, and a healthy offer from the Gold Coast. But Wally wanted to remain a Bronco and this prejudiced his reading of the tortuous negotiations to follow.

In his newspaper column Ray Price predicted as early as May that the Broncos would have to show the door to either Bennett or Lewis at the end of the season. That was sheer speculation by Price but then, on 13 July 1990, more authoritatively, Peter Frilingos in the *Daily Mirror* tipped a massive pay cut for Lewis if he stayed with the Broncos. Ribot denied it, and Wally believed him. "When you get a bloke who for years you've regarded as a friend, you tend to think you're amongst the troops," said Wally. So he told Gold Coast chief executive Larry Maloney, "Thanks, but all things being equal I'm not going to leave the Broncos. This year hasn't been so much fun for me and I'd like one more year here before I finish up."

As weeks went by Lewis could not get a 1991 contract offer from Ribot. He told his manager, Billy J. Smith, "You handle it Bill. I don't want to become a pain in the arse by keeping going in there." Smith approached Ribot half a dozen times with no greater success. "Either I'm not knocking loud enough or they're not listening," Smith told Wally. "And I think I know which one it is." In August, Ribot asked the NSWRL to exempt Lewis from their salary cap. Wally read that propitiously, as meaning the Broncos were keen to keep him. Not so Smith. "The way I read it, it was quite obvious the Broncos didn't want him. But Wally never accepted that. Right up until the death he expected them to turn around and say, 'We want you back.' I kept at Ribot because that was my job, to represent Lewis."

On 7 September the NSWRL refused Ribot's request to exempt Lewis. Five days later, Wednesday 12 September, when Wally and Billy J. Smith confronted Ribot in his Broncos office, Wally was in a buoyant mood. It was a big week for him. After 12 weeks out with his broken arm he was making his comeback for the Broncos that weekend, in a match which might lead to his first Sydney grand final. A good match would also prove his fitness for the 1990 Kangaroos tour.

Ribot savagely deflated him by declaring he could only offer a reduced contract. Despite all other speculation, Lewis' contract with the Broncos in 1990 was $145,000 plus bonuses of $1500 a win. Ribot then offered him $50,000 plus match bonuses for 1991. A good 1991 season made the offer worth about $70,000. I reminded Wally that at the time Ribot said the offer, in sign-on fee plus incentive and match payments, was worth a total of $100,000. "That's bullshit!" he said vehemently. "It was $50,000." Billy J. Smith agreed the offer was unacceptably low.

This was the final blow, his rejection from the Broncos. Smith argued Wally's case — the offer was an insult, they'd used Lewis and were now discarding him. Wally took over, "Come off it Reebs, that's not an offer. You know I can't accept that." All he wanted, he said, was a reasonable offer to give him one more year. He owed it to himself and to the Broncos, and the Broncos owed him that grace. All to no avail. Wally was angry and bewildered as he and Billy J. left empty-handed. Outside, Smith told Wally, "Mate, it's pretty obvious they're going to push you off."

Wally drove home and told Jacqui, his loyal confidante, "They want to dump me and they're trying to make me look like I'm to blame," he said. Wally imagined the public picking up the paper, reading, "Lewis Rejects Offer", and automatically thinking, "Gees, he must be greedy for money, that bloke." Wally told me, "That was exactly the opposite of what happened. The offer was meant to be refused. I'm 100 per cent sure of that." The more he thought about it the more it was the captaincy revisited. First they wanted "Wally Resigns As Captain" and now "Wally Refuses Offer". That way the Broncos came up smelling sweet. They had not learnt their lesson.

Wally rang Paul Vautin, "Fatty, you're not going to believe this..." The Broncos' puny offer of $50,000 was identical to that which Manly offered Vautin when they shunted him. Vautin could only reply in wonderment, "Mate, who would have ever thought this would happen to you." Wally hung up and recalled how some wise old heads had advised him, when he sang the praises of the Broncos, not to get too tied up with football clubs, because as soon as they used players up, they would spit them out. Wally hadn't listened then.

All the implications crowded in upon him. In his heart he wanted to play his last club match at Lang Park, where it had all begun. Like Greg Chappell, Dennis Lillee and Rodney Marsh, who all retired together, Wally wanted to retire with Geno and GD — despite the rift with Gene. "I couldn't imagine a better way to end my career than alongside those blokes," he said. Now those expectations were being snatched from him.

With his capacity for lateral thinking Wally devised a comeback. "I know what I'm going to do to these pricks," he thought. "I'm going to say 'Yeah, I'll play for $50,000,' and see what they say." So next day at 4 p.m., without informing manager Smith, Wally wound his way through a media scrum to Ribot's office.

However Ribot proved himself worth every cent the Broncos board paid him. Wally began to say he had been thinking about the offer. Ribot interrupted him. "If you can just hold on — we're not in a position to offer you a contract," he said. He explained that no matter what they offered Wally, under the NSWRL salary cap Wally was rated a $150,000 player. Wally was confused. "So what are you telling me?" he asked. Ribot delivered the coup de grâce. "Unfortunately we're going to release you." Wally sought desperately for some loophole. Since he hadn't played Test football in 1990 perhaps his salary rating might be reduced and he could show the ARL his contract. "Mate, no," said Ribot. "That's the way it is."

Wally left the office and headed for the training shed through a sea of reporters. Now he was really angry. Wayne Bennett's pre-season words kept reverberating through his mind: "I'm responsible for all the hiring and firing in this club." Wally had always admired Bennett in the past for his straightforward dealing with players who were to be cut. "He used to talk to me about it," said Wally. "He'd say, 'It's not a nice job, but I've just got to do it and the best way is with the truth.'

"That's how he cut my brother Scott from the club. If Wayne had come to me and said, 'Listen, I think you're finished, you're a bad influence, not worth two bob and I don't want you here next year,' I wouldn't have liked it, but I would have taken it on the chin a lot better than I did. I couldn't tell Wayne he was wrong for not wanting me at the Broncos, but I could for the way things happened. People may think it's unimportant but Wayne should have given me that news, not Reebs. And for that I was filthy on Bennett."

When Wally reached where the squad had gathered for their pre-training talk, Bennett asked him if he wanted to tell the boys of his decision. Wally at first ignored him and, when pushed, replied,

"I heard on the radio this morning I wouldn't be playing here next year, so if it's on the radio it must be right."

Bennett, exasperated, persisted, "Yes, that's the radio, but have you made a decision?" Wally said there was no decision to be made. Bennett, now cross himself, pressed ahead, "Yes there is. You were offered a contract and you were to give your decision to the club today." Wally looked hard at him and said that the club refused to offer him a contract. Bennett looked surprised. Wally left it at that, but at that moment, Wally lost all respect for the coach he had once so admired. First there had been the accusation of the feigned hamstring injury, then the loaded offer to play five-eighth after Kevin Walters had so excelled. Wally was convinced it was inconceivable that Bennett would not have known of Ribot's decision to cut him from the club.

As Wally jogged in training Dowling trotted up beside him. "Shit, looks like the old blokes are in trouble, are we?" he said. Then Alfie sidled over to say he was sorry to hear the news. Three or four more came over. It was the week of the Broncos final against Canberra. "Hope we win on Sunday and go on to the grand final," they said. "Might make it a bit easier for you." Not even this dramatic news was enough to bring Geno to Wally's side.

The 50 members of the media who had converged on Gilbert Park, Red Hill, turned Bennett's pre-final training session into a farce. Television cameramen chased as hard as the players themselves. "It's quite easily the most disappointing moment of my life," Wally told them. Such was Wally's media stature that this was sport's equivalent of the toppling of the former premier, Sir Joh Bjelke-Petersen — leviathans felled make great media spectacles.

Bennett told the media, "This club couldn't have started without Wally. We didn't want to lose him because of his services to the club. But name me the four or five first graders we should let go to keep Wally and keep within the salary cap." If Bennett, an honourable man, said he didn't want to lose Wally, he was to be believed. But so too were Ribot and the directors, they were all honourable men, and yet it was Wally's career which lay bleeding at their feet.

Wally and Billy J. Smith held one final meeting with directors Paul Morgan, Barry Maranta and Steve Williams, and manager John Ribot at Morgan's Mansfield hotel. The directors offered Wally a package worth $100,000 to retire. It was no magnanimous gift. Part of it undoubtedly was prompted by the Broncos' wish to end the Lewis saga cleanly. They wanted Wally off the front page and the Broncos onto the back page. Wally would have had to work for the $100,000—visit schools, give coaching clinics, lead club promotions, entertain guests at matches, become a management figurehead. The deal would have eroded his own revenue earning time and he probably would have had to resign his job with Channel 10.

Anyway, as Smith told the directors, "I thought we were here to discuss Wally playing, not retiring." Billy J. knew Wally wouldn't accept. "It was never going to succeed with him," he said. "Nor should it have either. His pride was too much for him and I believe he still had something to contribute as a player."

Ultimately, whether Bennett actually knew of Ribot's decision or not was irrelevant. Since the Broncos' inception Bennett signed everyone he wanted and cut everyone he didn't. By the end of 1990 the Broncos board had undoubtedly had a gutful of Wally Lewis, the "Letters to the Editor", the chorusing of columnists, the phone-in polls, the electronic media's investigations. The captaincy issue wouldn't die because Wally refused to capitulate. So long as he refused to lie down, the public lashed the club, and the Broncos never forgave him for that. He was a destructive influence and he had to go. Wally saw himself as refusing to compromise his principles, refusing to be a hypocrite. The Broncos interpreted this as manipulating public opinion via the media. A Broncos executive told me at the time, "I'll hand it to him, he was good at it, the best."

Thus by the end of the 1990 season the Broncos were ready to jettison Lewis. Far from Bennett having to cut him, it would have taken an act of intervention from Bennett to save him. Once Bennett indicated to the board that he sought no special leave to retain Lewis, the rest was foregone. Ribot divined the board's hostility, Bennett's antipathy and merely permitted natural financial priorities to do the rest. Ribot described it as the toughest decision he had made at the club, but by then the decision was easy. Delivering it to Wally and facing the public consequences were the hard parts.

Wally's final year with the Broncos had elements of a Shakespearean tragedy: the King's reign undermined and not allowed to run full term; his downfall plotted from within a small circle of men he trusted; being replaced as leader by his best friend; having his position usurped by a younger man; a media-led popular uprising failing to reinstate him, suffering injury. Finally he was rejected and cast out from his community, and a former brother-in-arms delivered the coup de grâce.

All these events occurred where Wally was most vulnerable, off the field. He needed one chance to demonstrate he was worthy of his reputation, one match to regain some ground, to let his natural gifts turn his fortunes around. He glimpsed the approaching Kangaroo tour as a parched man must a mirage.

8
A Medical Dispute

It seemed impossible that Wally Lewis' luck could get any worse, after a year in which he had been stripped of his rank and position with the Broncos, while plagued by a chronic hamstring injury, had lost an Origin series and then broken his arm. But during six days in 1990, from 13 September to 18 September, he reeled from one blow to the next as his fortunes plummeted to the lowest point of his life. As his wife Jacqui said, "I kept saying to him, 'Just hang on, don't give in and your luck will turn the corner.' Because that's the way Mum has always spoken. But then the corner would come and it was more bad news."

Wally fought against the tide of ill fortune that swept over him, believing that by sheer strength of will he could prevail. He displayed it in his efforts to repair his broken arm. He bought a $2700 electromagnetic pulse machine to promote bone calcification. "The bloke told me it worked on greyhounds and racehorses and reckoned Mal Meninga had used it too," said Wally. He strapped it on his arm watching television in the evening and wore the uncomfortable attachments all night. At breakfast he swallowed calcium bone growth supplements.

Injuries never diminished Wally's enthusiasm for his team. He attended all of the Broncos' home matches but after flying with the team to the first away match was left off subsequent free flight lists. He turned up to training sessions and worked assiduously on his fitness with Kelvin Giles. To avoid jarring his arm he ran distance work on a computer-driven treadmill which could raise its angle to allow him to run uphill. He later graduated to repetition sprints while Giles rode shotgun on him with a stopwatch, pushing him harder. "It wasn't much fun," said Wally. "I put lunch on the grass a couple of times."

The week before Wally was cut from the club, the Broncos played their semi-final against Manly. For this match, on 8 September, they lost Greg Dowling and Dale Shearer with injuries. Gene Miles was receiving pain-killing injections for a foot injury. Giles had assured Wally he would be fit for the following match but Wally approached Bennett at training. "I know I haven't played for a long time but with all these blokes out we haven't a lot of experience out there," he said. "This match is sudden death. I'm making myself available if you want to use me."

Bennett looked surprised. Wally got the impression the coach had presumed that his ex-captain was content to sit the season out and cheerfully depart with the Kangaroos. Bennett raised one eyebrow, "Do you think you'll be right?" Wally said he would be short of match fitness, but he would do the best he could for as long as he could. Bennett nodded and Wally began to prepare mentally. But on Saturday, Bennett ruled him out. Giles did not consider him fit enough. Wally exclaimed, "Wayne, fitness is not going to make any difference to me whether it's this week or next week." Still no go. The Broncos scraped home without Wally to set up the final against Canberra.

A few days later Ribot delivered his verdict on the Lewis contract, cutting Wally from the Broncos. All the joy and expectation of playing in the Sydney final drained from Wally. Of the first graders who gathered for training that week, he was the odd man out and everyone knew it. Wally was like a boxer suffering successive crashing knockdowns but refusing to stay down. Once more he got off the floor and put a brave face on his pain.

At training he proved his arm's strength by exchanging tackles with Chris Johns, Michael Hancock and Paul Hauff. Footballers hate risking injury at training. Johns asked Wally not to tackle him too hard and he'd do the same for Wally. Paul Hauff complained, "Wayne'll kick my bum if I'm hurt doing this." Wally had his own problems trying to work out how to envelop Hauff's giraffe-like stride. And Michael Hancock? "The usual," said Wally wryly, "Straight at me, hard as the bastard could go." Wally's wrist stung a little as it bent at angles it hadn't taken for three months, but he had no trouble hitting the ground and Bennett pencilled him in the squad.

Canberra officials insisted on examining the arm protection Wally would wear. Later Wally chided Mal Meninga, "Fancy checking me, George. What about that stove-pipe you used to wear?" Meninga laughed and replied, "Yeah but I don't have to wear it any more."

In the final at the Sydney Football Stadium, Canberra produced their trademark exhilarating form and the Broncos wilted. After 20 minutes trainer Giles called out, "Wally, get up, stretch, warm up." Wally's heart beat quicker. He was on! The packed stadium spied him jogging up the sideline and cheered him as they had never before. False alarm. He sat down and got the call again after 30 minutes. Same thing. At half-time Giles warned Wally and the other reserves, "You fellas keep stretching, you might be on early in the second half." Righto, Kelvin. Several changes were made but after 20 minutes, when Giles called, "Stretch up again," Wally just glanced up at him disgustedly. Giles looked down apologetically and said, "I'm sorry. I can't do anything." Wally waited with increasing misery until, with 14 minutes left, down came the message from Bennett to send Lewis on. "Go out and play your best," said Giles. "Help yourself along."

The Broncos were behind 22-nil. Wally knew from their stony faces and slumped shoulders the team was beaten. His one consolation was that with Geno switched back to the centres, they might be able to pull a few tricks and score a few points. "We'd played a thousand times together and we had our very own teamwork," said Wally. On the sideline he asked Giles who he was replacing. "Geno," said Giles. Wally plucked out his mouth-guard in disbelief, turned to Bennett in the stand and shook his head in disbelief — separating him and Geno to the last. Gene had been his last hope to make an impact, and now that was taken away from him too. "Mate, I didn't want to replace you," said Wally apologetically as he passed Geno.

Miles was aware of the tactical loss of their teamwork but told me, "I had to come off. I had a bruised bone in my foot, had it injected for all three finals. But I remember Wally was given a loud ovation and I was booed off, and that's the first time that ever happened in Sydney."

Wally heard the crowd's applause too, and initially thought it must have been Mal coming off. No. He looked for a Mexican wave, but no. Did he have a sign on his back — what was the story? Then he heard the unmistakable chant, "We Want Wall-ee!" He had little time to impress in the game but after several tackles remembered his arm — it had not hurt. "I wasn't on painkillers and not one ounce of pain came through," said Wally. "I had complete confidence in it."

Wally had presumed he knew Bennett the coach, if not the man. He had thought once the Broncos were in trouble Bennett would send him on early in the second half, because above all Bennett wanted to win the final. "He gave me a consolation run, that's all, just to show the Kangaroo selectors I could play," he said. "But it wasn't even good for that."

Greg Dowling thought Wally was lucky to get a run at all. "But I still think in that game we could have done with him earlier," he said. "We could have done with a bit of Wally magic and variation out there. Even if he'd only lasted 20 minutes he'd have lifted the guys' spirits because we all know what he does on the paddock."

Wally's surgeon Dr Peter Myers told me he had passed Lewis fit only for head-bin reserve in the second half, or, if nothing happened, to play the last ten minutes. That was his advice to Wayne Bennett, he said. Coaches often give in to pressure from players to exceed medical advice, but Bennett followed Myers' guidance almost to the minute.

In the dressing room afterwards Wally glanced around the dispirited faces and thought, "All these guys are just about ready to jump off the bridge, but I've got nothing to be sad about. I didn't have much to do with today's loss and I won't even be here next year. For them it's the end of the season but for me it's the end of the club. I'm going to cut myself off from this disappointment." He dressed quickly and in a neutral voice addressed the room, "Fellas ... I'm out of here. I won't see much of you any more, bad luck about today, thanks for the season, watch out for the sidestep next year." Several looked up and waved, some said good luck or held a fist, little finger and thumb extended near their ear, to indicate they would phone him. Miles and Bennett, deep in conversation, did not look up. Captain and coach were subdued; Wally understood that.

About two weeks later, 28 September, Wally signed to join the Gold Coast Seagulls, who had been chasing him for months. It was quite a day, for that evening he paid his last visit to the Broncos clubhouse, their black tie end of season presentation night. Wally's signing that day guaranteed the evening would have its tense moments. Wally and Jacqui sat at a Channel 10 table and listened as the night proceeded without any acknowledgment of Wally's contribution to the club. His name was not mentioned in any awards or honours. Wally told me, "A couple of the directors sort of glanced at me and then looked away. I thought 'There's no end to these blokes. They give us talks on how to handle pressure, they could do with a lesson themselves.' "

Ironically Kevin Walters, who had usurped Wally's five-eighth spot, broke the ice. Voted the club's best and fairest, Walters told the auditorium, "I'd just like to thank Wally. He's given me a lot of advice on plenty of occasions. I'm proud to say that I played in the same team with him. He's the best footballer I've ever seen." The praise put many in a quandary. To clap or not? Wally was quickly moving beyond caring.

He stood at the bar with Peter Jackson, who was leaving to join North Sydney, and ordered up. The barman asked what they wanted. "Red wine," said Jacko. What kind? "The most expensive," said Jacko, with impeccable taste. Wally stood and drank and watched. Some met his gaze, others ducked.

"It was obvious the place was divided over how to treat me," he said. "I decided I'd wait and if people wanted to talk to me they could." One by one they drifted over, GD, Kevie Walters, Alfie and Kerrod ... but not Geno. "He thought I was still filthy on him," said Wally. "Porky Morgan came over and then right at the end — I was just about full up to my ears with this wine Jacko had ordered — Bennett came over. He didn't talk about football, about work and I just answered him. I didn't want to spoil the night, or be objectionable. But I didn't ask him anything."

Remembering that final evening Wally felt the injustice of his treatment by Bennett all over again. "People say he was jealous, that I was detracting from him, that he couldn't handle big names," he said. "But he got rid of me, not Reebs or the board. Why? I don't know. He's the only bloke who would know why. I went out of my way to get on with him. I changed so many different attitudes to go along with his plans, changed my opinions on how the game should be played. I changed all that and after I did, I got the flick." For the only time in our hours of conversations I couldn't bring myself to proceed with my next question. Wally was still so plainly hurt it showed in his eyes. I sat and waited as he gazed past his balcony towards the canal water at the bottom of his garden.

Wally and Jacqui have not been back to the Broncos clubhouse since. "That was the club Wally never thought he'd leave," said Jacqui wistfully. "It was a time that made us realise that all the people you thought were your friends, weren't. It made us very wary."

Much later, when Wally was a Seagull, horse trainer Bruce McLachlan approached Broncos director Paul Morgan at Eagle Farm races. "Why the hell would you blokes ever get rid of Lewis?" he asked. Morgan trotted out the usual reply, Lewis was disruptive, he was this, he was that. McLachlan stopped him. "Know what? If I had a horse that was disruptive, kicked the stablemate and was cantankerous with the jockey, if he won for me every Saturday, I'd feed him every day of the week." Morgan laughed, and said with a wry grin, it was a shame they hadn't all got on.

Though profoundly sad, Wally was relieved when the the Broncos saga finally ended. Now he could concentrate on the final phase of his fateful season and, as he had so often on the football field, seek to conjure a triumph from Kangaroo selection to turn around this ignominious year. He and Mal Meninga would become triple Kangaroo tourists, joining such elite names as Churchill, Gasnier, Raper, Irvine and Langlands.

Yet even on that front storm-clouds were gathering. On 24 June, when Wally broke his arm, ARL chief Ken Arthurson encouraged him to presume he needed only to obtain a medical clearance to lead the Kangaroos. Six weeks later, on 2 August, this assurance had contracted to Wally having to prove his fitness. Arthurson was quoted as saying: "To be honest I couldn't see him making it without having a match beforehand."

Wally had suffered so much that year, his emotions were so exposed and raw, that he rushed to embrace Arthurson's cruel doubt. "I'd be wiser to let the tour go then, wouldn't I?" he said bitterly. "Make sure the arm is 100 per cent for next year." It was his depression talking — stuff the tour, stuff football, stuff everyone!

A phone call from coach Bobby Fulton restored his spirit and he realised he shouldn't be worrying at that stage, because the medical was not until late September. At home Jacqui watched Wally's progress anxiously. "He used to pick the kids up and swing them around and throw them in the air," she said. "You just don't do those things if your arm is giving you trouble. He was pretty happy with it."

Yet rumours persisted that Wally would not tour. Wally's own suspicions went on red alert after a Sydney function where he stood in a group which included a senior NSWRL official, made garrulous with drink. "Do you know if you go on this tour you'll break the great Clive Churchill's record for Tests as captain?" the official said. Wally agreed it would be a great honour. "And you'll break the great Reg Gasnier's record for Tests played?" Wally said it would be a big tour for him. The official, swaying unsteadily, eyed Wally and said, "Well I hope you don't go, because you're not half the footballer either of those blokes were." Wally was speechless. Others in the circle looked equally amazed as the official wheeled and walked away. It was such an outlandish remark Wally decided to ignore it. He recalled that old Ronny McAuliffe had once described the official as an anti-Queensland crank.

But on 17 September, the day before he was due to fly to Sydney for his tour medical test, Wally's phone ran hot with media tips that he was no show to pass the medical. Genuinely daunted, he rang ARL general manager Bob Abbott and said that if his exclusion was inevitable the ARL might as well save itself the air fare. Abbott reassured him he'd be given a fair go. Wally rang Fatty Vautin, who immediately asked, "What does Fulton think?" Wally said Fulton had said he would attend the medical with him. "Ah well, if Bozo goes along with you, you know you're in," said Fatty. The next morning Wally flew down, full of foreboding, stretching his arm and wrist nervously. Abbott met him at the airport and Wally once more expressed his doubts. "Nooo mate, nooo!" said Abbott assuring him he had every chance. They drove to a clinic for X-rays and then to the Sydney Football Stadium. Wally looked around for Fulton. He was away on business, a bad omen for Wally.

The ARL doctor, Dr Nathan Gibbs, examined the X-rays and then told Wally to prepare for a fitness test. Wally was not keen on any strenuous test but was buoyed up because Gibbs did not immediately comment on the X-rays. No news was good news.

Gibbs put Wally through a series of exercises — wheelbarrow walks, punching a bag — designed to test the suspect arm's strength and flexibility. Afterwards a group of media representatives congratulated Wally; it seemed obvious he had successfuly completed the tests. Abbott and Gibbs walked off the field into a dressing room, reappeared a minute later and called Wally over. They were seeking a second opinion on the X-rays from Dr Merv Cross, a leading orthopaedic specialist. Cross arrived from his Crows Nest surgery, studied the X-rays, gave his decision to Gibbs and departed. Wally, chatting to the media, gathered there were two views — that he looked to have passed the physical fitness test but that a strong rumour still existed he would fail no matter what.

Wally could bear the waiting no longer. He walked downstairs to where Gibbs and Abbott were sitting at a table. As he approached Abbott stood up and said, "Mate, we're sorry. Unfortunately we're going to have to rule you out. Dr Gibbs doesn't believe there's been sufficient growth in your arm ..." If Wally had been the fainting type he might have done so right then. All year people had been summoning him into rooms and gravely delivering death sentences to his football career.

He burst out, "There's nothing wrong with my arm!" He appealed to Gibbs, "You look me in the eye and tell me I've got something wrong with my arm." Gibbs was visibly upset at having to convey the awful news, and replied that he was sorry. Wally repeated his question. "You look me in the eye ..." Gibbs walked away with his head down. Wally asked to see Dr Cross but Abbott said Cross had already left the stadium. Abbott killed further conversation by announcing to the media that Wally had failed his test. Wally stood aside, tears welling in his eyes, more distressed than he had been by anything else that awful year. He exclaimed to the media, "If there was something wrong with me I could accept it, but this is a set-up."

After the media melee cleared, Abbott said to Wally, "C'mon mate, I'll drive you to the airport." Wally told him to get stuffed. Sydney radio identity Peter Peters offered him a lift and Wally used a portable telephone on the way to ring Jacqui. She was distraught. She knew how it would devastate Wally and how it would affect the whole family.

"I didn't say a word all the way home on the plane," said Wally. "I switched the car radio on and ended up turning it off because every station had it on their news. I was sick of it. I drove in and sat out the back and just didn't want to talk to anyone. I had tears in my eyes and then Mitchell came out and said, 'Why are you crying, Dad?' That did it. I couldn't hold it off any more. I just broke down."

He wept for the missed tour, for his humilation by the Broncos, for the sense of despair he felt about himself. He put his arm around his gentle son and held him close.

Abbott later announced that if Lewis could prove his arm had healed, he would be given a second chance. Wally then offered the ARL the same chance Christ gave the doubting apostle Thomas. Wally would have the arm surgically opened and invite Abbott and medical specialists to examine the healed bone. Abbott declined.

Wally failed his medical on a medical moot — two respected orthopaedic surgeons delivering contrary opinions on the degree of healing in a broken arm. Wally's surgeon, Dr Peter Myers, believed the fracture had healed sufficiently for Lewis, with the protection of an armguard, to go on tour. He thought it unfair for Wally to be ruled out by interpreting X-rays of the arm.

Before Wally's test, ARL chief Ken Arthurson had rung Dr Gibbs and told him that, given Wally's stature, he was to receive the benefit of any doubt about his fitness. With this leeway, from Gibbs' subsequent statements, it seems he may not have failed Lewis solely for inadequate fitness or flexibility. He based his ruling on his opinion that the X-rays revealed insufficient healing in the bone at the point of fracture.

Dr Gibbs, who is not a specialist, would have been outranked in any medical debate with Dr Myers. Thus the consulting role of Dr Merv Cross was crucial. He prefaced his comments to me by saying that Lewis was the best footballer he had ever seen. "What happened was an absolute tragedy," he said. It was a tragedy to equal that of Wayne Pearce, who had been ruled out of the 1986 Kangaroos by the ARL doctor even though Dr Cross, then Pearce's specialist, had passed him fit.

Cross told me that the X-rays showed Wally had no solid union in the fracture. "It would have been dangerous for him to play," he said. "Being the champion he is, if he tried too hard he could have broken the arm with the steel rod in it. And it's one hell of a job to get a rod out of a broken bone." Cross said the Lewis ruling was one of the easiest clinical decisions he'd ever had to make as an orthopaedic surgeon, but the hardest to make as a team doctor. "I knew there was a tremendous amount at stake for Wally," he said, "yet I was thinking about him. I would never have prejudiced his health that way. If you look at the literature on forearm fractures, particularly of the radius, like Wally's, they are renowned for their slow healing."

Wally was ruled out on Tuesday, 18 September, and that following weekend, in Brisbane, Dr Cross attended a conference of the Australian chapter of the International Society of the Knee — known as the Australian Knee Club. Dr Myers also attended this meeting and showed X-rays of Wally's arm to several colleagues. He said they supported his opinion.

When I informed Dr Cross of that he said, "I don't think he'd get too many agreeing." Dr Myers and Dr Cross are friends. Their conflicting opinions meant there was a genuine doubt about Wally's fitness but, contrary to Ken Arthurson's request, Dr Gibbs did not give Wally the benefit of that doubt. At another medical conference, in Canberra, the day after Wally's test, doctors brandished the morning newspaper and engaged in heated argument over Wally's arm.

The debate was all academic; the patient's hopes had died. He sat out the back of his home, inconsolable. One of the first to phone was Wayne Pearce, who said he felt sorry for Wally because he knew exactly how he felt. Wally told him, "Junior, everyone knew you were fitter than any bloke on that touring party in '86." David Fordham rang and invited the Lewises to his home for a barbeque wake. Wally was insecure, needing company, but only that of friends. Fordham and Billy J. Smith commiserated with and counselled Wally that evening. "It was like a big dream had been shattered," said Fordham.

That night Wally lay awake, wide-eyed with shock. "You're not asleep, are you?" whispered Jacqui. No, he said. "C'mon, try and get some sleep," she murmured. While she dozed he rose and watched television until dawn. Next day was Jacqui's birthday but joy had deserted the Lewis house. "He'd lost himself," said Jacqui. "Had he still been Broncos captain, or if the Broncos had retained him, he might have coped. But this was the last straw. It was hideous. I didn't know where to start. I didn't know what to say any more, I'd said it all before."

In desperation Jacqui rang Wally's friend Peter O'Callaghan who was holidaying in a rented unit at Palm Beach on the Gold Coast. She told him, "Peter, he's in his room, he won't answer any phone calls, he won't talk to anyone, will you speak to him if I switch you through?"

O'Callaghan invited Wally and Jacqui to stay with them on the coast. "Come on down, lose the media," he said. "Nobody'll know where you are. Give yourself a couple of days to get yourself together." They did, walking the beach, playing with the children. O'Callaghan told Wally during a stroll, "We all get our kicks in the backside over the years, you've been on top, on top, on top and suddenly you're getting all yours in one go." They didn't dine out on Jacqui's birthday; Wally didn't want to face the public.

Wally's faithful followers in Queensland, those who just a year before made the Broncos' lives hell, were aroused by the Brisbane *Sun*'s headline, "Wally's Only Crime Is Being A Queenslander". A phone-in poll by the paper, asking whether Lewis had been given a fair go, resulted in 3589 saying "No", and only 325 saying "Yes". Wally's army turned their venom upon the ARL, faxing and phoning more than 300 protests, often couched in strong language. ARL manager Bob Abbott was shocked at their vehemence. Dr Gibbs' Sydney surgery was also bombarded with abusive calls.

Sometimes Wally himself needed to be saved from such support. The following Saturday he ventured out to a birthday party thrown for Jacqui at a Wynnum restaurant. Wally was amongst familiar faces, including his brother Scott, but a sympathetic public would not be denied. Over his shoulder they came, "Mate what they did to you, we ought to protest", and "We knew this would be on once they won the Origin, eh?"

Wally ate, went to the toilet and vomited. "He said it was the meal but we ate the same food and we weren't sick," said Jacqui. "It was nerves. All my friends were there and I had their support but he wasn't ready to be out. Everyone was looking at him. He was this big high man who had been knocked down."

The next day Peter O'Callaghan took Wally and Jacqui to watch the local Brisbane grand final at Lang Park. Jacqui was delighted. The Kangaroos flew out that day and she dreaded Wally moping around the house. They sat in the Powers box and at half-time Wally was bombarded by autograph hunters. Most had a kind word for him and as the second half started, he told the few still waiting, "OK, I'll sign the rest after the game."

A large woman in the group insisted on him signing there and then. Wally politely demurred. The woman rounded on him. "Big head! Too good for ordinary people eh?" she said angrily. "No wonder the Broncos sacked you!" Jacqui held her breath, as did everyone in the box. This was the reddest of rags, surely Wally would snap. He didn't. At the final whistle the woman returned, shoved out two books and demanded, "Sign 'em now!" Wally absently signed.

Jacqui told me, "I was amazed, because I'm forever telling him not to blow up, but that time he should have told her to get lost. I thought, 'You poor bugger'. He couldn't even be bothered defending himself. He wasn't even thinking about her, he was off in that plane somewhere with the Kangaroos."

From the moment the Kangaroos left, Wally followed their every move, caught every news bulletin, special report and match replay. The tour overtook the house. Jacqui couldn't believe it. She told him, "What are you doing to yourself? Do you want me to give you a knife?" She didn't know how she would get through these next three months of the tour. "It was a real trying time," she said. "He wanted to be there. He still hadn't come to terms with it. People wouldn't understand. To them it's only a game, but it isn't only a game to Wally."

The first Test was at Wembley, on 27 October 1990, and Jacqui prepared to watch it with her husband, the first in six years when he was neither playing nor commentating. She organised a tennis party on their newly finished court and, with understanding neighbours, played late into the night until kick-off. Jacqui later realised that Wally didn't like to watch Tests in company. He became too involved, knowing too much about the game to enjoy amateur comments, even from friends. But she got them through that night.

Faced with the unacceptable, Wally channelled his agony down an unhealthy path — a conspiracy theory. He was convinced he had been set up, that the ARL had decreed that because of anti-Queensland envy or his past misdemeanours, his reign as Australian captain should end. His evidence was the rumours — the NSWRL official who wished him out of the tour and a second, less easily discarded incident. After the Canberra final a respected Brisbane journalist, talking to a senior official in Sydney rugby league, commented that Wally's arm had held up through the match. The official replied, "He'll never go to England."

The journalist does not wish to be identified, nor will he name the official concerned. I asked him how seriously he took the remark. "I was intrigued," he said. "A lot of those things are said about Lewis day to day. But given the assurance with which he said it, and in the light of what happened, it took on grander proportions."

After Wally failed the medical the journalist told him, "It didn't surprise me because I was told on the Sunday ..." Wally's ears pricked up. Understandably suspicious after his black year, he cast about for an outlet for his paranoia. He picked up the conspiracy theory and the media ran it for him. The problem with the theory was that it would have required the collusion of Drs Gibbs and Cross. Wally didn't see Dr Cross arrive at the stadium to check the X-rays. Was he even there?

Dr Cross assured me he did indeed drive from his Crows Nest surgery to the stadium and although Wally did not see him, he saw Wally. Medical ethics prevented him approaching Lewis, he said. He had been consulted only for an opinion on the X-rays, not to examine Lewis or conduct the fitness test. "I was there, believe me," he said. That apart, it seems fantastic that Dr Gibbs would risk his future as a sports physician and Dr Cross his orthopaedic specialist's reputation, to wipe Lewis — a player they both admire and against whom neither held any grudge — upon the whim of the ARL.

Wally's indiscreet comments brought him a letter demanding an apology from Dr Gibbs and the anger of Ken Arthurson for bringing rugby league into disrepute. Widnes rugby league club in England, ever alert for a money-spinner, rang Wally and invited him to make a guest appearance for Widnes in their tour match against the Kangaroos. Name your own price, fly first class, chance to prove your arm was fine, they said. They were talking to the wrong Aussie. He dismissed the idea of such a traitorous act.

Wally flew to England for the second and third Tests. Jacqui would rather he had stayed home. "To me it felt like he was punishing himself by going over," she said. But Wally was not there as a tour follower. Murphy's Law — that if anything can go wrong it will — was well and truly in ascendency in Wally's life by now and had extended into his testimonial year.

9

Money Matters

Billy J. Smith, professional master of ceremonies, stand-up comic and television sports commentator, became Wally's manager after they worked together for Channel 10 at the Seoul Olympics in 1988. Some colleagues considered Smith a curious choice for manager because with his own wide diversity of employment and relaxed attitude to life, they thought Smith needed a manager every bit as much as Lewis did. However Smith knew Wally well and was innovative, always throwing up ideas and, with Wally's retirement in mind, he unilaterally declared 1990 Wally's testimonial year. ARL chief Ken Arthurson gave it the go-ahead and Smith put together a high-powered committee to run the Wally Lewis Testimonial Fund.

The committee included Channel 10 (Qld) general manager Mike Lattin, David Fordham, Doug Ryan from the Mayfair Crest hotel and the QRL Origin team manager Dick "Tosser" Turner. Various meetings were attended by Queensland Newspapers managing director Ron Richards, advertising executive John Garnsey and former Test cricketer Ron Archer. They first met on 29 January 1990, and appointed an impressive group of three as fund trustees: Jack "The Slasher" Butler of the retail food chain; Barry Paul, chairman of the Kern Corporation, property developers; and Sir Robert Mathers of the Mathers shoe empire.

The goodwill felt towards Wally was shown by the willingness of those eminent people to volunteer their time for him. Testimonial funds are complex financial structures and Bruce Hatcher, an accountant, as well as chairman of the Lang Park Trust, was asked to advise on taxation aspects. Billy J., as Wally's manager, assumed the onerous role of fund chairman.

The committee, with Wally present, got off to a roaring start. Power Brewing agreed to provide beer for functions and Australian Airlines would assist in flights. Caricaturists were to be contacted to produce drawings of Wally for sale. A Lewis family barbeque day was suggested, as was a golf day and a race day. Merchandise was to be produced to be sold all year round: T-shirts, golf shirts, caps and portraits. A show bag was to be sold at the Brisbane Exhibition and Tyrrell's Wines were to be approached for a testimonial port. The committee was unanimous that a series of country and city dinners was a high priority.

They met in the Channel 10 board room or at Ryan's Mayfair Crest hotel and an attractive logo was produced. The design, printed on the letterhead, was a small bar and medallion, the size of a 50 cent coin. The bar, in maroon and gold, was inscribed "1990, Wally Lewis Testimonial Year". The medal carried Wally's portrait and around the perimeter ran "Queensland. Australia. For Services to Rugby League".

The fund was officially launched by the QRL at Lang Park on 7 February 1990. Bernie Power of Power Brewing weighed in with $50,000. Wally was astonished. Powers, who sponsor the Broncos, had used Wally as the linchpin of their inaugural advertising campaign. During drinks after the launch Wally told Bernie, "That's terrific, but you don't have to do that." Bernie replied that it was a gift, in return for what he'd done for Queensland. Bernie joked with him about Wally's closing line in the Powers television commercial, "Sorry Bondy". Bernie knew Wally had felt a bit strange about doing that. Wally had been. Alan Bond was not a man to take on lightly in those days. The testimonial gift was quite separate from any commercial arrangements Powers had had with Wally in the past or might have in the future. The QRL — backed by Fourex — contributed $35,000. Within a week or so of opening, the fund balance was approaching $100,000. The committee's initial estimation of a return of $250,000 looked eminently attainable. Wally thought it might even reach $350,000, a comfortable nest egg for his retirement.

The show moved south in May for a launch attended by a galaxy of rugby league stars at the Sydney Football Stadium. They included Johnny Raper, Frank Hyde, former Test team-mates Wayne Pearce,

Peter Sterling and Steve Mortimer and Wally's Queensland comrades, Gene Miles, Paul Vautin and Allan Langer. The highlight came when singer Jackie Love, glamourously clad in a no. 6 Test jersey and black fishnet stockings, danced with an embarrassed Lewis and sang the league's theme song "Simply The Best". Said Wally, "I've never seen an Australian jersey look so good on anyone. The only saving grace for me was that no matter how red my face looked, not many people were looking at me." As he danced with Love, Wally thought, "What do I do here? Dance toe-to-toe or steer clear? Either way I reckon I'll get stick from the missus when I got home."

A few early committee plans fell down. The race day was killed because the clubs' schedules were fully booked. Discussions on the show bag put it in the high-risk category — a lot of work for little return. The committee also encountered a minimal, but evident, resistance from some people who asked, "Why should we contribute to this? He got paid very well for what he did, didn't he?"

The first testimonial dinner was at the Mayfair Crest on 8 June 1990, with a good line-up of speakers, including Allan Border and Hayley Lewis. Seagulls marketing manager Ron Morris remembered being surprised at the empty seats in the ballroom. Too late the committee had realised that the date coincided with the huge Stradbroke luncheon at the same hotel. Some guests stayed at the luncheon and then came to Wally's dinner at night. Others passed, or passed out. Wally drew about 247 people where he might have had 500.

The oversight convinced the committee, which had been strong on spontaneity, less so on organisation, that testimonials were labour intensive and that Billy J. Smith, as their sole active employee, was becoming overburdened. But they were too late there as well.

In March 1990, Smith informed the committee he had ordered 20,000 Wally Lewis calendars. If marketed properly they would repay the fund handsomely, he said. Smith originally negotiated with the calender company, John Sands, on a sale or return basis. But in the final contract every calendar had to be sold or paid for. It was a huge liability and had the potential to wipe out most of the contributions already received. The enormity of the deal dawned on the committee. It was irreversible and the committee was jointly responsible. "What terrified us was that it was a fait accompli," said a committee member. "We saw that if we didn't sell them we were in strife. That became a nightmare, an absolute nightmare."

As a marketing concept the 1991 calendars were in the risk venture category. Calendars by internationally known Elle McPherson or nationally known Larry Pickering, sell well. But the majority of calendars are given away, paid for by the calendar's advertising. The Lewis calendars arrived in April 1990 and moving them would have been a full-time job for an experienced sales staff. The committee had neither the staff, nor the expertise nor the time.

Smith, attempting to meet his own career obligations, to manage Wally and to direct the testimonial, became snowed under. By August he had missed a few meetings and was tardy in providing accounts. The committee wrote to him: "It is now six months since the launch of the testimonial and the delay in completing formalities is unacceptable." Even so, with so many Channel 10 personnel involved — Smith, Fordham and Lattin — the committee assumed matters were in capable hands.

Wally became concerned that testimonial ideas, such as the country dinners, were not progressing to events. Smith organised for Wally to be on the Brisbane Bullets stand at the Brisbane Exhibition to sign calendars. "I sold about 100 over two days," said Wally. "No one wanted to buy them. They'd come up with something they'd bought at the Broncos stand or another sample bag and ask me to sign that."

In late September, a committee spokesman rang Wally. "How do you think your testimonial is travelling?" Good, said Wally, should be around $150,000 by now. The spokesman said, "How does $5000 sound?" Wally asked if he meant $5000 more than $150,000 — $155,000. "No, $5000 all up," said the committee member. Wally was incredulous. He'd received $85,000 from Bernie Power and the QRL in the first week. "You'd better come in," said the committee member. The fund indeed had $85,000 in fixed assets, but had received a letter of demand for $60,000 from John Sands, and other liabilities were assessed at $20,000. Wally was shocked at his testimonial's plight.

Billy J. Smith had flown to England where he was to oversee two Lewis testimonial dinners set down for Manchester and Leeds. Events now moved quickly.

On 23 October the committee faxed David Howes, executive

officer of the English RFL, inquiring about bookings for the two dinners. Howes faxed back within hours, "Apart from an initial discussion here in this office we have had no details of date, venue, time or price of tickets or the actual menu and speakers. Therefore we have made no attempts to promote this event." That reply was in turn faxed to all committee members. The next day, 24 October, the committee met and on the advice of legal counsel, appointed a new committee with accountant Bruce Hatcher as chairman. Invited to become troubleshooters on the new committee were retired bank manager Milton Samios and professional fund-raiser Col Thompson.

The following day, 25 October, the committee faxed Smith a crisis letter outlining balances, debts and informing him of the new committee. Smith faxed back from the Royal Hop Pole hotel in Gloucestershire, "In reference to the arrangements for the accounting of the testimonial, I sincerely apologise to all concerned. Maybe the fact that I endeavoured to do things myself did not work out." Privately it was a relief for him to be free of what had become an enormous burden.

A series of exchanges then ensued about the UK testimonial dinners in which Smith advised that Manchester had only 87 bookings and Leeds just 17. The prospects for increasing the numbers to 250 to make each viable were not good. He wrote, "I realise that some people may not react favourably to a cancellation but in view of the circumstances it may be the only realistic solution." The solution meant tracking down and refunding about 100 Australian tour followers the $100 a head they had already paid to attend the dinners.

With the dinners cancelled Smith advised against spending money to fly Wally over. Already the fund was up for a 500 pounds sterling late cancellation fee for the Old Trafford Function Centre in Manchester. Smith told me, "The overseas dinners were never a financial possibility once Wally was not in the Kangaroo side. We sent letters out to all the Australians on supporters tours and the demand just wasn't there. I told them it was not feasible for Wally to come over because it would cost him thousands in air fares and accommodation alone."

My own impression was that the UK dinners may have succeeded with English fans, despite Wally's omission, provided the dates had been pushed hard by the English Rugby League for weeks in advance. The committee asked David Howes if he would accept the position as chairman of the UK fund-raising committee. Howes faxed back, "While being a great admirer of Wally Lewis I regret that …" Howes was flat out running the 1990 Kangaroos tour. The committee again found they were one step behind events.

Wally was seething. He insisted upon flying to England anyway and left on 7 November. It was an unhappy Lewis I met in the foyer bar of the Ramada Renaissance hotel where the Kangaroos were staying in Manchester. He was there ostensibly to resurrect the testimonial dinners but soon found they were beyond rescue. Jacqui wished he had stayed home. "To me it was like he was punishing himself by going over there," she said.

Unsponsored by the ARL or Channel 10, every day in England was costly, but Wally could not have stayed away. When the Kangaroos first arrived in Manchester the selection saga was still with the team and they de-Lewised themselves at training with jokes. When an elderly man arrived to watch them train, Benny Elias sang out, "Hey, Wally's here after all, g'day Wally!" Several others took up the joke, until it became a matter of wonder that someone's absence could command such attention.

By the time Wally arrived the first Test had been lost and the tourists had bonded for survival under Meninga. Alfie Langer invited Wally to the team hotel for a drink one evening. Wally told him, "I don't know whether I can mate, after the blow up I've had with Gibbs and the ARL and they're all staying there." Langer reassured him; he'd be right. That evening in the bar I witnessed a sad spectacle. Wally spied ARL chief Ken Arthurson at the bar and headed straight for him. Arthurson, seeing him, picked up a drink and turned away to ignore him. When I spoke to Arthurson later that evening I saw how offended he was by Wally's persistence with the conspiracy theory over the Kangaroo medical. Wally had never once blamed Arthurson for his omission, but Arthurson felt any slur upon the ARL was a slur upon his stewardship. Such is Lewis's media power, that he has a scattergun affect. As the Broncos learned to their cost, being in conflict with Wally Lewis meant combating also the avalanche of public support which rumbled in his wake. Even those on the periphery of the controversy, like Arthurson, got sucked into the bickering.

After the tour, on 4 December 1990, Billy J. Smith tendered his resignation as chairman of the testimonial fund and offered to cooperate with the new committee. "I tried to do too much," Smith told me. "Tried to be a one-man band and I shouldn't have. I had a job, I was fielding media questions about Wally, I was performing professionally and calling Channel 10 footie. I'd have had to be superman." And the calendars? Smith sighed. "I pretty much made that decision, I've got to say that," he conceded. "The original deal didn't end up being the eventual deal, but it was my decision, no risk about that. But I did my very best for them."

The new committee prepared for a final assault on the public's generosity. They sold calendars through the *Courier-Mail* newspaper, at BP service stations and promoted them on radio. The QRL merchandised them, newsagencies pushed them and John Sands even took 3300 back to sell at their retail outlets. In the final accounting the calendars recorded a loss of $37,358.

Thankfully other schemes, had borne fruit. From Bookworld came $20,000 for Wally's *How to Play Rugby League* book and from Tyrrells $24,000 for a commemorative port. A golf day at Indooroopilly on 3 December 1990, where guests paid $50 a head to hit off and companies paid to sponsor certain holes, returned nearly $19,000. The committee decided to extend the testimonial into 1991. Wally hit the guest speaking circuit in earnest but found public enthusiasm waning. "We were pushing it uphill," he said. "We ran into people saying, 'Hey, hang on, we've been supporting this for six months already.'"

Dinner and a golf day in Townsville netted only $1500. "I told the committee we must go to Mt Isa, the greatest sporting town in the country," said Wally. "But a couple of nights before I arrived there was a big cricket carnival night we didn't know about. Everyone had gone to it so cash was scarce for mine." Mt Isa actually made a loss of $1126.

Cairns enthused Wally when he heard that the Brothers football club had faxed down: "We've got people climbing through the windows to get tickets, selling like hot cakes." After costs the evening netted $3000. New Zealand sports fans, if not their media, have always admired Lewis and an Auckland luncheon brought in nearly $7000.

By February 1991 Wally was well and truly a Seagull and their livewire marketing manager, Ron Morris, inquired how the fund was proceeding. At that stage it was struggling towards $60,000. "It was unbelievable," Morris told me. "I always said if you couldn't make a million out of Wally Lewis you weren't trying, because he's the total marketing product."

Morris proceeded to organise a testimonial dinner at Seagulls. He booked entertainers, obtained memorabilia from Sydney clubs — socks from St George, a jersey from Parramatta, boots from Balmain — and had young women model the gear on stage before auctioning it. He sold corporate tables, promoted the night, drew over 800 diners and made nearly $18,000, one of the fund's largest single contributions. Despite everything, the community was still fascinated by Wally Lewis.

The fund-raising finished with a gala $75 a head dinner in the grand ballroom of the Hilton hotel, Brisbane on 2 March 1991. Graced by the deputy premier, Tom Burns, with Olympic swimming coach, the eccentric Laurie Lawrence as guest speaker, the night netted just over $7000.

In the final analysis the testimonial, which was supposed to last a year, ran for 15 months. Testimonials don't come cheap. Without the calendars and all the other losses, including Wally's abortive UK trip, which cost over $7000, the fund would have topped $200,000. If the new committee's energy had been spent generating fresh funds instead of dreaming up new ways to flog calendars, $250,000 might have been raised. Wally couldn't thank the new committee enough for rescuing the fund and giving his disastrous year a more cheerful conclusion.

The committee was happy with the result. "When you consider the setbacks and the tight economic times, it wasn't bad," said a spokesman. "It was bloody hard work, grinding it out is how we did it. Wally took a front-line position and worked hard too. He picked it up and ran with it at the end of the day."

The testimonial committee held its own private wind-up luncheon for Wally. "Here's a good cheque for you," they told him, and added some advice which in summation ran: "Forget about making any criticism of Billy J.Smith — it's unfounded. There was no impropriety. He took on the job in good faith, did it because he was a friend of yours and because he wanted to help. He stood to gain nothing from it himself. That it was beyond him, or any other single person, was as much the fault of the entire committee as it was of Billy J. That's all you can say against the guy. There's nothing to be gained from being bitter. Get on with your life and give people what you're capable of giving. Don't look back over your shoulder, that's all finished."

Lewis and Smith have scarcely spoken since — his second close friendship severed in the space of a year. The problem with sports managers is that few have the necessary skills in business, taxation, law and sport. There's not too many you'd feed. That's why the top US management groups take as much as 30 per cent of their clients' earnings, but they're usually worth it because they produce the deals. Wally's managers accepted the position partly because they were friends. But part of their motivation was that although stars themselves, being associated with Wally, especially in his earlier years, made them even bigger stars than they were.

Ron Morris of the Seagulls, a shrewd observer, told me, "Wally's a very intelligent man, you only have to hear him talk, but he has these blind spots. Bad management and missed opportunities have seen a lot of dollars go astray. I don't think he realised how valuable he was. For ten years he had more pulling power than any other sportsman in Australia, yet he was never fully exploited. He should have been a multi-millionaire. I believe his profile demanded that."

I noted to Wally that his first part-time, manager-friend — radio personality Wayne Roberts — had not adequately forewarned Wally of a crippling taxation debt. Now his second part-time, manager-friend, Billy J. Smith, had bumbled his testimonial. Was there a lesson in not having friends manage him?

Said Wally, "I reckon the lesson it's taught me, more than anything else, is that if you're going to be involved in any business, employ someone from that trade to do it professionally, rather than try and convert somebody. That was me being stupid and I blame myself. But at the same time my criticism of myself has always been that I've been too trusting of my friends. I reckon there wouldn't be five people now I trust in this world — wouldn't be more."

One man he had trusted — as much as a Queensland rugby league player can trust a NSWRL executive — was Ken Arthurson. "He was as close as I ever got to having an ally over the border," said Wally. "The only other bloke I ever got along with was Bullfrog [Canterbury's Peter Moore]." Wally always appreciated the difficulty of

Arthurson's role, having to placate the NSW and Queensland rugby leagues. He'd watched Arthurson cool tempers when Wally's erstwhile benefactor, the late Senator Ron McAuliffe, was vehemently defending Queensland's honour. "Ken would chip away and Ron would give a little until they came up with something acceptable," said Wally. "Mind you, it was not always easy to detect how serious old Gunsynd was. Ron would fly off the handle at NSW and walk out leaving the media shaking their heads. Then he'd wink at me and say, 'Was I harsh enough? Or do you think I should go back in and give them a bit more!'"

McAuliffe was forever telling Wally, "If anybody should tell you Queensland gets a fair go, don't believe them. Ourselves, we know what's going on." Before McAuliffe died, he told Wally with uncanny presentiment, "Arko's the only bloke who will give us a bit of a hand. Just make sure you always stay onside with him." Yet here it was, in the new year of 1991 and Ken Arthurson wasn't speaking to him, hadn't since the Kangaroo selection blow up five months earlier.

Wally unwisely kept sniping away at the ARL, not volunteering criticism but readily answering leading questions if they were asked. On 10 February 1991, on Channel 9's "Sunday Sport", he reopened the Kangaroo wound, reiterating his allegations that a senior rugby league official had prejudiced his tour chances. It became a running sore until the ARL ordered him to appear before the board on 22 March to substantiate his claims. But on Sunday, 17 March, Wally walked into the Powers box at the Gold Coast Indy race and there was Arthurson. "I had no idea he would be there," said Wally. After some hesitation Wally approached and held out his hand. "Arko was a bit stand-offish at first, which is understandable," he said. "We chatted, but we didn't mention the tour."

The next day Arthurson rang Lewis. "We've got to talk," he said. "This hasn't been much of a year for you, I'll agree, but I've got to give you a rap over the knuckles for what you've been saying. A lot of people are jumping up and down wanting to know who this mysterious ARL official is you're talking about." Wally flew down on Wednesday, 20 March, two days before the scheduled ARL board meeting. At the ARL headquarters Arthurson said, "Instead of talking about it here, in these four walls, let's go and have some lunch."

They adjourned to the Hilton grill over the road. Wally said he knew Arthurson was disappointed with his stand but recounted the incident where the NSW official had said he hoped Wally didn't tour. "That bloke, is it who I think it is?" said Arthurson. Wally named him. Arthurson assured Wally it would have been a personal view. He could not have been speaking with the authority of the ARL. Under pressure, Wally agreed with Arthurson, but insisted he did say it. He then told Arthurson of the second incident, where a Brisbane journalist was told Wally wouldn't tour. But since that journalist refused to be named, let alone to name the source of the comment, Wally could take that no further.

Two days later, at the 22 March ARL meeting, Arthurson announced the board had accepted Lewis' apology for any embarrassment he may have caused the ARL. "Mr Lewis unreservedly withdraws any implication of impropriety by any member of the ARL or its management," said Arthurson. Wally told me he had made no such admission but at least he was back on side with Arthurson, and the ARL chief had extracted his pound of flesh for the six months of aggro Wally had caused him.

I asked Wally whether, given that he had based his conspiracy allegations on the words of one drunk official and another unnamed mystery official, he regretted pushing it as long and hard as he had? "I made comments if I was asked about it," he said. "I didn't call a press conference about it and go beserk, but I wasn't going to lie down about it either." Even though it probably irrevocably damaged his reputation? "Doesn't worry me if it did. If it got me offside with people I couldn't give a damn. If, in giving my view, I upset people, that's bad luck. I wasn't going to change my mind just to stay in line with them." I said that the view existed that Wayne Pearce, when he was dropped, had copped it sweet compared with Wally who was now perceived as a whinger. Wally replied heatedly, "If people think that Junior lay down and meekly accepted it, try talking to him now, seven years later. Just ask him. Ask Junior!"

10
Sun, Surf and Seagulls

Wally Lewis' run of bad luck, which was of almost biblical proportions, ended early in 1991 when he led his family out of the wilderness of the Broncos into the land of sun, surf and Seagulls. Their lives were transformed from the moment they took a drive one weekend to look over the Tweed Heads-based club.

As a teenager Wally had spent his summers on the coast; he was a lifesaver with Nobbys surf club, and on Saturday nights invariably ended up with friends at the huge Seagulls club. "I knew the place backwards," he said. Later he invested in a holiday unit on the beachfront at Burleigh, and throughout the summer of 1990-91 he gradually spent more time there as he tired of driving to and from Brisbane for training. By January the family had moved there as well and Jacqui's delight helped to banish gloom from Wally's mind. After maintaining a vast 50-square home, tennis court, pool and large gardens in Brisbane, she now had a two-bedroom unit overlooking the beach. The surf was her salt-water pool which she never had to chlorinate.

"Jack loved it," said Wally. "Grab a towel, 30 seconds to the beach, she could see the kids for 100 metres up either side of where she was sitting, they loved it, smiles all around." Wally began work at Sea-FM radio at Southport, starting at 6 a.m. with the morning crew and back home by 10 a.m.. "Jack would call out, 'Mind the baby,' and she'd take the boys to the beach for a couple of hours. The change in her was remarkable."

They were a young family joining the fastest growing urban area in Australia. With the coast's substantial population of Victorian retirees, the Bears Australian rules side equalled the Seagulls in popularity, though Wally's presence was soon to change that. The Rollers basketball squad was the coast's third major sports team and Wally knew players like Larry Sengstock and Ron Radliff from the Brisbane Bullets.

Wally himself dropped back a gear, propping his feet on the balcony rail, contemplating the surf and the seabirds, slowly shedding the disappointments of the worst year of his life. He heard that a Broncos director had said when Wally signed for the Gold Coast, "Well that's it. We'll never hear of him again." His blood stirred but he put his anger on hold and let the Gold Coast work its healing balm.

The experiences of the past year had shaken him to his core. The hurt inflicted by the Broncos had resulted in a huge loss of self-esteem. When signing with the Seagulls, his financial adviser had told him they should push for several small concessions. "If they don't adjust the contract we get up and walk out," the adviser said. Wally was reluctant, terrified the club would object and he would have no contract, no club. He was a vastly reduced man to the player who boldly took on Kerry Packer in negotiations to join Manly in 1986. "We were just dotting the i's and crossing the t's," said the adviser. "But when the Seagulls agreed I could see the relief spread over Wally's face."

Wally introduced himself to Mike Pahoff, the Seagulls physiotherapist. "OK, I've had my couple of weeks of being depressed," he said, with some understatement. "Now I want to get back on line." Pahoff went through Wally's injuries with him, and decided he was an orthopaedic disaster. The upshot was that in April 1991 Wally had an arthroscopy on his left knee — another hospital "holiday".

Peter O'Callaghan joined him on the coast while he recuperated. "It was one of the funniest things," said O'Callaghan. "He was hobbling up the beach and some old ladies stopped him. 'We're with you, Wally,' they said. I grabbed him and said 'C'mon mate, let's keep walking,' because I knew how he hated it. But he said: 'No, no, I really need this at the moment, I've had so many boots in the backside I need to hear people say that.' So he stood there and chatted to these old women quite happily."

Jacqui found the children were welcomed at Seagulls as they

never were at the Broncos, and the boys were swift to ditch their Broncos jerseys for the Seagulls colours. Watching television one day, a Broncos commercial came on and Mitchell, Wally's eldest, grimaced and said, "The Broncos suck". Wally cuffed him lightly over the ear and asked him what he'd said. Mitchell replied, "Well they do, I heard Poppy say so." Wally looked at Jacqui, who was laughing behind her hand. She would speak to her father, she said.

Seagulls player Chris Close, star of Queensland's first Origin win in 1980, welcomed the Lewises south. "I'd known Choppy since I was 16, so that made things easier for us," said Wally. "He was one of the Origin family. Whatever anyone says, the Origin boys dig deep." Broncos reserve grade hooker Ray Herring had transferred to the Seagulls as well and Jacqui personally knew Seagulls forward Keith Neller and half Geoff Bagnall from pre-Broncos days. There was no shortage of familiar faces.

By August 1991, Wally found the three flights of stairs to his unit too hard on his knees, especially as he was usually carrying the boys, after they had fallen asleep on the way home in the car. He bought a canal-side house at Broadbeach Waters, installed a pool and erected his trademark flagpole. That was always quite a ceremony. "The kids love carrying the flag down and helping haul it up," he said. The coast is also a burglar's paradise so Wally bought a purebred bull mastiff pup as a guard dog. "He was that shy at first if you looked him in the eye he'd dig a hole and bury his head," said Wally. "And when he first barked he scared himself. But now if he barks the trees vibrate. When he lets them go nobody in their right mind would enter the yard."

Wally left Channel 10 with their blessings and his own fond memories of three years with David Fordham and Billy J. Smith in the sports department. "We got on a treat, the three of us," he said. "But if someone rang you with a news story, 99 times out of 100 you'd be suspicious because we were always setting each other up, phoney accents, phoney interstate calls ... your first reaction was, 'Where's Fordo?' "

The pranks had started the first night Wally read the news. Drymouthed with nerves, he noticed other staffers in fits of laughter. He mimed a question from the set — What's the joke? Sports reporter Terry Kennedy asked him how was the tennis story. Wally looked at his sheets and blanched. "They'd pulled out every Czech and Rus-

1989. Wally with defeated Blues captain Gavin Miller. (Photo courtesy Peter O'Halloran)

1989. Third Origin Lang Park — happier days than those to come. Wally with Gene Miles (left) and Tony Currie. (Photo courtesy Peter O'Halloran)

1989. Wally congratulates Sam Backo, the powerhouse in so many Maroon victories. (Photo courtesy Peter O'Halloran)

1989. The Blues' Des Hasler with a dilemma as Wally and Geno scheme. (Photo courtesy *Courier-Mail*)

1990. Winner, Celebrity Challenge race Australian Grand Prix, Adelaide. (Photo courtesy Live Action)

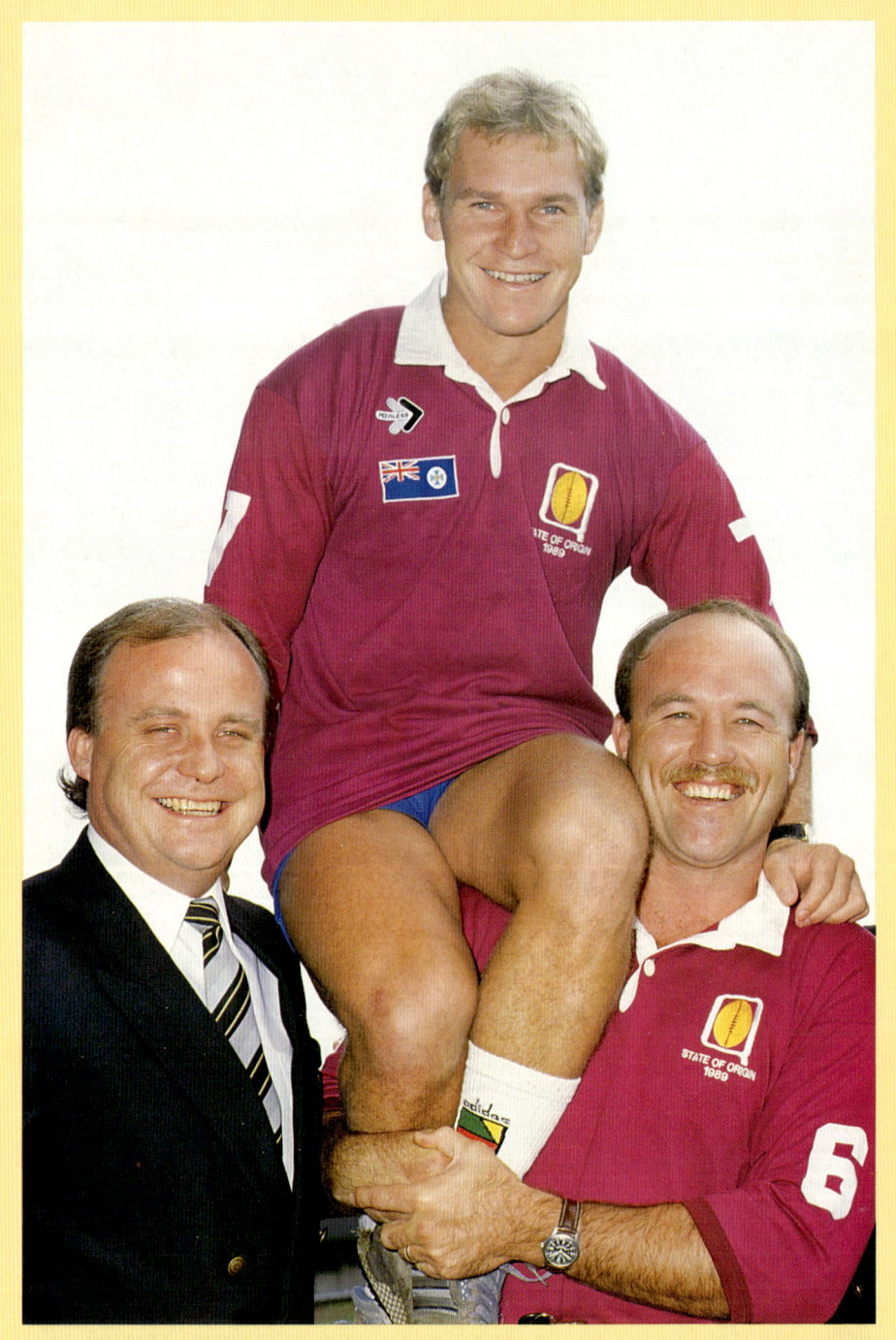

Wally with friends David Fordham and Allan Langer. (Photo courtesy *Courier-Mail*)

1990. Wally at an auction night for his Testimonial year with Broncos director Paul Morgan. (Photo courtesy Peter O'Halloran)

1991. Queensland Origin manager Dick "Tosser" Turner shows his genuine affection for his retiring captain at Lang Park. (Photo courtesy Peter O'Halloran)

1991. Lang Park pays tribute. (Photo courtesy Peter O'Halloran)

1991. ARL chief Ken Arthurson with the player he ranked among the greatest ever. (Photo courtesy Peter O'Halloran)

1991. Wally and friends salute his final Series win.

1992. Martin Bella and referee Eddie Ward follow Wally's kick-off to start his final game in Queensland — the celebrity challenge in his honour at Seagulls stadium. (Photo courtesy Double PR Photography)

sian name they could find," he said. "Navratilova, Cherkasov, Zvereva, Ivanisevich ... I practised them all to myself quickly but I got 'Ivanisevich' wrong every time. And then I was on. The blokes were roaring laughing and I started to smile too because I thought, 'Here they come' and I read, 'Meanwhile Goran Ivanisevich won through in straight sets', and I thought, 'Gees, I got it!'" As the segment went to video footage Kennedy was laughing and clapping. Wally called out, "You bastards, I didn't think I'd get that Ivanivis ... Ivanisch." And he couldn't say it again.

After a year on the news he had become sufficiently confident one evening to adlib as he read an item. However he neglected to tell the autocue operator who, as she heard the unrehearsed words, halted the autocue and wound back searching for them. That lost him. No worries, he looked down at the typed copy that newsreaders always keep in case of autocue problems. No! For some ridiculous reason he'd put the story on the bottom of his sheaf of notes and couldn't find it. A second's silence ticked by, which is like a minute on live television. Said Wally, "I looked up and went to say something and stopped. I thought 'What do I do?' And I remember thinking, 'On the football field I'd know what to do.' And then the nerves just hit me, bang! Like a lead weight. It's the only time in my life where I can say definitely that my nerves were shot."

The autocue finally caught up and Wally paused for a moment — again it seemed like an eternity — to find where he had left off. "I started to read again but I was gone because I knew I was screwing up," he said. From his peripheral vision he could see the camera operator giving him the wind up, hurry up signal. It wasn't over yet. "I made another mistake three or four words later and I could hear my voice starting to quake," he said. He stumbled over several more words before the segment mercifully ended.

As he uttered his last word he slumped back in his chair and stared wildly around. Newsreader Chris Collins calmed him: "Settle down, settle down, you'll be right." Wally gulped the glass of water in front of him, then drank Collins' water and her co-reader's as well. Collins told him, "You forgot the golden rule, always keep your copy in front of you as a back-up." Being Wally Lewis, his balls-up made the day for television gossip columnists but, on his own estimation, he eventually became a comfortable, if not skilled, news presenter for Channel 10.

When he first joined Sea-FM, the Gold Coast's top-rating station, the morning staff waited anxiously. Station manager Craig Denyer said that people had told him Wally was arrogant, prickly and unhelpful. Morning host Suki (Susan Mead) commented, "We found those rumours were absolute garbage. He was just so reliable. One morning he came in battered and bruised from a State of Origin the previous night. He was limping and one eye was almost closed from a broken cheekbone. He could hardly focus and he read the news with one hand holding his swollen eye open. We couldn't believe it. That same morning another of our staff rang and said he wouldn't be in, his wife had kicked him out of bed and he'd hurt his back!"

Wally knew he was winning friends with his punctuality. He sensed he needed to repair his name, sullied by the endless Broncos saga. He compiled and read sport in five newsbreaks from 7 a.m. to 9 a.m.. The morning crew warmed to him and helped hone his radio style. He read with the singsong voice inflection he had adopted for television. "Forget the ups and downs, just talk it," Suki urged him. "Pre-read it, underline the words you want to emphasise." Wally walked the corridors reading aloud and gradually relaxed his delivery. The morning crew occasionally took matters in hand. "Just as he was about to read the news we'd open a *Playboy* or *Penthouse* centrefold in front of him," said Suki. "You couldn't fluster him, that's his football experience, but you'd hear the smile come into his voice."

Suki soon discovered his Achilles heel — foreign names. "He'd Australianise the names of the French Grand Prix drivers," said Suki. "He'd call Jean Alesi 'Gene' and Alain Prost 'Alan'. Bjorn Borg was another. We'd go into hysterics. He'd try a few times, then say 'Oh that guy'. Or he'd say, 'Take your mouth-guard out Wally,' or at the end, 'Give yourself an upper-cut.' One day he read some tennis results and said, 'So it looks like all the big names have been knocked out.' We chorused, 'Lucky for you Wally!'" Wally denies such lapses but, paradoxically, the more he showed himself to be fallible, the more listeners warmed to him.

Wally rang his children every morning from the studio before they left for school. "OK, love you mate, have a good day at school," he'd say, then on to the next. The morning crew listened to this daily ritual, at first with disbelief, and then with growing respect. Even then they half-expected him to fail eventually in this paternal duty, but he never did. When Lewis says he is committed to his family it is no pretence, no propaganda. One morning, at the end of his call, he added, "Is mummy there? Put the old boiler back on."

Overhearing, the crew blasted him, "Wally you can't call Jacqui that, even as a joke, your children will grow up with no respect for women. It's outdated, it's disgusting." They collected a few more Wallyisms, like "All sheilas like to work on their suntan" and "Any sheila likes shopping all day long," and the crew set about exposing Wally the chauvinist.

On their star-crossed lovers segment they cross-examined him as a typical Sagittarian. With inside information from Jacqui they said, "Wally, Sagittarians are supposed to so love sport that they'll happily sit back and watch football on television while their wives are out mowing the lawn and washing the car." Untrue, absurd, said Wally confidently. The crew suddenly patched through Jacqui: "It's true, absolutely true," she said. "When I was at my most pregnant, Wally was lying on the couch while I was out there!" Jacqui was in hysterics, the crew were falling about. Wally had to laugh.

He told her, "You'll keep, you'll keep, wait until I get home!". This was all on air.

Wally has a very quick wit and a droll sense of humour yet the morning crew found he'd drop his best one-liners the moment he switched off his microphone. His DJ, recovering from laughter, said, "Wal, why didn't you say that on air?" Fatty Vautin, when he joined the electronic media, recklessly exploited his own spontaneity on air, risking the risqué. Wally, after a lifetime of controversies, was careful. He always avoided anything even a little dubious.

When Vautin flew north to promote his biography he invited both Wayne Bennett and Wally to a book signing in Brisbane. Wally declined. Fatty later drove down the coast where Jacqui chided him, "You didn't bring your driver with you?" Vautin looked blank. Huh? "You know, your mate Wayne!" said Jacqui. Fatty chuckled but had his revenge.

Wally joined him to sign Vautin's books at a Lowe's clothing store. A woman approached Wally apologetically, "I don't know you but I'll get your autograph too, young man. I know this fellow from the 'Ray Martin Show'." Fatty grinned gleefully at Wally — such was the power of television.

To overcome Wally's aloof, cautious style, Sea-FM instituted a promotion to bring him to the people — the Wally Patrols, where listeners rang and asked him to perform a task for them. Girls rang up and sang requests and others made up rhymes, but the station always chose the most outrageous dares. He had to hose out the fur seals cage at Seaworld: "Afterwards, no matter how I scrubbed, my hands and under my nails just stunk from this rancid cage," he said. He was asked to change the dirty nappies on twins but drew the line. "Lady, I've got three kids and I've changed three nappies in my life," he said. "That's it, no more. I'll dress them for you." During the requests Wally and a co-presenter kept up a running commentary on air, full of Wally asides and jokes.

The Wally Patrols were a sensation, reported in the newspaper and on television. Sea-FM reaches 100,000 on the Gold Coast and the audience loved this new, easygoing, accessible King Wally. Oddly enough, Wally enjoyed it. From a working-class background, he had always had an affinity with rank and file fans, always possessed the common touch. Gradually he changed from Wally Lewis sportsman-sportscaster to become a radio personality. When the station asked for messages of good luck to Wally in the State of Origin camp, the switchboard lit up with wellwishers.

Two years after Wally joined, the breakfast session's ratings had soared from 20 to 29.5. More important, to Wally, he became part of the labour force, and enjoyed the companionship and the satisfaction of the work. "He's fun to work with," said a staffer. "When he's away it's like there's some big part missing from the show."

The staff also witnessed how Wally would not suffer fools gladly. "He either puts up the brick wall, or goes on the offensive," said Suki. "I've heard him on the phone to some people, and boy, I wouldn't want to be on the receiving end. He can't stand people trying to make publicity out of him. He calls them crocodiles." An organiser once offered to donate $500 to the charity of Wally's choice if he would do a bungie jump. He was interested until he overheard the organiser crow that it would be great publicity for the organiser. Without a word Wally got in his car and left.

Help was at hand to vet the crocodiles. In January 1991, fully ten years after he first captained Queensland and ascended to national fame and glory, Wally finally acquired a fully professional agent. Peter Hickey was looking after champion iron-man Trevor Hendy and Test cricketer Craig McDermott when — post Billy J. Smith —

Wally's testimonial committee sought him out. "I knew it would be a challenge," said Hickey. "Then when I met him I thought, 'I'll never get close to this guy, he'll never open up.' " Hickey decided to do his job, never get upset, and if Wally complained, tell him take it or leave it.

He set out to alter Lewis' market appeal, to shake the controversy-ridden footballer tag. "I had to put him in the best light," said Hickey. "Move him from being a hero to a legend, from Mr Trouble to Mr Nice Guy." Hickey nurtured Wally's business — returned calls, followed up bookings — "Everything OK? Wally on time? Good speech?" — and was politeness itself when he declined unsuitable requests. "I'd tell them he had family commitments that night," said Hickey. "And they'd say, 'Oh, isn't it nice that he's like that.' The funny thing, it was often true. He doesn't like to stay away overnight. Hardly happened in two years. He'll even forfeit bookings if he can't get back."

Informed of this, Sydney and Melbourne television celebrity shows frequently booked Wally in early, and choppered him from the airport to the studio and back again to catch the evening flight. Once, when he landed too late for any connecting flights from Brisbane to the Gold Coast, the television station choppered him from Brisbane to his home.

Wally was on a recorded game show in Adelaide one day with Test cricket opener David Boon when the director revealed that it was a knockout quiz with quarter-finals, semis and finals. Wally calculated, "Gees, we'll be sitting around here for another eleven hours!" He led Boon in the head-to-head quiz until the final question when he unaccountably faltered, saying, "Ohh, ahh, no, sorry I don't know."

"David Boon's the winner! Thanks for playing Wally, we'll go to a break now," said the compere. Boon turned to Wally and hissed, "You bastard!" Wally grinned and congratulated Boon, saying he was just too smart for Wally. Boon said, "Too smart my arse, you'll be on a plane home and I'll still be sitting here tomorrow morning."

Professionally organised, given responsibility and respect, Wally responded in kind. "He became a great guy to work with," said Hickey. "It was rewarding to attend a function to watch him perform because everything I'd told the organisers about him would be true, and more." One of Wally's best speaking performances was in New

Zealand and the trip got off to Wally's usual hectic start. He rang Hickey an hour before his plane was due to take off from Brisbane airport. He was still on the Gold Coast, he said. "You're what!" exclaimed Hickey, because it's an hour's drive to the international terminal. Hickey rang for the the Seaworld helicopter. "This is the best part of managing Wally Lewis," Hickey told me. "The King's in trouble, everyone comes out. It's great. Anybody else you couldn't do it." Wally sped to Seaworld, choppered to Brisbane, clearances were prepared and he made his flight by minutes. "Every time there's an emergency, you mention Wally and the barriers come down," said Hickey. "It's the debt that everyone feels they owe him for putting himself on the line for Queensland. He never abuses favours and returns them with personal appearances."

On this visit to New Zealand, Wally and Peter Hickey arrived at the tiny Mangere East Hawks rugby league club, near Auckland. The hall was so packed they had to eat in the kitchen. "Must have been 500 people there," said Wally. Peter Hickey had never seen such a cross-pollination of sports types. "High society graziers to Maoris in thongs, Mercedes Benzes to clapped-out bombs, three-piece suits to labourers in singlets," he said. "They loved him, just in awe of the bloke." Wally spoke for an hour, bringing the house down with well worn jokes about those front row intellectual giants, Steve Roach and Sam Backo. He wound up, walked backstage and heard the applause turn into slow hand clapping. The club manager rushed up to say the audience wanted an encore. Wally returned to roars of approval and answered questions for another 45 minutes, departing just in time to catch his Brisbane flight.

Wally rarely has time now for evening engagements and when he does he usually performs gratis for charities. For luncheon engagements Hickey used to charge anything from $2500 to $3500 for a Lewis speech, $1000 to $1500 for a guest appearance. Yet sometimes he would halve it, depending upon the financial circumstances of the client. "He could command more," said Hickey. "But he doesn't want to get the reputation for being too expensive. He's in it for the long haul." Hickey often assisted the inexperienced. "They ring up and say, 'We'd like Wally but we can't afford him.' I tell them to sell seats at their head table and Wally will sit there for the evening. That way they collect his appearance fee. They say, 'What a great idea,' and usually ring back within a few hours and book him."

Wally really earned his money during one visit to a western NSW country town. "It was the day of their big street parade," said Hickey. "Fans camped all night along the main street for vantage points. They had a big semitrailer filled with hay and on top was a king's throne and Wally had to sit in it. He vowed and declared he wouldn't, but he did. We went up the main street slow as could be, lined with thousands cheering and waving, and at the end Wally says, 'Thank God that's over!' But before we could get off, the truck sped around the block and did it all over again!"

Hickey has fielded some strange requests on Wally's behalf. One girl had a boyfriend who she considered devoted too much time to sport — touch football two nights, indoor cricket one night, squash another night, gym another, training another. She wanted Wally to join her and her boyfriend for dinner so that he could explain that as heavily involved as he was with sport, he still made time for his family. Another family rang Hickey to say they were just down from Mackay and were planning a barbeque at Broadbeach. Would Wally like to come — don't worry, they'd bring the sausages and eggs. "It was no joke," said Hickey. "They felt that fondly towards him, he was like one of their family."

On a graduated scale of income, football was Wally's main earner, followed by Power Brewing, Sea-FM, then his own endorsements and appearances. The Queensland beer wars always disturbed him, contracted as he was to Powers personally, but aware of what Fourex had done for the Origin series and the Kangaroos. Soon after joining the Seagulls, Fourex offered Wally a reputed $250,000, spread over several years, to defect from Powers. "It was a lot more than I was getting from Powers and I felt flattered," Wally told me. "But I didn't think it would do me or Fourex any good to switch. People would say, 'Oh, he's taken Powers money, but now he's not with the Broncos any more he's deserted back to Fourex.'

Wally mentioned the Fourex offer — not the precise amount — to brewer Bernie Power, who inquired, "How much have I got to beat?" Wally demurred and asked about his future with Powers. When reassured, he told Power he was content with his lot. Power said, "Well you shouldn't be expected to stay for a figure that's a lot less." Shooting blind, he boosted Wally's money to just below the Fourex figure. They shook on the deal. "Good to have you back on board," said Power.

Wally, noting the change in ownership of Fourex, first to Alan Bond's Swan Brewery and then to New Zealand's Lion Nathan, suggested an advertisement to Power to follow his "Sorry Bondy" success. He outlined his concept. "I'm at a barbeque and a bloke asks me to get a beer," he said. "I go inside and a bloke at the fridge says, 'You want a beer?' and throws me a can. As it flies through the air you glimpse the yellow label. No prizes for guessing the brand. I say, 'No, I don't want one of those mate, give me an Australian beer.' He throws me a Powers, I open it and say, 'Ah, that's better, an Aussie beer.' Then I open a door and throw the yellow can out and say 'This one's for them' and through the doorway all you can see is hundreds and hundreds of sheep." Power roared laughing. He could count on this Queenslander.

Peter Hickey was invaluable to Wally in handling the hundreds of charity requests Wally received each year. He donated so much Origin and Test clothing for charities to raffle or auction that he ran out until the QRL obliged by supplying him with extra no. 6 jerseys. Donating jerseys was a breeze compared with the requests to visit elderly folk in hospital. "My father is dying and the one thing he wanted to do was meet Wally Lewis" — he received scores of such letters. Wally at first dutifully visited them all, shook thin, emaciated hands, looked them in the eye and tried to think of something cheerful to say. "What could I say?" he said. He was no glib conversationalist and the effort drained him emotionally every time.

Worse were the visits to Camp Quality or to children in hospital. Camp Quality, a centre at the back of the Gold Coast, is for seriously ill children. "I'd try and make it enjoyable for the kids, paint a face on myself to make them smile," he said. "They were all in a terrific mood usually, because they sort of realised they didn't have a lot of time left and whatever they had they were determined to enjoy. But you could see it in their eyes they were doing it tough. They were sick and some were balding from chemotherapy treatment. To be honest, I didn't like it, because when I left I felt so depressed, I'd have done so little."

On one hospital visit, Wally's arrival brought a smile to the pained face of a sick boy, who said hello quietly and shook hands. But after a few minutes talk the boy fell silent and turned away. His mother asked him, "Aren't you happy he's here?" The boy nodded, yes. "Then why are you crying?" Her son answered, "Because it hurts, mum, it hurts." His mother became tearful and Wally, helpless, beat a discreet retreat, tears welling in his own eyes. As he left the ward he could hear the boy's moans of pain. It was a profound shock to Wally, proof, if he needed it, that the brilliance of his own fame could never truly lighten the shadows of human suffering.

Even Jacqui didn't understand fully the impact of such visits on Wally until an old school friend's child developed leukaemia. Could Wally visit him in hospital? "Wally was really hesitant," said Jacqui. "But he went up and saw this sick little seven-year-old boy and it made the boy's day for him. He thought it was wonderful. But it really cut Wally up, took a big effort. And I suddenly realised I was doing what everyone else asks of him — to share his strength. But his strength isn't endless."

He never charged for charity appearances; indeed he demanded complete anonymity. He'd say there were to be no photographers, unless the charity needed a photo for fund-raising. They would say it was good exposure for him, and Wally would tell them, "I need exposure like a hole in the head. I've been in the paper enough times to make up fish and chip wrapping for the next 20 years." Did he mind if they put a small item in the newspaper thanking him for coming? "Thanks, but no thanks," said Wally. "I'm here, and I'm glad to help. Let's leave it at that."

Hickey protected Wally from the more heartrending requests. He devised a system of sending signed photographs to the elderly ill and memorabilia to young patients. "Would Wally do that?" the relatives gratefully asked. Yes he would, replied Hickey. But one request got through his guard, and then through Wally's as well. The Tamworth Truck Drivers Club approached Wally to visit Mathew Devins, a nine-year-old boy suffering from terminal leukaemia. Mathew required two transfusions a week to maintain a viable blood level. He knew his time was limited and he told his parents he wished he could meet Wally Lewis. During Wally's next Sydney trip he went out of his way to fly via Tamworth where the club members met him and drove to Mathew's home at 7 a.m.. When Mathew and his father opened the door the boy gazed at Wally for several seconds in surprise. His father cheerfully asked him who it was. The boy scowled in disgust. "I know who he is, but what's he doing here?" Wally laughed and gave him a football. He liked him from the start.

Mathew was a freckle-faced boy, with straight brown hair, a

cheeky grin and a worldliness natural to country kids who spend more time in adult company than with television. His illness had also made him mature beyond his years. Wally sat down to breakfast with the family while Mathew recounted his soccer exploits, 21 goals in a season. Wally told him they'd have to convert him to rugby league.

"I was there half an hour and he filled it with three hours conversation," said Wally. "He told me what the story was, how long he had to live, that he might survive to Christmas — this was November 20. He looked me straight in the eye, a terrific little kid, brave as they come." Mathew jumped in the car and rode to the airport with Wally, growing quieter by the block. "What's the matter with you mate, you're not as chirpy as you were?" asked Wally. Mathew told his father he didn't want Wally to go.

Wally put his arm around the boy, took him for a short walk on the tarmac and explained how he had to go home to see his own boys. "Mate, I think you're a brave little kid, you know the problems in front of you." Yeah, said Mathew, I know I'm going to die. Wally was once more stunned by such candour. "I started thinking, 'My God, how brave is this little bastard!' I told him, 'You've got to keep your chin up, when it starts getting you down and you're not feeling good, that's when you have to really fight and say you're going to hang on. When you wake up tomorrow you just say that you're going to wake up tomorrow too.' "

Wally kissed him lightly on the head, shook his hand and told him he'd call him in a couple of days. As the plane climbed away Wally looked down and saw the little boy's figure standing alone on the tarmac. A photograph of Mathew and Wally became the morning poster for the Tamworth *Leader* on 20 November, 1991, under the banner, "Dreams Do Come True" followed by "King Wally Visits Town".

Wally told Jacqui, "I'm going to invite him up." Peter Hickey organised a room at the Pan Pacific hotel at Broadbeach. "You can stay at my place if you like," said Wally, but Mathew was happy with seven television channels, video, and surf at his front door. Even in the space of a few weeks the disease had affected Mathew's facial nerves, giving him a lopsided grin. Wally told the Seagulls players Mathew's story and when he arrived at training, and later at a barbeque, each player welcomed him with a few friendly words.

Wally was proud of how his players responded; Mathew was prouder still.

Wally rang Peter Hickey to organise five tickets to Dreamworld — himself, his two boys Mitchell and Lincoln, Mathew and his father. Said Hickey, "I knew then how moved Wally was, because for him to take two days of his time was big stuff." The three boys got along famously. Mitchell and Mathew played Teenage Mutant Ninja Turtles and when Mathew beat the ever-competitive Lincoln in video games, Lincoln responded with his favourite saying, "Matty, give yourself an upper-cut!"

The visit ending, Mathew grew downcast and Wally told him, "Now come on mate, don't you go quiet on me again, you've had a good time and you'll be able to tell all your mates about it." Yeah, said Mathew, he'd tease them when he got back. He thanked Wally. "I guess I'm lucky really, not many kids get the chance to meet someone as famous as you," he said. Wally replied, "No Matty, I'm the lucky one, not many people get to meet someone as brave as you."

Wally rang Mathew at Christmas but never saw him again. In late January, his phone rang at 6 a.m.. "As soon as I heard it I knew I didn't want to answer it," he said.

It was Mathew's father. Mathew had died early that morning. Mr Devins said his son had been awake most of the night in pain and knew he was dying. But he had a last message for the Lewis family. "Tell Wally thanks very much, he'll always be my friend, tell Mitchell to keep practising Ninja Turtles and tell Lincoln to give himself an upper-cut." They were his last words.

Wally broke into tears on the phone. "Imagine the kid, that close to death, and he can pull a joke out like that," Wally told me. He sent one of his jerseys down and Mathew was buried in it on 21 January 1992, eight short weeks after Wally first stood at his doorstep in Tamworth.

Wally called the boys together for his first sombre task as a father. They sat there stony-faced as Wally explained. Mitchell thought it was sad. Lincoln had trouble in comprehending that he wouldn't ever get better. But a few days later Lincoln came to Wally tearfully; "Dad, I liked Matty." Wally replied that he had, too. He'd left his mark on Wally.

Jacqui insulated herself from the heartbreak. "I didn't want to get involved," she said. "It was Wally and the boys and that was sad enough without me."

From that day forward Wally decided to align himself with two charities each year and no more. He and Jacqui then closely screened any request which threatened to draw the family into such heartache. Wally was resilient enough to cope with just about anything, but he would never expose his family to such a tragedy again.

11
Track and Field

The evening of Saturday, 2 February 1991, Wally turned off the Gold Coast highway towards the Tweed Heads home of the Seagulls and struck a massive traffic jam. "Took me 45 minutes to travel under two kilometres," he said. "I thought the bridge must have collapsed or something." It wasn't a bridge collapse, but Wally's first match for the Seagulls, a trial against Canterbury. It was a record crowd of 13,189, only the second time in three years the Seagulls had filled their stadium.

Wally watched the preliminary games with club chairman Larry Maloney, who said with a grin, "Not a bad crowd." Wally gave a pained smile in return. It had crossed his mind when he signed with the Seagulls to incorporate a percentage of any increase in gate takings in his contract. This crowd was twice the normal turnout. "I'd have been a rich man in one season," he told me ruefully. Wally had signed for a reported $150,000 a year and in this match alone the Seagulls management were recouping half his fee in increased gate takings. Wally was a bargain for the struggling, publicity-starved Seagulls.

Wally was also a little nervous. The fanfare leading up to the game was overwhelming, even by his standards. Sea-FM advertised themselves as "the only station with Wally Lewis" and huge hoardings directed motorists to the Seagulls ground, "The Club Fit For A King". He had featured on the back page of the Gold Coast *Bulletin* most days, the expectation being that his mere presence would boost the Seagulls into semi-final contention. "The way it was building, anything less than winning would be an awful let-down," he said.

The scoreboard flashed "Welcome to Wally World", and spectators rose to greet him, some giving him their Emperor's genuflect. "Wallee-Wallee" chants broke out, while the piped music was the theme from *Superman The Movie*.

The Seagulls won a match memorable for Wally incidents: he scored a disallowed try from a bomb; he was sin-binned for a professional foul; and in an all-in brawl a spectator hurled a can of beer which hit him square on the forehead. "It turns out he was chucking it at the Canterbury bloke who was belting me," he said. "I remember seeing it at the last moment, just before it hit me on the melon." The blow cost Wally three stitches and the spectator a $1000 fine in court.

The crowd's reception consolidated the coast move for Wally. Although privately relaxed, to transfer from the high-profile Broncos to the down-table Seagulls was a culture shock professionally. The Broncos owners were all business men-of-the-world; the Seagulls directors mostly lived within a few kilometres of the club. The Broncos attracted national advertisers; the Seagulls could not. One moment Wally's coach was Broncos Wayne Bennett, an acknowledged innovator in the modern game; next it was the Seagulls Malcolm Clift, an innovator, but from the previous decade.

Originally Wally was to have become Seagulls captain-coach in his first year, 1991, but he delayed so long, waiting in vain upon an offer from the Broncos, that the Seagulls appointed Clift. Wally was contented. He told Jacqui, "This will be good, should make things easier." He was appointed club and first grade captain — his old Broncos positions — and soon got a taste of football, Seagulls style. He had heard that the coast's carefree holiday lifestyle had infected the Seagulls, although he could see no wrong in diving into the surf after long road runs in 32 degrees heat. Nor did he care much that players sported an odd assortment of training gear, from board shorts to cycling pants. However he did question the training regimes.

Coach Malcolm Clift, known as "Shifty", was unimpressed when Wally suggested new skills at training — bread and butter Broncos stuff. "You could tell he was thinking, 'We didn't need that in the old days,'" said Wally. He in turn watched Clift's more traditional methods — sometimes running up and down the field a few metres apart passing the ball — and asked Chris Close how the hell these were going to help them. Close laughed, grabbed some team-mates and said, "Gator's blowin' up about Shifty's style." Close told him, "Mate, down here you just roll with the punches and at the end of the day collect your cheque." Wally replied that he didn't want to do that — he wanted to win. Said Close, "Yeah, well so do I, but for now you just have to do as you're told and don't argue."

The week of the Seagulls' first round match against Wests, Wally was committed to practise for the Gold Coast Indy celebrity Grand Prix. A 4 p.m. Friday lap practice at the Surfers Paradise circuit was delayed until 5 p.m. but training at Tweed Heads was 5.30 p.m.. Wally was anxious to keep a clean slate with his new club. "I'm going to get shot," he thought, knowing he could never make it on time through the heavy coast traffic.

Enter manager Peter Hickey. "This time I got clearance for the Westpac chopper," he said. "We had it all worked out. It landed right beside the pits, Wally finished his three laps practice, jumped on board, straight to Tweed Heads." At 5.30 p.m. the players on the field at Seagulls were checking their watches asking, "Uh oh, first match, where's Wally?" They all knew the Seagulls management was watching for signs of training truancy. "Suddenly out of the sky drops this chopper," said Hickey. "They all stared up and then cleared a circle, thinking it was a TV news chopper."

The helicopter landed in the middle of the field and, like a scene from *Close Encounters*, out stepped the King, still clad futuristically in racing suit and boots. Wally walked towards Chris Close, who was laughing and shaking his head in disbelief. "Don't say a thing, Choppy," threatened Wally, looking sheepish. "Don't say a bloody word!" The arrival was a sensation at the sleepy, parochial club where most players rocked up to training in clapped-out utes.

Trainer Billy Johnstone joked, "You gave coupla the blokes a fright, Gator. They didn't know what the shit that was. Never seen one before!"

Wally always had a liking for fast driving and within weeks of arriving on the coast, the Gold Coast *Bulletin* newspaper was receiving indignant calls that Lewis' distinctive red Nissan 300 ZX had been seen zipping here, haring along there. "I like driving and I'm normally in a hurry," said Wally. The combination produced a memorable encounter with a police patrol at 2 a.m. near Beenleigh on the highway south. Wally, cold sober, returning home after a guest appearance, saw the flashing blue light in his rear vision mirror, slowed and pulled over. A furious traffic cop yanked him from his driver's seat.

"Oh, it's you!" said the officer, fractionally softening his manner. All the same, he hauled Wally to the police car where a high speed was locked on the dashboard, blinking accusingly. "That's when I managed to catch you," he said. "Before that I was flat out and you were going away from me!" Like us all, Wally has occasionally been booked for speeding but luck's a fortune. Queenslanders from the governor to the garbo would gladly forgive Wally one mistake to repay him for all the pleasure he has given them over the years. The policeman berated Wally, then noted the hour and that there was no other traffic, and said, "I'm going to follow you. If you go one kilometre over the limit I'll arrest you and throw you in gaol for dangerous driving."

In 1989 when the Broncos travelled to Bathurst for their Panasonic Cup semi-final against Souths, Wally, Gene Miles, Greg Dowling and Sam Backo had decided to kill a couple of hours by hiring a Commodore to take a spin around the Bathurst mountain racing circuit. Knowing Wally's driving, Geno and GD leapt in the back, leaving Big Sam to take the passenger's seat, all unknowing. Wally took the corners confidently but too fast for Backo, who nervously told Wally to slow down. That was his mistake. "Sam frightened a lot of players on the field but he was easy to scare in a car," said Wally.

Wally speeded up a little and Big Sam crouched down below the dashboard refusing to look ahead. Down Conrod Straight Wally revved up to 190 kph, by which time Sam, a very religious man, was praying, furiously crossing himself and equally furiously cursing Wally, in his hoarse gravelly voice. "Pull up! Bloodywell Pull Up, Willya! Wally! You'll kill us! I'll kill you! We're all gonna die!" Geno and GD roared laughing in the back seat as Wally finally eased down. When they returned the hire car, GD cheerfully advised the owner that he might as well sell the car, because it wouldn't be worth two bob after that run.

Wally may have preferred that I didn't mention these highway adventures, but it's him. He has the reflexes, the judgment, the skills to have been a racing driver. That's where he found himself back in 1988, in litre sprint cars at the Brisbane Exhibition showground where he and Gene Miles were invited for celebrity races. Wally won one race but the sprint cars weren't designed for Geno's long frame and legs. He couldn't even find a helmet the right size. "It was ridiculous watching him squeeze in," said Wally. "He was so cramped he didn't realise he had one foot permanently resting on the brake pedal and he did five laps with smoke and a shower of white hot sparks flying everywhere from his wheels."

In the second race Wally rolled spectacularly after slamming into the side wall. "I got out of the car and gave it a kick in the guts to show the crowd I was OK," said Wally. "They stopped the race, the ambulance came over and everyone rushed up to see if I was hurt. I noticed Gene on the opposite side of the track pointing me out to an official. This guy nods his head and then sprints 150 metres over to me, flat chat, arrives breathless and says, 'Gene wants ... puff, pant ... to know ... puff, pant ...' And I said, 'Yeah, yeah, I'm all right, tell him I'm OK,' and this bloke shakes his head and says, 'No, Gene wants to know ... puff, pant ... if you're finished with your helmet, can he have it?' I burst out laughing and told the bloke, 'Yeah, take it and tell Geno not to be so worried about me!'"

Wally's next motor adventure came in the BMW Celebrity challenge race at the Australian Grand Prix in Adelaide in November 1990. Wally, iron-man Grant Kenny and Hawthorne Aussie rules glamour boy Dermot Brereton stuck together, and with everything open 24 hours a day for the Grand Prix, scarcely slept in five days. "Every night was a big night and we usually ended up legless," said Wally. It was only a few weeks after the whole Broncos-Kangaroo debacle and Wally luxuriated in almost total anonymity away from the rugby league states. He said, "They flocked to Dermot, half-knew Grant and three or four thought they'd seen me on 'Wide World of Sports'. No one said a word to me."

The race field was a galaxy of sportspeople — Wally, Grant and Dermot, Wallaby captain Nick Farr-Jones, basketballer Phil Smythe, Kiwi cricketer John Wright, Olympic cyclist Gary Niewand, Olympic sprinter Jane Flemming, and a collection of politicians and television faces. Among them also was an English aristocrat, the Marquis of Blandford, immaculately dressed in professional racing gear, right down to his checked neck cravat. "Have a look at this geezer!" cracked Grant. Dermot asked what a marquis was. "A marquee's a tent," joked Wally, and they addressed James Blandford as "Tent" from then on, much to his mystification.

A serious contender for the race was an RAF fighter pilot who entertained the lads with derring-do yarns of flying at 1600 kph, of bailing out and of the emphasis placed on safety at all times. He showed his mettle in the practice laps by dwelling on the line and letting all the bunny drivers scrap away up front — one woman, a Melbourne newsreader, flicked her indicators at every corner. Without having to jockey for space, the pilot notched the fastest lap to snatch pole position from Grant and Wally.

On the eve of the race the terrible threesome followed their usual evening routine and were well away at a drivers and sponsors concert watching Normie Rowe. Next thing the boys were on stage too, Normie on one microphone, them on another, singing "Eagle Rock". By popular demand — "Idiots sometimes make good entertainment," confessed Wally — they sang a dozen songs from a lyric book, drawing more people onstage.

Eventually they looked over and saw Rowe, lazing back in a chair with a drink, declaring, "Keep going you blokes, this is the easiest night I've had for ages."

Next day at the race start Wally pondered how he'd get past Grant, one ahead of him on the grid. As the engines revved, in his rear vision mirror Wally saw a car take off through the pack seconds before the green light. "Don't know who it was, but I let go too," said Wally. Smoke poured from Grant's wheels as he took off as well. The offending back-marker who provoked Wally into a fractional fly start was politician Dr John Hewson. This gave Wally the jump on Kenny by the first corner, but he trailed the jet pilot.

The speedometers on all the cars were taped over to stop the amateur drivers worrying about their speed, but Wally wished he could have seen their top speed as he hammered down the long main straight in their BMW 318Is, probably doing 160 kph. All Wally knew was that everything was flashing by very quickly. About 300 metres from the corner he pulled out and surged almost level with the jet pilot. As they hurtled towards the bend Wally thought, "I don't know whether I'm going to get past this bloke in time." Then another thought flashed up — how the pilot had said that in aircraft he was trained always to put safety first. Wally thought, "Let's see if he goes into defensive mode." He delayed braking, delayed ... delayed ... in a terrifying test of nerves. The corner loomed up. "At the last moment I saw him suddenly decide he wasn't going to make it," said Wally. "He hit the brakes, screeched, locked up and went into a slide." Simultaneously Wally stood on his brakes, pumping with all his strength to avoid locking up, nosed into the corner, stole the pilot's line and emerged in front. The crowd at the corner roared excitedly as though it was the Grand Prix proper. That was it. Wally held his lead for the remaining four laps; Gary Niewand came second with "Tent" third.

Former world champion Jackie Stewart judged Wally's Adelaide drive as the best he'd ever seen by a celebrity driver, so Wally was firm favourite for the Gold Coast Indy celebrity challenge on 17 March, 1991. They were driving privately owned, turbo-charged Ford Lasers, not as quick as the BMWs, nor as stable with their front wheel drive. Iron-man Jon Robinson grabbed pole position, followed by Wally, surfboard champion Tom Carroll, artist Larry Pickering, iron-man Dwayne Thuys, MTV's Richard Wilkins, Grant Kenny and the usual array of personalities.

Wally was stiff and sore from the previous night's first competition match for the Seagulls, a loss to Wests. But the adrenalin started rushing as he pulled on his fireproof, orange driving suit, thick gloves and helmet. The race was a rolling start and Jon Robinson confided to Wally beforehand, "Why don't we get going early and leave the others for dead?" Wally told him they would be black flagged before they even reached the start. But forewarned was forearmed.

"I watched him and sure enough 100 metres out, he's had a glance at me and pissed off and I started laughing, it was so blatant," said Wally. "I went with him and then thought, 'I'll see if he scares, this iron-man,' and I swerved over on him. But he hardly backed off so I knew I'd have to go right to the wire with him."

Coming to the first corner they were dead level and again Wally made it a test of who would blink first. "I thought, 'I'll brake now,' and he didn't, and then ...' I'll brake *now*' and he didn't and then ... 'Shit, I'd better brake NOW!' " But a nano-second earlier Robinson flinched, eased back. Wally used his gears, double de-clutching to maintain engine speed while helping slow the Laser down. He slipped through into the lead, one wheel riding the chicane gutter, and held Robinson off until they stretched out along the beachfront. "At the next corner I saw Robbo drift to have a go on the inside so I stayed wide to get some pace off the bend," said Wally. He attacked the corner, stealing Robinson's space and the iron-man, his line gone, braked hard.

Close behind, Larry Pickering nosed inside Tom Carroll and, when Robbo suddenly braked, Pickering clipped his tail, spinning him into a safety wall of tyres. The entire field slowed to pass the prang and when Wally next glanced back he was 100 metres in front. Grant Kenny had emerged from the pack to be second.

"Wally, can you hear me?" asked Darrell Eastlake over Wally's helmet radio link to Channel Nine's live coverage. "Yeah mate, gotcha," replied Wally.

"Listen Wally, Jon Robinson just went spinning out behind, did you see the shot?" Eastlake said. "Yeah mate, bit of bad luck, wasn't it?" came the response. For the rest of the race Wally chatted to Eastlake, occasionally meeting and disposing of challenges.

"Tommy Carroll the surfer's coming up behind you through the pack, he's driven at Adelaide, had a bit of experience, so he might give you a bit of a run," said Eastlake.

"Yeah well, Tommy went like a mad dog in training yesterday, he was the real dark horse for the race. I'm expecting him to put in some work in the last two laps," said Wally.

But Pickering pranged Carroll as well and then Dwayne Thuys spun twice, leaving Kenny as the last challenger. "I expected that from Grant the iron-man," Wally told Eastlake. "If he tries to pass me I guess I'll have to use a little bit of elbow room."

Former world Formula One champion Alan Jones told viewers, "The ability to be able to talk to us while he's going through the corners is not an easy thing to do, I can tell you. You really have to concentrate 100 per cent. To have us screaming down his ear and answering back is no mean feat."

"Are the concrete walls a bit daunting?" asked Eastlake.

"Well mate, if they were made of something softer you wouldn't mind because ... WHOOOAA!" Wally stopped talking in a hurry as he misjudged a bend and narrowly missed a wall.

On the last corner of the last lap Dwayne Thuys managed to roll his Laser, but was unhurt. At the chequered flag it was Wally from Kenny and Carroll. Thuys had joined them for a drink and a laugh in the pits tent when Thuys suddenly exclaimed, "Oh gees!" The owner of Thuys' Laser was sprinting up the track, calling out, "Hey, hey you!"

Thuys said, "Shit! I'm in trouble, this bloke's going to hammer me for rolling his car." Wally told him not to worry, the owners all knew the risks when they lent the cars. The owner arrived. "You rolled my car!" he exclaimed. Thuys began an effusive apology.

The owner interrupted, "No, mate, no, I want to thank you. That will be front page exposure for me in every city in Australia. I couldn't buy that sort of advertising." Thuys laughed with relief and sure enough, next day, there was Thuys on his roof on most front pages.

In Adelaide, driving with Frank Gardiner, Wally noticed how, at 140 kph, Gardiner would ease the car into a corner, take it to the limits and ease it out again. "He was a genius driver, used to do stunt driving for movies," said Wally. On another occasion he went three laps beside Dick Johnson at Lakeside raceway. "He caned it, went 1.8 seconds outside the lap record with me on board, an extra 95 kilos," said Wally. "When we got back he said it was running a bit rough and I said, 'Dick, that might be because I had both feet pressed through the floorboards after one of those corners.'"

The experiences showed Wally that he could no more enter top class car racing at his age, than racing drivers could take up Origin football. "They absolutely fly, those blokes," he said. "The difference between them and normal driving can't be compared. I'd like to have a go at Bathurst, not in the big race, in a race for standard street cars."

Football was Wally's game but all his vast skills couldn't transform the Seagulls into Jonathan Livingstones. After they lost their second match of the season, to Manly at Brookvale, Wally sat in the dressing room, his nose bleeding and broken, and sighed, "It's going to be a long, hard year." He had put on a virtuoso display of cut-out, flick and inside passes, grubber, line and high kicks, all to no avail.

The Broncos saga gave one last lurch mid-season. Wally missed the first round match against his old club through injury. He was incensed when the Broncos, to draw a good crowd, continued to promote the match as though he would play. "It was dishonest to use me as a promotional tool," he said. "And hypocritical given their refusal to re-sign me." The second round match then became the great Lewis-versus-Bennett clash although, as Wally said, "As far as I know, Bennett isn't going to be on the field." Wally had an ordinary game, in fact his first 50 minutes were so shocking he took himself off. "I'd built myself up so much for the game, maybe I overdid it," he said. Though the Broncos won, Bennett excused their unimpressive form as being because they had been dragged down to the Seagulls' level. Wally said mischievously, "When I read that I thought, 'Looks like Wayne must still have some character building to do there.'" Perhaps Bennett was conscious that, in their first season without Lewis, the Broncos were heading for their worst premiership finish — seventh — since their inception.

At the Indy race Wally had begun the process of reconciliation with Ken Arthurson to open up the possibility of national selection again. An Origin spot was the first step. "I knew a few people were still crooked at me for blowing up about missing the tour," Wally said. "I wanted to get back in and show them all." He played his best for the Seagulls but at the back of his mind he was thinking about the Origins. He had so many points to prove.

The difference between Wally's fortunes with the Broncos and the Kangaroos, and with the Origins was that Queensland gave Wally the unquestioned loyalty, respect and faith he never received from the Brisbane club or the national selectors. There was never a doubt that Wally would be preferred to Kangaroo captain Mal Meninga to lead Queensland in the 1991 series. Meninga went south, didn't he? End of story. The pure maroon spirit that runs in the veins of the QRL selectors, general manager Ross Livermore and Origin manager Dick Turner, is the same that imbued the old warhorse himself, Senator Ron McAuliffe. Coach Graham Lowe comprehended that as early as January when he said he wanted Wally as skipper — no offence to Meninga.

The Lewis-doubters once more set up their caterwauling, reliably led by former Australian captain Ian Walsh. In his *Telegraph Mirror* column he called upon Lewis to retire with his reputation as a post-war legend intact. "He's in the Queensland side on a sympathy vote ... on form this season he's certainly down from Olympus to being a mere mortal."

When NSW chose Cliff Lyons to defend his Kangaroo five-eighth position and left Laurie Daley at centre, Wally breathed easier. He had accounted for both Cliff and Laurie before, but Daley had the potential to provoke battles on the scale that Wally once fought with Brett Kenny, except that Wally was now 31 — 10 years older than Daley.

In the first Origin of 1991, at Lang Park, NSW once more failed to live up to being perennial favourites. That they didn't may be attributed to one man, Queensland's 198 cm (6ft 6ins) fullback Paul Hauff, a replacement for injured Gary Belcher. In the first few minutes Hauff was the only player between a try and the electric speed of Greg "Brandy" Alexander on a clean break. Yet Hauff wrapped him up. Then in his second trial by speed, Hauff fenced in the equally quick Andrew "ET" Ettingshausen after a similar break.

"I've rarely seen a bloke more nervous than Hauffy before the game," said Wally. "When he saved those tries the blokes went to town congratulating him and he grew bigger and bigger with confidence. With his long legs he doesn't look like he's going that quick. Neither Brandy nor ET would have thought he'd cover them. But he did it easily."

Wally played a commanding role, growing in confidence himself, until just before half-time he essayed a big hit on ET. "He lifted his elbow up, like 99.9 per cent of blokes do to protect themselves," said Wally. "And he caught me in the left eye. Gees it hurt!" As they ran on after half-time Wally tried to clear his nose and knew immediately he shouldn't have. His cheekbone went "pop" and a sharp pain stabbed across his eye socket. "It was the worst thing I could do," he said. "My cheekbone started to swell, my eye closed and I had trouble focusing." His black eye was a fractured orbit, an injury similar to that he suffered to his right eye in the third Origin in 1989. He should have gone off immediately but he chose to ignore it. He had too much at stake on that field. He justified that decision 15 minutes from full-time when he and Mal Meninga demonstrated why any team including two players with 47 Origins between them should never be underdogs in any match.

Queensland had possession close to the NSW line. "I saw Blocker Roach standing out wide and I picked on him straight away as one bloke I could outsprint," said Wally, stating the facts, yet having half a dig at his friend Steve Roach. He outflanked Roach, committing the next Blues defender to leave his post opposite Meninga. Mal, unmarked, suddenly veered inside and with exquisite timing Wally dropped the ball in his arms. "It was a great pass," said Meninga later. "They always are. You expect that from him." Meninga now had a ten metre charge to the line with only Alexander to stop him.

Said Wally, "I turned around to watch Mal just as I hit the ground and I could see Brandy standing at fullback thinking, 'What am I going to do here!' If you've got a bus up against a Mini Minor you know which is going to give ground."

NSW scored a late try but Queensland led 6-4 as Meninga kicked off from halfway with a minute to full-time. He took three steps and effortlessly booted the ball straight over the dead ball line on the full — penalty NSW. Mal turned to Wally in anguished astonishment. "I didn't even try to kick it that hard," he said. All Wally could think was that after playing so well it could now finish a draw, 6-6.

Alexander raced up to take the kick. "We felt safer with Brandy than if Mick O'Connor had taken it," said Wally. "We didn't think Brandy would get the distance." Alexander didn't and Wally, positioned in front of the posts, caught the ball. As he did former Broncos team-mate Chris Johns tackled him and the final whistle blew. "You bastard!" exploded Johns, frustrated at having played in his fourth consecutive losing Origin.

Wally was voted man-of-the-match though Gene Miles, Greg Dowling and Barry Muir, and indeed Wally himself, all thought Paul Hauff deserved the honour. However the award reflected the sentiments of the crowd, players and the media. Mal Meninga thought Wally was getting better with age. ARL chief Ken Arthurson said, "To see him play like that and get such a wonderful reception from the crowd was magnificent." *Telegraph Mirror* doyen Peter Frilingos and former Test half Tommy Raudonikis, in the Brisbane *Sun*, both said they would have to eat humble pie for doubting Wally. Ian Walsh wrote exasperatedly, "Does NSW realise they let a one-eyed, one-armed man with a crook knee and short of condition treat them like puppets?"

Inevitably discussions began about whether Wally would reclaim his Test captaincy from Meninga. Arthurson summarised it, "Wally has a proven record as a captain, Mal is a champion player, an inspirational leader and nature's gentleman off the field." Meninga generously said he would step aside for Wally. "He would have been captain on the Kangaroo tour had he been fit," he said. The next sensational Origin at the Sydney Football Stadium settled all that.

NSW won it 14-12 on a waterlogged field after Michael O'Connor kicked a magnificent sideline conversion two minutes from full-time, tying the series 1-1. All that was secondary to the way in which the game changed Wally's destiny. Origin matches are played at high speed with hammer hitting and hot tempers, and heavy rain that night did not cool this match. New South Wale's forwards, notably Mark Geyer, asserted a dubious physical authority and Wally kept up a running appeal to Queensland referee David Manson, "Come on, Dave, they're going a bit high!" Manson assured him that he knew, and he'd look after it.

As the half-time siren sounded, hooker Steve Walters took the ball up and virtually dropped into Mark Geyer's tackle. Geyer, more intent upon maintaining aggression than inflicting real harm, swung a left arm at Walters' head as he went down and then half-chopped down on his neck as well. Andrew Gee stepped in and pushed Geyer away, Geyer swung an instinctive punch at Gee but missed. Then Wally interceded, spearing in to push Geyer away. Michael O'Connor jumped in between Wally and Geyer and absurdly, in the madness of melees, he and Wally ended up wrestling on the ground. "I didn't even know it was Mick until we got to our feet," said Wally.

By then the brawl had spread to anyone who thought they had a past grievance, although why Canberra club-mates, Ricky Stuart for NSW and Gary Coyne for Queensland, decided to grab jerseys shows how random brawls can become. Wally's first words to Manson when order was restored were, "That was totally uncalled for, David," referring to Geyer's chop at Walters. Meninga backed Wally up, yelling, "How about his elbow!" Wally fully expected Geyer to be penalised or earn ten minutes in the sin-bin. Geyer told Manson, pointing at Wally, "What about this bloke? He started it by rushing in." Wally exclaimed, "What! You used your bloody elbow, that's what started it!" Manson told Lewis, Geyer and NSW captain Benny Elias to shut up. Geyer accused Wally of trying to run the game. Wally stepped up nose to nose with Geyer and said, "You dog! You've been going high every tackle." Geyer screwed up his face in anger and flexed his fists as Manson separated them. Wally was infuriated that Manson, after general cautions, did not sin-bin Geyer.

As they all turned towards the dressing rooms Geyer and Wally were still exchanging insults and Geyer deliberately skirted captain Elias and stepped in Wally's path. Wally told me, "He turned around as if to say 'Come on, if you want to have a go, have a go now.' I wasn't going to walk around him so I pushed him out of the way." Geyer shaped up, Manson leapt in once more and Elias lightly held Wally back, telling him, "Come on mate, let's just get off." Wally seethed, "Benny, your bloke started it!" Geyer, white with anger, cursed the air as he ran off. Wally was cursed by the crowd as he departed.

In their change room the Queenslanders were incensed with Manson as much as Geyer. "It just seemed we were playing under a different set of rules to those we had every other week of the year," said Wally. "Our blokes were asking, 'What's going on here? There's high shots going left, right and centre.'"

Wally decided to bait Geyer in the second half. He told the team, "He'll come out and do something crazy. Just give the ball to me and I'll run at him. If he blows up he'll go for sure." Geyer brooded until 11 minutes into the second half and then, in another fit of ill-considered and overzealous aggression, he cocked his elbow and felled Paul Hauff with a blatant forearm jolt. Geyer hastily back-pedalled, Peter Jackson hurled after him, Gary Coyne punched him. Geyer was like a wounded lion at bay before jackals. "Jacko absolutely snapped," said Wally. "Very rarely see him go beserk. And Coynie, I don't think I've ever seen him lift a hand before that match or since."

Another brawl ensued but this time Wally ran from group to group, pulling his players away and screaming, "Get out of it! Get back! He's gone, he'll get 12 months for that!" Wally was still calming his players, "Don't worry, he's gone ..." when he heard Manson blow a mere penalty against Geyer. Wally turned to him, "David, you've got to be kidding! That's the worst thing I've seen since the Les Boyd thing." Manson ignored Wally as other players began hurling abuse, "You've got no balls, no guts David!" They all knew him and were amazed because Manson never allowed violent play in Brisbane football.

"Manson was responsible, completely," said Wally. "There's never been anyone sent off in State of Origin football. After the match our blokes were saying, 'Well we know what to do in the third match, we can do whatever we like and we won't get sent off.'" In Manson's defence he said he was unsighted on Geyer's charge at Hauff, rather like a linesman in tennis.

Queensland coach Graham Lowe called Geyer a "lunatic", and the QRL cited Geyer to appear before the ARL judiciary. After the game Wally was disturbed to notice prominent NSWRL officials clapping Geyer on the shoulder and congratulating him for standing up to the Queenslanders. Sure enough, it was Wally who began copping the flak.

One photograph did the most damage, the scene of a snarling Wally, nose to nose with Geyer, at the height of their half-time barney. The rain was pelting down, Wally's wet hair was flattened on his scalp, Geyer's body posture was that of a man on a hair-trigger. The look on Wally's face was so venomous that all others in the photograph — the two linesmen, referee Manson, Benny Elias, even Geyer himself — seemed to pale before his rage. Wally's expression promised terrible retribution, almost cosmic, as powerful as the elements themselves. Said Ken Arthurson, "Geyer has been cited and a Queensland player can consider himself very lucky not to be cited as well. I won't name the player, but I think it's fairly obvious who I'm talking about." NSWRL general manager John Quayle had no such qualms. In the Brisbane *Sunday Sun* on 2 June, he said, "We're not going to cite Lewis and get him on the front page which is exactly what he wants." Quayle himself should have been cited for such discriminatory remarks which demonstrated clearly the contempt he held for Lewis. No further evidence was needed to understand the depth of antipathy NSW felt towards Lewis and his uncompromising stance as a Queenslander. Geyer was suspended for six matches, missing the deciding Origin.

Yet Wally remained the culprit. "Lewis' snarling, inflammatory display ... will most likely see him struck off as captaincy material," wrote Ian Heads in the *Sydney Morning Herald*. So be it, said Wally. "I don't regret what I did," he told me. "I was standing up for one of my players. Perhaps I should have shut my mouth and moved away, but I don't believe I have to back away from issues like that. If it happened tomorrow I'd probably do the same thing all over again. Just remember — I was protesting against the foul, I didn't commit it." Later, on his video, *Long Live The King*, Wally was more conciliatory. "Maybe I should have had the common sense to settle down more. I guess that's part of my makeup," he said.

The third Origin would decide the series. The scene was set for yet another titanic finale to an Origin series. After the previous year's farce in Melbourne, Wally had made that promise to Tosser Turner: he wouldn't retire until Queenland regained the shield. He became especially focused as the media counted down the two weeks to the night of nights, already a Lang Park sellout. He ignored the controversy about the Sydney blow-up, he ignored speculation about the Australian captaincy, he concentrated on the event which for so long had been his showcase. As he went into camp with the team his club struggles with the hapless Seagulls faded into obscurity. Wally's creative genius only exploded into flower under the heat of fire. The older he got the greater the challenge needed for him to burn as brightly as the previous year. Well he had it now, the third Origin of 1991.

Yet just as Wally believed that nothing could surpass in importance this approaching night of personal justification, an event of stunning intensity overtook his life. It reduced the Australian captaincy, that acrimonious Sydney match and, yes, even this decisive Origin at Lang Park, into comparative insignificance. Football would never mean as much to him again.

12

Jamie-Lee Lewis

At 7 a.m. on Tuesday, 11 June, 1991, on the eve of the third State of Origin, Jacqui Lewis took her daughter Jamie-Lee to St Andrews hospital for tests on her hearing. The complex procedures meant Jamie-Lee had to undergo a general anaesthetic, a serious decision for the Lewises. Jamie-Lee, born on 7 June, 1990, was not quite 12 months old. Jacqui sat down with her mother to wait. Wally told manager Turner and coach Lowe of his daughter's tests and joined them in the hospital waiting room soon after. Though the Lewises were concerned about Jamie-Lee's hearing, the tests were being done to discover what, if anything, was impeding her ear canals; it should then be possible to remedy it. They were optimistic. There was no reason to be otherwise.

Jacqui had no problems in pregnancy and talked to her baby in the womb because, she says, babies can hear in there. She was careful of her health while carrying Jamie-Lee. She doesn't drink or smoke, doesn't take vitamins and is reluctant to swallow so much as an aspirin. Wally attended the birth, as he did with the two boys, and Jacqui breastfed her new daughter for nine months. In looks, Jamie-Lee is a throwback to the Ballingers, June Lewis' side of the family. Imagine a child with Jacqui's twinkling personality but Wally's solid build and tunnel-visioned determination. In that bundle of non-stop action, the King met his match. Jacqui said he wouldn't even rouse at his tiny daughter if she made a noise when he was putting at golf.

By the time she was six months old she rambled so much in baby language that Jacqui's brother-in-law told her, "Don't bring that kid over here, she talks more than you do!" Her favourite word was

"Mummumumum." Between seven and ten months however, she contracted successive flu viruses and began tapping at her head with her clenched fists. At her worst she screamed with pain and pointed at, or clawed at her ears. Wally and Jacqui began the usual parental round of doctors for antibiotics. Nothing seriously wrong, they were assured.

About that age they noticed Jamie-Lee would occasionally not respond to their call. Her brothers would sometimes tap her on the shoulder from behind to attract her attention. But at other times she responded so quickly, whipping around, ever alert, she allayed any concerns. "What worried me was that she didn't jump to the telephone and most kids do that really early," said Jacqui. Then came the smashed plate incident. All three children were engrossed watching television and the two boys swung around instantly at the shattering noise. "What's that?" they chorused. But not Jamie-Lee. She kept watching the screen.

That did it. Wally and Jacqui booked her in for the St Andrews tests. Shortly before, Jacqui had flown to Sydney for the second Origin. Paul Vautin's wife, Kim, picked her up from the airport. "Isn't it good that someone has finally listened to your suspicions," said Kim, when Jacqui was discussing Jamie-Lee. "In a couple of weeks it will be all fixed." Jacqui noticed that Kim's little boy Matthew, three months older than Jamie-Lee, was responding to a wide range of noises — doorbells, car doors, whistles. The contrast made her thoughtful. "You're really watching, aren't you Jack," said Kim worriedly.

Wally went into camp for the third Origin in Brisbane and had his hands full carrying out instructions from Graham Lowe, who was still in Sydney recovering from a blood clot in his leg. At one stage Lowe addressed the players from his hospital bed in a telephone hook-up. "He sounded surprisingly well," said Wally. "But you could hear his heart monitor going beep, beep, beep, in the background. It drew the blokes closer together because he was very much a players' coach. Some coaches you respect but you wouldn't talk to them if they weren't coaching you. For Lowie you'd do anything."

Ken Arthurson visited both camps to warn them the ARL would not stand for a repeat of the Sydney match's spite. Wally listened and permitted himself an ironic thought — "One moment the league bosses were congratulating NSW on standing up to Queensland, then suddenly it becomes a disgraceful performance." Wally gave up all hope of the Test captaincy after Arthurson cast doubt on whether he would even make the side. The communication lines were down once more on that friendship.

On the Friday night before the Origin the Queensland team enjoyed a traditional social evening out. Occasionally they would visit the Cafe Neon club, a nightspot within a good punt of Lang Park. The sight of this larger-than-life group usually produced a mixture of awe and bravado among other patrons. "A few come up and say good luck," said Wally. "An occasional young drunk will shoot his mouth off but if someone like Sam Backo turns around and says, 'What did you say?' it quietens them down."

This evening they drank at Rosie's Tavern in the city and as a woman passed, one of the players reached out and pulled the woman's dress zipper about ten centimetres down her back. It was a childish, provocative act, though not deserving of the end result. The girl's escort, a slim young Army lad full of Dutch courage, confronted Peter Jackson — 190cm and 99kg (6ft 3 ins, 15st 9lb). Entirely innocent, Jackson denied the accusation but mischievously pointed at a team-mate beside him. The soldier started swinging and it was on. Wally watched from the bar and stayed well clear, leaving soon after, but some players delayed and became involved in another stoush with security guards. One of the major antagonists, who was very drunk, belied his reputation for gentlemanly behaviour off the field, but shall remain nameless.

The Queensland camp drew close together under coach Lowe's influence. Apart from his technical knowledge, Lowe's great strength lay in his ability to touch each player emotionally. He had the ideal approach to the growing tension of this deciding Origin. Wally felt the team's fate was in safe hands as he drove to St Andrews hospital the day before the match and sat down with Jacqui and her mother to wait.

Jacqui: "We sat in this waiting room for an hour. A little boy went in for his operation after Jamie-Lee, got his tonsils and adenoids out and was back out before her. That's when I started to worry. I thought, 'Something's wrong, something's wrong.' I wanted her out of there."

Wally: "I got uneasy. Jacqui kept talking more and more and I tried to calm her down. After nearly two hours I just went quiet and tried to prepare myself for the worst. Then this nurse came out and said the doctor would see us around the back. My heart stopped and I started thinking, 'This can't be true.' We started walking and Jacqui was talking non-stop."

Jacqui: "We seemed to walk forever and it grew cold near the operating theatre. The doctor was standing there still in his operating gown and he said 'Come in here,' into this little waiting room. You could see the sorrow on his face, that he was going to tell us something sad and that he hated having to do it."

Wally: "He looked at us and after a little preamble, and I was holding my breath, he said, 'Your daughter is profoundly deaf.' Jacqui just collapsed. There was a couch and she just fell on to it weeping and saying, 'No, no, no!' I could feel the tears pricking the back of my eyes but I thought I'd better stand up here because she wasn't handling it too well."

Jacqui: "I fell into a heap but thankfully Wally kept his cool, he started asking questions because he wanted to know. I didn't know what 'profoundly deaf' meant. The doctor said you don't get any worse than that. I stood up and asked, 'Is there any chance she'll hear again? Is there any operation?' and he said, 'No, there's nothing we can do.'"

Wally: "I didn't hear the first 30 seconds of his explanation. Then I asked where she was. Could we go and see her?"

When they returned to the waiting room upstairs, Jacqui's mother took one look at Jacqui's face and burst into tears too. Jacqui ran to her, distraught, "Mum, she's deaf, she's never going to hear!" At 4 p.m. Jamie-Lee was discharged. Wally, who had returned from the team hotel, bought her a chocolate bar and a drink but she was cheerful enough. "It was funny," said Jacqui. "The little boy who'd had his tonsils out was crying and his parents smiling, and here's us crying and Jamie-Lee smiling."

Jacqui's sister Kaylene, who works with children with special disabilities, arrived and put Jamie-Lee's deafness in perspective. "Come on," she urged Jacqui. "There's children with far worse problems than Jamie-Lee's." Wally and Jacqui knew that, but it would take them a little time to adjust and they knew they would have to endure it all over again when the news became public.

"I knew what to expect later because even our doctor was shocked," said Jacqui. "He reacted like a person off the street would.

You know, 'Wally Lewis's kid deaf? King Wally's kid with a problem? No, no, no. This is the man that's got everything.' Even the doctors were a bit in awe of Wally. They weren't immune either."

Wally wanted to stay with his family but returned dutifully to afternoon training, which was winding up at Lang Park. As soon as he arrived, television camera crews zeroed in — why had he missed training? Wally flew at them and then apologised. How were they to know? Manager Turner stared hard and asked, "Everything all right?" Wally began to explain but stopped, looking down, tears filling his eyes. "Oh, no," said Turner quietly. "It can't be, the poor little kid."

Turner whispered to Graham Lowe, who called the retreating players back and said, "Listen fellas, we're going to train for a few more minutes yet, let's get back out there." The players light-heartedly complained but word spread quickly among them and they drew Wally into their midst. The waiting journalists heard too and to Wally's relief acquiesced to his request for no interviews about Jamie-Lee.

Back at the hotel Wally put his training gear away, sat down, picked up the framed photograph of his family which he always placed on his bedside table in camp and gazed at Jamie-Lee. All the emotions he had kept pent-up, so he could be strong for Jacqui and carry on his role as State captain at training, suddenly welled up and he wept quietly. He felt somehow guilty. Maybe he was responsible. But then the boys were fine. It didn't make sense.

There was a knock at the door and one of the team trainers entered and offered his sympathy. Wally accepted his words politely, wishing he could be left alone. The trainer then added that he knew how Wally felt. He had a lad with a terminal illness who might not reach 20. From his charity visits to hospital Wally knew how the trainer must feel. Wally pulled himself together. "Gees, I'm sorry to hear that, I didn't know," he said. "Yeah", said the trainer. "It's the way it goes, it's not a real fair life sometimes, is it?" No, it wasn't, Wally agreed. Such a sad confession dwarfed his own burden.

The trainer left and Wally pondered how random fate could be. "There I was feeling sorry for myself and here's this bloke far worse off," he said. "By coming in he made me feel better but it probably didn't help him, reminding himself." So Wally, having stepped onto the ancient road of grief, guilt and relief, dressed and joined his team-mates for dinner, but he couldn't stay. He drove to spend the evening with Jacqui and the children at her parents' house at Hawthorne and returned late to the hotel.

Next morning at 7.30, the phone rang in Wally's darkened hotel room. It was Sydney talkback host and football coach Alan Jones. He'd like to talk to Wally about Jamie-Lee. Wally started to grind his teeth. He'd always got on well with Jones and thought, "This is not like Jonesy, he'd respect my privacy, surely." Wally replied that he'd prefer to keep it quiet. Jones told him, "Mate it's everywhere, it's news." I could not find any report about Jamie-Lee in the Sydney or Brisbane morning newspapers of that day. If it was already news it must have been the electronic media which released it. Few media incidents have upset Wally more than the use of that story on the day of the Origin. He knew it must emerge eventually but this was too soon. He was distressed that his intimate family life should become public by such instant exposure.

Perhaps the unfairest, and most grotesque, slander ever spread about Wally was the pub talk that he had exploited his daughter's disability to satisfy some supposed craving for publicity. An occasional letter berated the Lewises for their concern about their daughter. "My God what's wrong with these people, she's only deaf!" The Lewises were not allowed to be normal. They were expected to live up to a media-made image of the perfect family unit. Neither parent ever reacted excessively or said it was the end of the world for them. As great as their private sorrow was, the early media exposure forced them to overcome their grief rapidly to cope with the public's curiosity. After the initial shock, the Lewises bounced back bravely and didn't feel sorry for themselves thereafter. As Jacqui told me, "I never once thought, 'Why me?' Because I wouldn't want it for anyone else's child either."

Jacqui slept badly the night following Jamie-Lee's tests, and in the morning drove to the hotel to deliver Wally's football boots, which he had forgotten once again. He'd slept poorly too. He rang Jacqui several times that day. They had so much to discuss. They were learning a great deal about Jamie-Lee and how she had come to respond so often as if she really *could* hear. She had learnt "Mum-mum" by instinctively lip-reading and she had seemed to respond to people calling her name by using senses other than sounds. She felt floor vibrations when people walked near her, felt breezes when doors opened, saw shadows of people approaching, followed other people's gazes. Sometimes she had turned by chance, just as her name was called. When Jacqui had taken her to clinics she moved all their bells and guessed at all their noises because nobody bothered to hide their actions from her eyes.

Friends later asked the Lewises, "Surely you must have been able to tell she was deaf?", but Jamie-Lee's other faculties were supersensitive. She had a keen eye and an educated peripheral vision, and she had deceived everyone, including doctors. They had treated her for a variety of ear infections and conditions which, they said, could explain her variable hearing. They also interpreted her lack of speech as the "third child syndrome" — the youngest who doesn't bother talking because she cannot communicate at the same level as the older children, or because they speak for her. Jamie-Lee's declared deafness was a revelation to Wally and Jacqui. Everything which had been puzzling them fell into place.

"Jacqui was saying we'd have to do this and that and what deaf program we'd follow and what was available," said Wally. "All I could think about was Jamie-Lee. I didn't think about football even though I knew I had to start preparing for the game. We had a team meeting and I was listening, but in the middle of my head there was a fight going on — what was going to stay in my mind and what was to be rejected. And I was rejecting the football."

Wally didn't immediately realise what a momentous confession he had made to himself. For the first time ever a wedge had been driven between himself and the game that was his life. Once made, the split swiftly widened. Arriving at Lang Park, he completed his final pre match television wrap-up and afterwards the interviewer consoled him, "Thanks Wally, bet you'll be glad when this Origin's over and you've got more time to spend with your kid."

The words stayed with him. His thoughts went back to his talks with Jacqui and how much more of their time Jamie-Lee would need. And suddenly he knew what he had to do. With 15 minutes to kick-off he found manager Turner and said earnestly, "Toss, this is the end of the road for me, mate." Turner looked carefully at Wally. So much emotion had flowed in the last 24 hours that it was becoming difficult to distinguish drama from melodrama. Wally could hear the weight of his own words as he spoke, because he was about to end a decade of almost religious custom. "This will be my last game," he said. Turner knew his decision was genuine. He replied, "Yeah, family comes first, always." He grabbed Wally by the shoulders, the player with whom he had spent so many years upholding Queensland's Origin honour, and said huskily, "Well we'd better make sure this finishes the right way."

Wally asked him to tell QRL chief Ross Livermore to make an announcement whenever he saw fit. Turner hedged. "What about if we're not in front?" He remembered from the losing 1990 series that Wally had vowed he would not retire from State of Origin until he'd won back the shield. Wally said, "Makes no difference Toss, whether we're in front or behind mate, it's my last game."

While Wally tossed the coin with NSW skipper Benny Elias, Turner broke the news to the Queensland dressing room. With tears in his eyes, and voice trembling, he urged the team, "This bloke has been State of Origin football. You're all here because he's made tonight what it is. So how do we send him off? You all know. We can't lose tonight, it means too much. We owe him this one." Wally's last Origin was always bound to be a sentimental night but the Jamie-Lee news made it redolent with bathos. Neither the discovery of her deafness nor Wally's sudden decision to retire from Origin football was premeditated, but as motivational material it was empowering. No Queensland team spent a more electric last few minutes in Lang Park's concrete bunker than on that evening of 12 June, 1991. As they filed out, all the players shook Wally's hand and Mal Meninga, his Kangaroo successor — but not usurper — grabbed him last of all and said, "This one's for you."

For Wally, the National Anthem was a tense 45 seconds as it gave him time to think. In the stand he could see Jacqui and the two boys and his attention started to wander to Jamie-Lee. Then the whistle blew. Tosser Turner and Ross Livermore consulted and decided to wait until the second half to announce Wally's retirement. They hoped Queensland would be in front, but while Martin Bella was off, sin-binned, NSW scored to lead 12-8 with 15 minutes to go. Livermore told coach Lowe, "We might let it go now, gee the crowd up." Lowe said to wait until Queensland were attacking.

Livermore hurried downstairs to the dressing room where Turner was talking to sin-binned Bella. "We're getting close, we'll have to do something soon," said Ross. Turner nodded. Livermore raced to his office just in time to see, on his closed circuit television, Dale

Shearer cross to level the scores 12-12. As Meninga lined up the difficult conversion, ten metres in from touch, Livermore told the ground announcer, "When Meninga kicks this, wait two minutes because the crowd noise will be out of this world. Then let it go." Such confidence! But then Meninga is a pressure performer, always as likely to kick the improbable as the probable. Unerringly he made it 14-12, as he said, to ensure Wally went out a winner. As NSW kicked off the ground announcer "let it go" and the crowd buzzed with added excitement.

The last minutes of the game, the match aftermath, indeed the next few days sank beneath a sea of sentimentality, accolades and reminiscences. "If I could write a storybook ending, the last chapter couldn't have been more perfect than that last night," said Wally. "I got the chance to retire from State of Origin the way I wanted, at Lang Park, in front of a crowd that appreciated Queensland's success." And more. The match equalled the most watched progam in the 32 years of Brisbane television, rating at 65, the same as the 1982 Commonwealth Games opening on the ABC.

Wally thanked all his Queensland fans that night, lapping the field with his two boys. Scarcely a spectator left until Wally completed his circuit, giving him a standing ovation as he progressed, like a slow motion Mexican wave. "People asked why I took my boys with me," said Wally. "They'd been victims of me spending a lot of time away from home for football. The eldest, Mitchell, once said to me, 'I'm happy when you play good football Dad.' So I wanted them to be part of that special moment for me."

Presenting Wally with the Origin shield, Ken Arthurson received a hostile reception from the crowd and jokingly remarked that if that was how the crowd felt when NSW lost, "What would have happened if we'd won!" Those words, from the supposedly neutral ARL chairman, quite unfairly convicted him of parochialism in the eyes of diehard Queenslanders. The truth was his later defence: "If anyone from outside Queensland has done more for Queensland rugby league [than me], I'd like to meet him."

Before a crush of media swamped him, Wally folded his no. 6 jersey and presented it to Tosser Turner. Ross Livermore was sorry he couldn't have marked the post match supper with some presentation but, like everyone else, he'd been taken by surprise. "The scenario, the script, he proved to the knockers he could come back, it was just genius timing," he said. Livermore was already thinking of a Wally Lewis medal to be awarded to the player's player of future series. Long-time admirer, columnist Lawrie Kavanagh, had bigger plans. In the *Courier-Mail* two days later, he wrote, "The least we can do to honour Lewis would be a bronze statue of the man erected at Lang Park by public subscription. Anything less would not be fitting for the greatest rugby league player."

A giant front-page picture of Wally holding the Origin Shield aloft appeared in the *Courier-Mail* newspaper the morning after the match. The next day, when Kavanagh's column appeared, the newspaper devoted an entire page to tributes to "King Wally, The Peerless Player". Ten writers gave their opinions of, and experiences with, Wally over the years, while some of his Test colleagues — Miles, Vautin, Murray, Pearce and Fulton — spoke in glowing terms. The next day a picture of Wally was front page news again, this time holding Jamie-Lee aloft. For three days Lewis dominated the radio, television and newspaper news.

Yet perhaps the best tribute Wally received was not published. It came second-hand, via a conversation a journalist had with Paul Hauff and Willie Carne, both of whom had just played their first Origin series. Neither had played under Wally's captaincy at the Broncos. "We learnt a big lesson in this series," they said. "You should never be influenced by what other people tell you about someone. You should learn it first-hand. Wally was an absolute inspiration to play under. We couldn't fault him."

In the *Sydney Morning Herald* respected writer Ian Heads commented, "It is unarguable that Lewis has been State of Origin football's Bradman." He wrote also that if the Australian selectors were to pick a five-eighth strictly on 1991 Origin form, they'd pick Lewis. The Geyer incident had removed the captaincy from Wally's reach. A newspaper poll in Sydney returned 61 per cent favouring Meninga remaining captain and 39 per cent Lewis. Those proportions would have been reversed in a Brisbane poll.

Wally's chances of regaining the leadership might have improved but for a queer ruling by the NSWRL. Michael O'Connor wanted Mal Meninga cited for a brutal tackle in the third Origin, which concussed him and broke his nose. A bitter O'Connor said part of his motivation to cite Meninga was that his young daughter had been upset when she saw his swollen and bruised face. The NSWRL supinely accepted Meninga's public and private apology to O'Connor. Wests coach Warren Ryan wondered aloud in his *Sydney Morning Herald* column whether the ARL had been swayed by their desire to keep captain Meninga's reputation unsullied. Ryan's logic? The ARL blackballed Lewis for snarling at Geyer, who was subsequently outed for six weeks. Meninga was acquitted unscathed after busting up O'Connor.

Wally returned from rugby league oblivion to be selected as five-eighth for the Test against New Zealand on 3 July, 1991 in Melbourne. It would be his thirty-third Test, making him equal fourth in Test appearances with Johnny Raper, behind Graeme Langlands and Clive Churchill (34) and Reg Gasnier (36). If he played in all three Tests against the Kiwis he would jump to 35 Tests. With two more Tests to come that season against Papua New Guinea, the record was within his grasp. However with 22 Tests as captain he was still one behind Clive Churchill's record of 23 and he was not likely to equal that.

Wally was thrilled to be back in the bottle green and wattle gold national colours. It was disappointing not to be captain but he knew he was on probation just being in the team. "One bad game and there's enough people in high places who wouldn't need too many excuses to question my place," he said. He almost got it right. It was not one bad game from him, but one bad game from his team. As happened several times during Wally's career, a relaxed and complacent Australia, languid post-Origin, was hustled and harried by the fired-up Kiwis who bolted away 24-8 in the first Test, played in Melbourne. Coach Fulton afterwards pointed to defensive lapses "out wide", well clear of Wally.

"I didn't think I played badly," said Wally. "Maybe missed two tackles, didn't drop a ball, didn't make any tactical mistakes, had a try disallowed." But this was Australia's biggest Test loss in 20 years and in front of new patrons in an alien city where rugby league was on show. Both the ARL and Bobby Fulton had lost face and they needed a scapegoat. Wally rang Jacqui that night. "I think I'm a Garry Goner," he said. No, no, said Jacqui, you went OK. She hadn't felt the stares in the dressing room nor heard the scuttlebutt. Graham Lowe sensed the poised axe. "It would be a huge mistake to drop Lewis," he warned. Wally waited to hear from "Bozo" but the usual friendly phone calls didn't come. His hopes dwindled.

Two weeks later David Fordham rang Wally at home with the team for the second Test. Wally listened and remarked resignedly that he could see the arrows pointing. Jacqui looked up. More bad news? She was surprisingly calm. "Oh well, they didn't surprise you this time, as least you knew it was coming," she said. Fatty Vautin was soon on the phone. "He's got you eh?" he said. Wally knew who he meant. Vautin said that if Bozo hadn't been ringing Wally up, he was never a show.

Wally told me, "It hurt. It was a hollow feeling. First time I'd been dropped from a Test side. In 1982 in England I simply didn't make the team. This time I wasn't committing suicide over it. Jamie-Lee had forced my retirement from one arena, the ARL from another. It let a bit more air out of the tyres, but they were pretty flat by then anyway."

Of course he would have loved to have gone out in a blaze of glory, as in the Origins, although he had already defied the odds making it back into the Test side. Wally candidly told me, "There was one bloke who had an absolute shocker in that backline yet he kept his position for all the Tests." Wally's logical replacements, Laurie Daley and Cliff Lyons, both disagreed with his sacking. New five-eighth Peter Jackson mused that he was chosen because selectors saw certain things in him that Wally could not offer. What could they be? I asked Wally. "Well, hair for a start," he joked.

Wally commentated on Channel 7 for the next two Tests and predicted, "They'll thrash the Kiwis. In the first Test it was the conditions, complacency, the place, and New Zealand played well on the night. But they've woken Australia up." Australia won the next two, 44-0 and 40-12. Those who dislike Wally listened in vain, as they had when he missed the Kangaroo tour, for comments from him bagging the Australian team. Wally dismissed any such nonsense. "None of those blokes sacked me from the team," he said.

Thus ended Wally's Test career, not with a bang, nor with a whimper. Because a loss is only as painful as it is missed and Wally had already altered his priorities that Origin night weeks before. He had turned his focus, his energy and his capacity to inspire, upon his daughter's well-being. During the first week the Jamie-Lee news broke Wally and Jacqui received twenty letters, the second week fifty, the third week and for weeks afterwards, hundreds, always encouraging and many from parents with deaf children.

One delightful letter came from Anne Ferrato, aged 15, of Kentlyn, NSW, who had a hearing loss equal to Jamie-Lee's. She wrote, "My mother has told me that those early days of finding that you have a deaf child and not knowing what the future holds, are really hard." Some parents sent vidoes of their deaf children's achievements, some posted presents to Jamie-Lee. Wally was shopping in Pacific Fair, Broadbeach, one day when a mother sent her little boy up with flowers for Jamie-Lee. One of the few light-hearted moments came when Wally rang Fatty Vautin and told him about Jamie-Lee. Fatty groaned on the phone. He had just sent Jamie-Lee a birthday present notable for its capacity to make noise. Wally roared laughing. "It's got whistles and drums and makes one hell of a noise," he told me. "Thank God she can't hear it otherwise she'd have loved it and driven us all batty with it."

At the end of the 1991 football season he and Jacqui took a brief holiday to Cairns. They had to sort out Jamie-Lee's future — whether she should learn sign language, have cochlear implants (a bionic ear) or whether to attempt the Shepherd Centre method of natural speech. As always, word of their presence spread quickly and on the second day in Cairns they received a note from a local — would they like to meet his deaf daughter? They agreed and for an hour Wally and Jacqui were at first astonished and then entertained by 17-year-old Wendy Smith. "She was profoundly deaf like Jamie-Lee," said Wally. "She'd attended the Shepherd Centre, in Sydney, wore hearing aids and scarcely missed a word we spoke. She'd attended a normal school and even learnt the piano. When she left Jacqui and I just looked at each other in disbelief."

Jacqui and her sister Kaylene flew to Sydney in November to visit the centre which basically renounces the deaf world of signing with hands in favour of lip-reading and acquired speech using powerful hearing aids. Jacqui listened to a profoundly deaf boy have a detailed conversation about cars. "I thought, 'Wow! This is what my child's going to be like,'" said Jacqui. "But then we saw a boy with only moderate hearing loss and he could hardly say anything. It was up to the individual and the parents."

Jamie-Lee was tested at the National Acoustic Laboratories in Southport. If she was as deaf as was suspected, hearing aids would not help her and the Shepherd method would be out. Audiologist Linda Forsythe taught Jamie-Lee a process whereby if she heard a noise and looked up, a hand puppet (operated by Forsythe) would light up in a window. Wally watched nervously through a one-way window as Forsythe turned up the sound and pitch levels. Nothing. Further. Nothing. Once more. "Suddenly Jamie-Lee looked straight up and pointed at the puppet in the window," said Wally. "They did it again and Bang! up she looked again with a big smile. Jacqui and I were both laughing with tears because it was the first time we could see that she could hear." Forsythe gave them the good news — she could wear hearing aids.

From then on Jamie-Lee's every day was an education lesson from the family. "We tried for a week to get her to say 'Up'," said Jacqui. "We used a jack-in-the-box, jumped up ourselves and the boys helped. Then Wally came home from training one night and she suddenly said, 'Up!" and we said, 'Yeahhh, up!' and we were all yelling and laughing at the same time."

Jamie-Lee has sensory neural hearing loss which means that there are some sounds, no matter how loud or what pitch, she may never hear, even with hearing aids. How well she learns to speak will depend upon her eventual range of detection of sounds. She began lessons with speech pathologist Dimity Dornan at the Hear-And-Say centre for deaf children in Brisbane, which uses the basic Shepherd techniques. "Children who are on this program pick up lip-reading without us ever having to teach it," said Dornan. "I'm teaching her to listen. She's not going to get any more hearing. I'm trying to stretch that little bit of hearing she has a long way."

Jamie-Lee will always be disadvantaged by the distortion which occurs in any hearing aid. Background noise at parties will interfere with the clarity of conversations and her aids will amplify electronic noises above speech. Jacqui wants her to learn sign language as well, just so she can occasionally rest from the intense concentration required for listening and lip-reading.

Jacqui has already experienced the peculiar disadvantages of looking after a deaf child when compared with a hearing child. Shopping one day, Jacqui took her eyes off Jamie-Lee for a moment, looked back and she was gone. "I just panicked because your first instinct is to yell for her," said Jacqui. "I went straight for the front door and this attendant said 'Are you looking for a little blonde girl?' And there she was trying clothes against herself. She hadn't moved five yards away but she wouldn't have heard me if I'd called."

When Jacqui was pregnant and read bedtime stories to the two boys she always patted her stomach and included Jamie-Lee as the third pig in the Big Bad Wolf or the third goat in Billy Goats Gruff. To Jacqui, she was the third child listening. Exactly when Jamie-Lee became deaf remains unknown, and no longer matters. Except, as Jacqui's sister Kaylene quipped later, "You might have wasted nine months chatting." Sometimes, when Jamie-Lee's progress seems to have slowed, Jacqui and Wally become discouraged — but only temporarily.

Therapist Dimity Dornan said, "She's a very lucky little girl. She's got a mother who's very chatty and with her lots of the time, a father with a nice deep voice with whom she has a good relationship and two brothers who talk to her. That's exactly the environment she needs." It's an odd description for a deaf child — a very lucky little girl — but then it's true. When Wally told his eldest boy Mitchell about Jamie-Lee's deafness, Mitchell thought for a moment and said determinedly, "I feel sorry for her, but we'll help her, won't we dad?"

Further confirmation that Jamie-Lee was lucky came from the amazing Bradley Wolf, the little Queensland boy with cerebral palsy who, at the age of 13, used a computer suddenly to begin communicating with his parents and the world in mature prose and poetry. He met the Lewises and poignantly wrote, "Wally and Jacqui, many may have deserted you over the years and I don't want to intrude into your private life but I just wanted you to know through my own personal experiences that God didn't desert you, as He only gives special children to special people."

13

Bronzed Aussie

Summer waned and the last great adventure of Wally's playing career began, his 1992 season as captain-coach of the Seagulls. They had finished last in 1991, winning just two matches. Gold Coast fans had expected more from Wally's presence. Good judges, like Bobby Fulton, now warned that the dual role of captain-coach was beyond anyone in the modern era. It would not be easy. In the Seagulls, Wally was leading a side which would have been no match for the last team for which he had been captain-coach, his Wynnum-Manly club which won the Brisbane premiership in 1986.

Greg Dowling and Gene Miles were two of the Wynnum stars. GD retired at the end of 1991, and Geno, playing with Wigan in England, followed a few months later. Of the three old warhorses only Wally, probably the least physically sound of the trio, was saddling up for another tilt at the formidable Sydney competition. The Australian selectors had intimated he was too old and too slow for the demands of international football. Trainers estimate the modern game improves in all facets by 5 per cent each year, and that older players slow by 5 per cent each year. Wally, aged 32, would have to lift his fitness by 10 per cent just to keep up.

Enter Darryl Leahy, a Gold Coast gym proprietor and sometime triathalon competitor. Leahy brought swimmer Lisa Curry back to Olympic fitness levels and contributed to Clint Robinson's Olympic kayaking gold medal. He had watched Wally struggle through 1991, thought him unfit and lacking zest in club football. He presumed Wally had been given the best possible advice from training experts.

But as Lewis' experience at the Broncos had demonstrated, this was not always true.

Leahy contacted Lewis' manager Peter Hickey and in November 1991 enrolled Wally into his Centrepoint gym. "He only had limited time, as most superstars do, so we had to devise a really hard program that was safe and would only take him an hour to complete," said Leahy. He added a psychological program complete with dire motivational slogans such as "Winners Do What Losers Don't" and "If You're Not Training, Someone Somewhere Is". He wrote to Lewis: "Wally, if you play again in 1992 you must come back fitter, stronger and mentally tougher than ever before. You have been a tremendous ambassador for your state and for Rugby League. Now be an ambassador for yourself."

He checked his diet — Wally still ate some fast, fatty foods — and turned him from deep fries to fish, fruit and salads. He wrote to him, "It's pointless having a new Porsche motor car and putting kerosene in the fuel tank." Wally had suffered constant stomach upsets since moving to the Gold Coast. Leahy knew from previous experience with iron-man Guy Leech that it might be the coast's water. He contacted ex-Wallaby, Greg Cornelson, who ran a company called Springbrook, and had fresh water delivered to Wally's home. The stomach upsets disappeared.

Leahy summoned an osteopath to straighten Wally's spine and a masseur to dissolve the knots in his hamstrings. He introduced him to relaxation techniques and prescribed amino acids and vitamin supplements — in short the holistic approach to New Age health. Immediately they began training Wally complained of pain in his left wrist. Leahy sent him off to surgeon Dr Peter Myers who found that the steel nail in his left arm had backed out a few centimetres. In January 1992, Myers removed the nail from the arm that had ruled Wally out of a Kangaroo tour.

Back in the gym, Leahy devised techniques of lifting and pushing in slow motion so that Wally's damaged knee and shoulder joints never jarred or locked. He nursed Wally along, standing beside him at each exercise machine, encouraging him, holding Wally's mobile phone, which rings every few minutes, telling callers, "He won't be a moment, he's got ten more lateral pull downs to go — nine, eight, seven ...."

Leahy cons his athletes. He would tell Lisa Curry he wanted

twelve reps of whatever exercise he'd planned and when Lisa got to ten say, "OK, only five to go." Lisa would duly deliver. Not Wally. If twelve was the number requested he'd finish twelve and if Leahy said only three to go, Wally would say, "Darryl, it's just as well you're not a bank Johnny, you'd send the bloody joint broke."

Leahy did often push Wally hard, at times until he vomited from exhaustion. "We didn't mess around," said Leahy. "But he wanted to do it. Hard to believe from his reputation, eh?"

When the football season started in March 1992, Seagulls officials became concerned that Wally didn't seem to be putting in at the club's training. They rang Leahy and said they wanted Wally for strength testing — bench presses and thigh squats — shoulder and knee joint stresses that Leahy had deliberately avoided. Leahy asked what the average club five-eighth was bench pressing at Seagulls. The official said about 130 kilos. "Don't worry," said Leahy. "Wally's bench pressing 160 kilos in sets of 10!" He was actually pressing all of 45 kilos at this stage. The Seagulls official was astounded. "Really!" he said and from then on Wally gained the reputation at Seagulls of being fit and superstrong. In a way it became a self-fulfilling prophecy.

Wally could no longer be superstrong in his arthritic knees, or in his mended shoulders, but on the torso machine he was twisting 70 kilo repetitions. When he finished that exercise one day he said to Leahy, "Gees, that's hard work, that one." Leahy replied in admiration, "Wal, you're moving the stack — there's no more weights to put on it." Leahy had seen others twist that weight with several repeats; Wally was doing it 15 times. Leahy rated Lewis the strongest man in the torso he had ever tested — that's strength between the thigh and the waist — hip flexors, abdominals and glutimus maximus. It's where a tackle often started and faltered on Wally, and why he could stand and off-load with players hanging from his waist.

For years he had been going to training and been told, "Wally, you're slack, you're fat, you don't train hard, you're slow." Leahy did the opposite. He told Wally he was topping the charts in the gym; he was burning up his exercise cycle; he was eating and drinking better. No one was asking him to pound out arduous ten kilometre road runs which pained his joints, or do sharp sprints with suspect hamstrings. He wasn't being asked to match strides with 20-year-olds in macho field workouts. Wally estimated that at the Broncos he achieved only 70 per cent of the fitness he achieved under Leahy.

Before the first game of the season Leahy wrote, "Wally, remember you are the greatest player in the game today. Use your skills and experience as only you know how. Be aware that you will be stronger than your opposition."

Wally didn't play in the first game, the World Sevens, but coached the Seagulls to become the only team to defeat the eventual winners, Wigan. Before the final match in the pool Wally asked an official what happened if the three teams, Wigan, Cronulla and the Seagulls, tied with one win each. He was told it went to the team with the best for and against record. With a minute to go against Cronulla, the Seagulls, though behind 10–6, led the pool on the for and against countback. Wally sent out instructions to play out the clock. He said, "Our blokes jumped up and down, Hallelujah, you beauty, and then Arthur Beetson came over and said, 'Ah well mate, bad luck for both of us. Wigan are through.' I said, 'No, no.' And Artie said, 'Yeah, it goes on tries, Wigan have six, we've got five each.'"

Wally was astounded. He frantically sought out the misguided official but to no avail. "Our blokes just about went beserk when they found out because they'd heard the original bloke's assurances. They didn't blame me, it was the official's error. He apologised later, little bloody good it did us!" The first radio comment Wally heard afterwards was, "Already the pressure of coaching and playing in the Sydney premiership is getting to Lewis; he's made his first blunder."

Strike two for Wally in the eyes of his critics came in the Seagulls Challenge Cup match against the Broncos. Wally played down media hype about the "Clash of the Titans". As coach he didn't want the 'Gulls building themselves up for one game a year. But now his dual player-coach role had overtaken his relations with the Broncos as a favourite target for the media. This time, with the Broncos leading 12-10 seven minutes from full-time, the Seagulls were awarded a penalty within easy kicking range. Instead Wally took a quick tap and although the Seagulls went desperately close to scoring the Broncos held on to win. Asked afterwards why he hadn't taken the shot at goal, Wally said a draw would have been no use because the Broncos had scored the first try. He was crestfallen when told the match would have gone into extra time and the first try rule applied only if the scores were then still deadlocked. "It's my fault then, I didn't know the rule," he admitted.

Wally insists he'd have made the same decision whether he'd known the rule or not. He told me, "The way our blokes were finishing I thought we were a big chance. Toddy [Brent Todd] and three or four others yelled out, 'Take the tap!' We thought we'd score." Nor could he say whether he'd have ordered a goal kick had he been off the field as coach. He said, "I wouldn't have known how everyone was feeling on the field at the time. How fired up they were. Often that's a decision only the captain can make on the spur of the moment."

The Seagulls backed up against the Broncos four weeks later in the premiership — Wally's last match at Lang Park. It should have been a time for pleasant nostalgia because he had played his first match there, a primary school grand final in 1967. He estimated he had played some 200 matches there since then. "It may sound funny when people say I know every blade of grass on the ground but it's true in a way," Wally told me. "When you're out there you can see the field curves down to the sidelines and if you kick towards the edge of the field it's naturally going to run downhill. Just common sense."

Wally made no special pleas to his team before the match. "There were no violins playing before we ran out," he said. He was greeted by thunderous cheers from a crowd of 23,000 with "Go Wally" flashing on the scoreboard. I found myself sitting behind his mother June Lewis and was amused to hear her shout in the first half, "C'mon Blondie, run!" That was her personal nickname for Wally as a youth and she was still using it on this 32-year-old balding father on the field. In the opening minutes of the second half Kerrod Walters hit Wally so hard in a late tackle that Wally lost control of his speech, his vision and even his bladder. He staggered off and when he returned hit Kerrod in a thumping tackle and the pair came up cuffing each other.

"I went in to hit him as hard as I could and he went off at me," said Wally. "I said, 'What's up with you? It's all right for you to belt me, is it!' The Seagulls once more narrowly lost the local derby and as Kerrod and Wally shook hands they exchanged further harsh words. Kevin Walters called out, telling Kerrod not to worry about it. Wally bellowed, "Kevie, I'm the bloke that got knocked out!" It was an unhappy conclusion and Wally almost forgot to wave to the crowd. "I wanted to say thanks to everyone but I was too disapppointed to think about it," he said.

The last thing Wally wanted was bad blood with past friends, so he entered the Broncos dressing room and found Kerrod. "Listen, I'm not picking on you or anything," he began. Kerrod interrupted, "Are you going to cite me?" Wally was astonished. It never entered his mind. Kerrod was either joking or misguided. Whatever, Kerrod softened, "Wal, the hit wasn't meant, I was just trying to charge the kick down, that's all." Wally was appeased. He'd always got on well with the twins. He said, "OK, we'd better have a beer then, eh?"

Now Wally could attend to the media's requests for nostalgia. What were his best memories of Lang Park? "My first and last Origin matches," he said. "The last for obvious reasons, the first because I had hair in those days."

Wally had one last bout with the Broncos in the second round but by then the Brisbane side were in the form which carried them to the premiership. Specifically he put it down to the Broncos' strength training under Kelvin Giles. "They do an amazing amount of weight training," he said. "Playing against them it was obvious they were the strongest and hardest team in the competition. They didn't have as many big blokes as other teams, but their individual strength was ridiculous. They've all got it, even their little guys." Wally had seen it begin in Giles' first year at Red Hill.

He had seen no evidence of steroid use, he said. The only occasion he knew of a player popping pills was back in his early days with Brisbane Valleys. "A bloke was complaining about feeling flat before a game and our coach Russ Strudwick gave him some pills and said, 'Get these into you, you'll have a blinder.' The bloke did and he came back in roaring, 'That's me! that's me! You better give me a couple more of those pills.' Struddy stayed real calm and said, 'Yeah? How were those salt tablets, all right?' And then he said, 'Forget the pills. Now you know you can do it, get out there and do it every week!' "

In the Seagulls' third round game, against Illawarra, they suffered a blow from which they didn't really recover all season. They were incensed when Brent Todd was sent off in the first minute. Wally raced over to his forwards and yelled, "If you blokes weren't in the right frame of mind before the game I'll bet you are now! Let's show these bastards what we're made of!"

At half-time Wally gave instructions on how to rotate the replacements to keep 12 fresh men on the field. "Mick [McLean], work your guts out for 15 minutes and when you're dropping, give me a shout and I'll bring another bloke on, then in eight minutes the next tiredest goes off and Mick comes back and so on ..." But the Seagulls lost players through injuries and all four replacements were on the field when Clinton Mohr was ordered to the blood-bin. A fifth replacement ran on and the Seagulls pulled off a courageous 18-8 win.

The match even finished on a humorous note for Wally. With both prop forwards injured he had to pack into the last scrum in the front row. His Illawarra opposite, Craig Izzard, a centre turned second row, looked up and laughed. "I never thought I'd see this," he said, shaking his head. Wally grinned and said, "What about you up here too!" As they leaned heads Wally growled, "I always said I'd turn it up rather than play front row." Izzard replied, "Too right, you can't get any worse than this." So it is no myth that prop forwards do have gentlemanly conversations in scrums.

When Brent Todd was suspended for four weeks the Seagulls were still sufficiently elated to josh Wally, "Gator, what happens to Toddy if you're not our coach — ten in the bin, penalty maybe? We'll have to get rid of you!" But the smiles disappeared when their use of the fifth replacement was questioned, and turned to dismay 11 days later when the NSWRL docked the Seagulls their two competition points. Two rules governed the case. One clause allowed a maximum of four replacements but the following paragraph stated that a blood-bin replacement "shall not count as one of the four replacements referred to in the preceding paragraph ..." The incident should have been used as a precedent to clarify which rule took ascendancy, with no penalty against the Seagulls.

Wally darkly addressed his players at training, "Fellas, we didn't get any points for our Illawarra win. The rules are in black and white, but apparently now it is a matter of interpretation." His team was shattered, more than he could have imagined. "Gator," they asked seriously. "What have you done to these blokes down south? Why are they putting this shit on us when we're just battlers?" Wally didn't say so but it was because ten years ago he stole their crown and they had never forgiven him.

"It upset the blokes for a long time," said Wally. "I had that many meetings about it, telling them to put it to the back of their minds. I thought up new challenges to make them look ahead but every now and then you'd hear the comment, 'Oh, what's the use, they'll find some reason to knock us.'"

Wally's own form was an inspiration. With just over a week to the first Origin, the Seagulls defeated Canberra and State selector Hugh Kelly sought out Wally in the dressing room. "You feeling itchy?" he said. Wally looked up. "Hughie, I'm itchy all right, I was itchy five minutes after I retired last year." Kelly then asked him if he was thinking of changing his mind. Wally shook his head. Kelly wasn't asking him for sentimental reasons, or because Wally might add some mystical energy to the Queensland team simply by his presence. His form warranted selection. Mike McLean, Wally's Seagulls and erstwhile Origin team-mate, said to him, "Mate, the way you're going, why not?"

After Queensland lost the first Origin in Sydney the Queensland chairman of selectors, Dud Beattie, also asked Wally if there was a chance he'd change his mind. Wally remained retired. "It's like dying, you only do it once," he said. For a player not in either team, he cast a huge shadow over the series. "Wally Gone But Not Forgotten" wrote Sam North in the *Sydney Morning Herald*. It was so true. Would he make a comeback? Would he assist Graham Lowe in coaching Queensland? Was he to be Lowe's successor? NSW coach Phil Gould warned about complacency in Wally's absence. Stories about Queensland players focused on how they would fill Wally's shoes — Mal Meninga as captain, Allan Langer as play maker, Kevin Walters as five-eighth.

Most noticeable in that first Origin was how it lacked an identity, lacked parochialism, lacked a provocative personality ... lacked Lewis. Columnist Debbie Spillane said it for many: "It's just not the same any more. Whether he's too old or retired, pick Wally so we can have it all over again." Jeff Wells, in *The Australian*, agreed. Even the NSW fans recognised it, he wrote: "A mob of them stayed to let the stadium ring with a rousing, affectionate chorus of his famous anthem, 'Wally's A Wanker'." Radio comic H.G. Nelson called on Queenslanders in their thousands to join a demonstration march from Tweed Heads to Lang Park demanding Wally's return.

The second Origin was famous for more reasons than one. After Wally's last Origin in 1991, *Courier-Mail* columnist Lawrie Kavanagh had suggested a statue should be erected in his honour. Kavanagh listed Wally's Origin contribution as one of three events which took Queensland from state adolescence to national maturity in the 1980s. The other two were the 1982 Commonwealth Games and the 1988 World Expo. The statue idea caught on, the *Courier-Mail* donated $1000 towards a public appeal for $10,000, and it was off and running. The statue, in bronze, would be a life-size sculpture, moulded by John Underwood, whose Artbusters studio created the lifelike street figures for the Expo.

"As much as it was a compliment it was an embarrassment at first," Wally said. "Aren't statues usually reserved for dead people?" He preferred the QRL's idea of a Wally Lewis medal for player-of-the-series. He didn't know much about statues. "The only statue I've ever taken any notice of is the soldier outside the church halfway to the Gold Coast from Brisbane," he said. "As far back as 1975 when we were driving down to the surf club we'd all salute that bloke as we passed."

As the donations and letters rolled in, and Wally took in their tone and content, he was won over. I hesitated to tackle the stack of hundreds of letters which resulted from the appeal, but once I started I couldn't stop. The outpourings of affection for Wally were worthy of a hero of Bradman's status. The residents of a Redland Bay nursing home, with an average age of 85, even took their cue from the old phrase, "He's our Don Bradman", except as they passed around the latest newspaper story of Wally they'd say, "He's our Wally."

The donations came mostly from Queensland, but many from NSW, and some from Melbourne, Tasmania and even New Zealand. Melbourne donors wondered whether they should set Dermot Brereton or Ron Barassi in bronze. Most letters were small gems, embodying what Wally had meant to each contributor. An architect wrote in suggesting the budget be raised from $10,000 to $100,000 and the statue made twice life-size to match Wally's exploits for Queensland. He also suggested the proper place for the statue was the Queen Street mall, in the centre of Brisbane. Kerrie Rowe of Goondiwindi, a true fan, wanted the statue cast in gold instead of bronze!

The Jendra family of Wishart, Brisbane, said their three young children had included their pocket money in the family's contribution. Some donations were as large as $100 but the majority were between $5 and $20. The appeal was no corporate jaunt; it was funded by the very smallest, rank and file rugby league fan, like the Stephan sisters of Windsor who sent their donation on behalf of their father, a pre-war front row forward. They wrote, "We salute Wally's spirit of determination, and his pride in himself, his jersey, his state and his country."

Some contributors were wry admirers. A doctor from north Rockhampton wrote, "Wally can be a pain in the neck sometimes, but he's OUR pain in the neck!" Similarly Jean Hunter of Maryborough wrote, "If the lazy bugger had trained a bit more we could have been seeing him at the top for a few years more. But we are all human!"

A few letters opposed the appeal. One initialled, but unsigned, included a small plastic sachet of cow manure to indicate what the author thought of the appeal. Another said Kavanagh was guilty of seeking to place Wally above the game itself. A halfpenny was taped to one letter signed, "A cockroach". So Wally was still polarising people, even as a bronze statue.

Several letters proposed that instead of a statue the appeal should assist handicapped children, and Wally would have been glad to go along with that. Gillian McLelland of Taringa, Brisbane, suggested that instead of a statue they design a medal for the best under 18s five-eighth. She imagined herself sitting back in a rocking chair in later years, watching some fresh faced youngster receive the award and thinking, "You'll need to be good son, you'll need to be very, very good."

It was fascinating to read how deeply Wally had reached into the hearts and homes of Queenslanders: some had Wally memorabilia boards hung over their bars; many kept scrapbooks of articles about him; yet others named pets after Wally — their dogs, cats, a goldfish and even a huntsman spider. Some burst into long, heroic verse of which these random lines are but a few short examples:—

Thanks Wal for all the fun,
the hype and rev of football on the run,
may the years to come be kinder than the few,
that pinched the cake and took the icing too!

and —
King Wally ranks among the best,
and led Australia through,
to record-breaking victories,
as Captain Kangaroo.

and —
You gave your all for club, state and country,
a champion of champions, to put it more bluntly.

One poem became a memento, preserved in a frame beside a photograph of Wally in the pose that was later to become his statue pose, holding aloft the Origin shield. Jacqui put the poem over their own lounge room bar. It concluded:

For ten years now he's been the King, in the greatest game of all,
It didn't matter who he played, they were sure to fall,
So we'll end this tribute, to the man we've dubbed the King,
"Thank you Wally", in our ears your name will always ring.

The donations came with tributes on ornate cards and on scraps of old paper, typewritten and in spidery handwriting, on letterheads and with illegible signatures, from an enormous range of people of many different ages, both men and women. Two suggestions common to many letters were that Wally be sculpted with his hands on his hips — his querulous pose when confronting referees — and that he be given his hairline from the mid-1980s. Above all, in nearly every letter, love shone through, like that expressed by Mrs Wood of Wynnum West, just widowed, who wrote, "Wally, on the football field, was an inspiration in my troubles; many of us miss him very much."

Wally became involved in some of the appeal fund–raising, visiting Boggo Road gaol to collect a cheque for $204.67 from the prisoners' meagre earnings. Prison surroundings did not daunt him. "They were very down to earth," he said. "If the prisoners don't like you they'll tell you. They'd say, 'G'day Wally, you bloody baldy-headed old bastard' and I always found they appreciated it if I talked just as hard back to them. What surprised me was when they said, 'Give it to those Broncos bastards, leave Alfie alone he's a good bloke, but bash the others.' Probably because Wayne was an ex-copper."

At his first modelling session Wally stripped to his togs, was covered with thick petroleum jelly to protect his skin and then swathed in strips of water-soaked plaster of Paris. The pose chosen was of Wally holding the real, solid timber, Origin shield triumphantly above his head. "My arms began to sag after a few minutes," said Wally. "They reckoned I had to stand there for 20 minutes at least while the plaster dried. I said, 'Mate, you try doing it with this

10 kilo shield!' " Hooks were screwed into the shield and ropes used to hold it aloft but, even so, as the plaster was layered on, Wally's arms grew unbearably heavy. "By the end, when they took the cast off and I dropped my arms, I had this terrible sensation as the blood rushed through them," he said. Then came the hardest part, half an hour of scrubbing in a shower to get the grease off.

Later they did his face as well. He closed his eyes and breathed through a straw as the petroleum jelly and plaster were applied again, over moustache, hair, ears, the lot. When Wally saw a preliminary cast he noticed his hair was plastered flat on his scalp. He thought, "Gees, I haven't got much but I've got more hair than that." He asked them if there was any chance they could drop a bit more hair on. They did, but according to Wally the statue still ended up looking rather flat on top.

About 60 of the 600 people who donated to the appeal were balloted to attend the final pouring of the bronze into the moulds at the Artbusters studios. Wally moved among these ardent fans and met a couple who had donated $7.64 on behalf of their daughter who was killed in a car crash in 1988 aged 19. She was a devoted Wally fan and later when her parents found her piggybank with that amount inside they knew she would have wanted it to go towards the statue. "It was very moving meeting them," said Wally. "As you get older these things touch you more. They made me feel that playing was worthwhile, despite all the insults, injuries and disappointments."

Wally didn't see the statue again until the night of the second Origin, 20 May, 1992 at Lang Park. He, Jacqui and the three children all walked out under the glare of the floodlights and flashing camera bulbs. Jacqui exclaimed, "Oh God, you'd think we were the royal family!" Lawrie Kavanagh replied that in Queensland, to the football followers, they were. Or as H.G. Nelson hilariously told his listeners, tongue in cheek, "There they go, the King, Mrs King and the three little Kings ..."

"Your policeman is here," Wally was told and he was escorted from his television commentary box through the applauding crowd down to the ground. Premier Wayne Goss pressed a button and the statue rose comically, rather than majestically, from a giant crown on wheels in the centre of Lang Park. The crown was coloured royal purple and maroon, and studded with red and green lights, with silver trimming. Wally kept the whole performance well in proportion, wondering whether the statue would topple from its seemingly precarious perch. Then Premier Goss told the 33,000 people in the stadium, "Not too many people in the world have this sort of honour." That got to Wally. "People might laugh at this, but it was a humbling experience," he said. "I stood there and despite myself got goose bumps."

In the crowd, Jacqui's mother overheard criticism of the Lewises for exposing the children to the public glare of that evening. Said Jacqui, "It was their night as much as his, because they lost him to football for so much of their early years. And the next day Mitchell told everyone at school how, as the statue rose, Jamie-Lee was going, 'Up, up, up!' Now that's therapy for you."

The statue now stands beside the scoreboard at Lang Park, overlooking the scene of so many of Wally's triumphs. I feel it is lost there, hidden from the view of ordinary tourists and passersby. It belongs around in front of the QRL's headquarters at the main entrance to the ground. Perhaps the QRL do not feel the statue itself is sufficiently inspirational to deserve such prominence. In that I would agree. The statue is faithful to its commission — it is life-size and life-like, but to do justice to Lewis' performances he needed a heroic sculpture.

Wally's appeal must be difficult to capture in art. The QRL commissioned Hugh Sawrey to paint a portrait of Wally after his last Origin in 1991. Sawrey had painted "The Man From Snowy River" as a wedding gift to the Lewises. Wally stood for his portrait at Sawrey's Gold Coast home and the result was a William Dobell-type, impressionistic painting, completely the opposite of the realistic Artbusters statue. Sawrey asked Wally what he thought. It put Wally on the spot. What could he say? "I don't know Hugh, the head looks a bit small to the rest of the body," he said tentatively. Sawrey explained how the body was in front, ready for battle while the head was withdrawn for planning.

The painting was formally presented to Wally at the 1991 Origin team's victory dinner. Sawrey was a guest at the dinner but Peter Jackson was never one to mince words. "What about the size of the bloody head!" he exclaimed. "It was that big when he was eight years old!"

After the bronze statue was unveiled at Lang Park, Wally made his way back up to his television commentary eyrie to watch Alfie Langer unveil a little known talent for field goals, booting Queensland to State of Origin victory just 66 seconds from full-time. I sat behind Wally as he commentated for New Zealand television. Contrary to popular belief, he did not utter the joyful magic word as Alfie's kick sailed between the posts. But he did rock so far back in his chair, willing the kick through, that he nearly fell over, shouting, "It's there!"

Before the match, television caller Graeme Hughes had noticed a Laurie Daley fan with a placard reading "King Laurie". He told Wally on air, "I didn't know you'd relinquished that title." Wally replied, "I've been carrying that around for far too long, take it away Laurie, it's all yours!". After Alfie's kick newspapers hailed Langer as the new "King", so the pair could fight out the title between themselves.

Wally always liked Alfie. "Quiet sort of bloke, but at the same time can be a real cheeky little bastard," he said. "He's like a laugh waiting to happen, Alfie. I think he'll captain Australia. He's got extra jobs with the Broncos now and is more responsible. In attack he's not quite as fast as he used to be, maybe lost half a metre, but he's made up for that in brains and strength. Where once he would have taken off to score himself, now he'll drag the defence in and try to create something for the bloke backing him up. He picks his time when to run and he's a good judge."

Wally said that in club matches he'd told his players to run straight at Langer rather than around him. "That way he can't get his feet across in front of you to bring you down," he said. "I've seen it work with limited success. To me his tackling style is suspect, I've got to admit that." Because his feet sometimes got there before his hands? "Of course they do. Not always. It happens so quickly refs can't pick it. He's not being penalised so congratulations to him. He does it in a very effective way. Other players used to get into trouble because they did it to hurt people. Alfie's saving grace is that he does it just to bring people down."

The 1992 representative season concluded with the visit by Great Britain. Of interest to Wally was that they included Ellery Hanley as captain even though his injuries restricted him to very little play on tour. De facto captain Garry Schofield quipped to Wally, "Bet you wish you had our doctor for the last Kangaroo tour."

14
Exit the Emperor

Southern crowds disliked Wally primarily because he was so good, and as his last year wound down they were sorry to see a player of his brilliance depart. In the second half of the season every match was a farewell game for him at some NSW ground. From Penrith to Cronulla, north to Newcastle, clubs promoted their Seagulls match as the last chance to see King Wally, and every time the home-town spectators responded with applause. Wally in turn farewelled some of the players he had opposed for a decade — Mick O'Connor retiring from Manly, Steve Roach retiring from Balmain, Brett Kenny talking about retiring from Parramatta.

In his last match against Canberra, Wally managed to run head-long into Mal Meninga in a tackle. "I plomped backwards and he landed on top of me. I said, 'Will you get off me, you big unit!' and he started laughing. As he got up he put one hand in my guts and another on my head and put all his weight on me and I started laughing too." Wally was glad of Meninga's friendliness because he sensed some inevitable hangover of tension from the Test captaincy issue the previous year. "At the end of the game a photographer asked us to put an arm around each other and Mal sort of hesitated, but I said, 'Well mate, I'll have this photo, can you get me one? I'll have it blown up and put it in my bar.' Then Mal asked the photographer for one as well."

Under Wally's stewardship the Seagulls crowds jumped 21 per cent from the previous year, twice that of the next best, Illawarra, whose attendances rose by nine per cent. The season was frustrating to Wally because the Seagulls were narrowly pipped in match after match. They won six games, compared with two games the previous season, and finished with 11 points — it would have been 13 but for the Illawarra disqualification. However they still finished last. That was the reality of life in the world's toughest rugby league competition.

Wally himself had one of his most consistent seasons, missing only one match through injury, and his form, despite his age, was equal to any earlier in his career. Much of it must be attributed to his fitness. One newspaper voted him as having the competition's most under-rated season. Seagulls physiotherapist Mike Pahoff said Wally had come to a stage in his career where he knew what he could take, physically and mentally, preparing for a season of football. Said Pahoff, "Any coach who is a stickler for everyone having to conform, who doesn't allow for individualism, is crazy. It amazes me when I hear, 'Oh he wouldn't train.' I think, 'For God's sake, it didn't do him much harm, did it?'"

Darryl Leahy felt vindicated because Wally's last season was free of injury. He told me, "The Broncos were the strongest team in the competition, so Kelvin Giles did a fantastic job in conditioning them. But everyone is different and we all need different ways of motivating ourselves to train. To get where he had, Wally had to have the right attitude somewhere. The fact that everyone said he was hopeless at training didn't matter to me, because I know what most club trainers are like. I believe they're the ones who are hopeless because they're not reaching the talent that's obviously there. Wally turned out to be very good in his training. I just wish I had met him ten years ago."

Seagulls trainer, Rudi Meir, remembered Wally's last season because of his regular glimpses of classic Lewis brilliance. "The ball seemed to accelerate whenever it reached him," said Meir. "He was like Gene Kelly or Fred Astaire, every move he made was crisp and sharp." I saw what Meir meant when I watched Wally in the week leading up to his last competition match against Penrith at Seagulls Stadium. At training he threw a series of passes to reserve grade coach Graham Eadie, starting from 10 metres and working his way out to 30 metres. He bounced the ball once and fired it off at Eadie, no arc, dead flat trajectory. Eadie's return passes were lobbing high in the air at 30 metres, but Wally's were still arrow straight. He called the squad over for final instructions. Most intriguing was his prediction about Penrith's super half, Greg "Brandy" Alexander. "There'll come a stage where I'll call someone else in to five-eighth and I'll cover behind you," said Wally. "Brandy will be getting ready, he'll hold out, hold out and when he sees us tire he'll start to run. I'll have a look for him."

Driving down to the coast for that last game I heard Wayne Bennett and Allan Langer interviewed on ABC radio. Both agreed Wally was the best reader of a game they had ever seen. Bennett conceded he and Wally hadn't parted in the best possible way, but he did say that Wally had played some great matches for the Broncos." Langer praised Wally's inspiring leadership. "He's always led by example," he said. "He's still the Emperor and it will be sad to see him step down." He added mischievously, "Don't lose too much more hair, the old King, hope you go out on a winning note." It was a tough task against the reigning premiers, Penrith.

In the coach's box, sprint trainer Larry Corowa was calling reserve grade tackle counts to a statistician — "Number 34 tackles, 53 assists." Corowa made a joke about pre-match nerves. "Nerves? What are they?" laughed Wally. Graham Eadie walked behind him and joked, "You don't get nerves when you're 38!" Just before half-time a strapper arrived and tapped Wally on the shoulder. Wally gave a start, as though he'd been in a trance. The strapper carefully applied white plaster in strips to Wally's shaved ankles and departed. Wally went back to gazing over the field of his football dreams. Nobody said a word to him for the next 45 minutes. Nobody dared to. He was building like a Test batsman before a crucial innings. Below him lay the sights and sounds of so many Sundays of his life. The green field, the white lines, the crowd's constant buzz, children screaming with streamers, the ref's shrill whistle, the prancing cheer girls, the call of confectioners, the hot, sweet smell of tomato sauce and meat pies.

He was the last into the dressing room where he was met by Ken Arthurson. Wally was confused. He had not expected to see Arko, hadn't see him for months. From being totally inwardly focused he had to assume his ex-national captain's mantle. Arthurson shook his hand, wished him luck and asked about Jamie-Lee. It was unnerving, being pleasant to Arthurson, yet still thinking about how he intended to nail Penrith's Greg Alexander!

Wally followed his last pre-game ritual. Gold neck chain off, watch off, handed those and wallet to trainer. He tucked his socks in his shoes and put them in his locker, then hung his trousers and T-shirt on a hook. A pair of light blue, tight togs went underneath the shorts and then the Seagulls strip, two pairs of socks and a brand new pair of boots. He tied black tape around the sock tops to keep them up and over the bootlaces to keep them done up.

While Wally was outside tossing the coin with Penrith captain John Cartwright, Graham Eadie addressed the team. "Eight minutes to next year fellas," he began. "This is Wally's last ... I can remember my last game and it's a bloody big thing. Wally's done a lot for this game. Let's give him a send-off the right way."

He didn't need to fire up the boys. Brent Todd told me later, "That was as tense as any Test dressing room I've been in. It was a big honour for the guys. No one said a word you noticed. Never been like that before. They'd have given their right arm for him, I tell you."

Wally rushed back in, his concentration now converted to fast-release adrenalin. "Listen, I can tell you, these Penrith blokes are turned right on. They're out there belting things, crashing each other, they think they're still a big chance for the semi-finals." For the next few minutes he berated them with instructions — "We've won the toss, no penalties first six, no penalties second six, I want an absolute bloody overdose of talk!"

Eadie shook Wally's hand, "All the best Gator." The Black Flash, Larry Corowa, followed suit. A Seagulls official delayed Wally's exit by ten seconds as the announcement was made, "Ladies and gentlemen, playing his last Winfield Cup match, after 30 State of Origin games, 33 Tests, 23 as Australian captain, the King, the Emperor Wally Lewis."

He ran on as he always did, ball in one hand, mouth-guard in the other, acknowledging the prolonged applause. It was 29 August, 1992 — 14 years and four months from when he played his first A grade game for Valleys. Seagulls marketing manager, Ron Morris, describes Wally as the greatest Aussie actor since Mel Gibson. "He really is. He plays to his audience," he said, "If it's a full house and it's a big occasion, the bloke gives you an Oscar winning performance." That evening the Seagulls Stadium was like a mini-Lang Park, and with Penrith leading 8-6 in the second half, Wally improvised on a script that wasn't developing as he wished. Near the Penrith line on the fifth tackle he grubber kicked through, fell on the ball, rose and bullocked through Steve Carter's tackle to plunge over. Seagulls 12-8.

On Channel 9, Darrell Eastlake yelled the facts: "I think the King's gone in! Look at the crowd, they've gone absolutely off! The King's gone in, you wouldn't believe it!" Co-commentator Fatty Vautin chimed in, "Well that'll do me. He's a genius! I said before the game I hoped old Baldy got a try and he's done just that."

Wayne Bennett, in his brief ABC radio comments, had included praise of Wally's front-on defence. With 15 minutes left Greg Alexander fulfilled Wally's prediction, suddenly gliding through the Seagulls' tiring backline, on course for a match winning try. Then he met Wally, so well positioned his cover defending tackle became a front-on body slam. Fatty Vautin wanted to make Wally man-of-the-match. "He's gone out in style as he would have wished to have," he said as Wally began a victory lap. "Queenslanders love him and he's just an out and out champion, a great bloke and a real good friend." Wally rated those comments way above any match award.

Penrith captain John Cartwright embraced Wally, Greg Alexander shook his hand. The crowd gave him three cheers and for the last time Jacqui and the children joined him on the field, while his parents Jim and June Lewis stood back from the melee, teary eyed. The crowd packed around him chanting, "Wall-ee's A Legend". Said Wally, "At first I thought it was the other chant and I thought, 'Oh no, don't tell me I'm getting it from my own mob too!'" As he entered the dressing room Graham Eadie called for three more cheers from the players.

Wally suddenly sang out, "Guys, do you mind if I just have a word alone with the players a minute?" Everyone — trainers, strappers, physios, doctors, myself — filed dutifully out. I left my tape cassette running in a corner and it recorded an emotional Wally telling his silent players, "Fellas, thanks for the finish. There's probably lots of ways I could have finished my football career, but here at home with all my mates in my own team, I couldn't finish in a better way. Probably meant a lot to you blokes to win that game out there tonight, but let me tell you, it meant a fair bit to me too. Thanks for the year, now let's get on the piss together!" The players broke into a rousing cheer, "Good on yer mate!", and then the cry went up, "Song Toddy, song!" Brent Todd, yelling like an army drill sergeant, led them on the team song and added a final verse:

Gator played his last game today,
And showed Penrith how to play,
Yeah! On yer boys.

The doors opened again and we flooded back in. Ken Arthurson walked across and knelt in front of Wally where he sat. They spoke quietly and shook hands. It looked like they were mending fences once more and it impelled Wally to make another short speech, thanking Arthurson for his attendance, a special honour for the club. But of course Arthurson, by his mere presence, was honouring Wally, inviting the prodigal five-eighth back into the ARL fold.

Then came the media and it was an undeclared truce. "I know I've been a bastard to work with," Wally said. No reporter was game to second that. "Now I'm just a coach I might not be so cranky, but I'm not guaranteeing anything."

Jacqui told the media, "The short kick, the chase, the try — not much has changed over the years, has it? As my son Mitchell said, 'Daddy kicked, tackled, scored a try and finished football all in one night.'" Her admiration for her husband brings out the eloquence in Jacqui. "He's so skilled, he makes football a work of art," she said. "But the reason he's a champion is that no matter how often he's kicked down, he always bounces back. A champion father and husband too."

Wally was the last to leave that room filled with scattered ice, dirty bandages, spilled beer and soggy sandwiches. Outside the crowd was still drifting away from a memorable night. Wally walked across to the Stardust room in the leagues club and spontaneous applause broke out the moment he entered. He was immediately swamped by fans and it stayed that way until after midnight. He had hoped to join his players for a long drink but soon saw it was a forlorn hope. "All I did was sign things and talk to people," he said. "So I said to the missus, 'Let's get out of here.'" At home he began to muse over the years, but it had been a hard day's night and sleep overtook him.

Over the next few days phone calls and faxes flowed in from friends and the famous. One fax said, "It is impossible to compare players over many years but I am certain of only one fact — there has never been a greater player than you. Bullfrog." That was Peter Moore, chief executive of Canterbury-Bankstown club. Bob Abbott sent one on behalf of the ARL, though Ken Arthurson, by his presence at Seagulls Stadium, had already surpassed that. Another thanked Wally, "for the years of entertainment you have given us as the greatest rugby league footballer in the world. Sincerely, Chook and Family (Johnny Raper MBE)." Yet another came from Queensland Premier Wayne Goss: "Congratulations on your last game. A classy way to go out — a win and the winning try!"

Thus ended Wally's playing career, except that before the Penrith match he was bothered by the idea that a serious competition match should be his last game. It narrowed the interest to the two clubs involved, whereas he felt like reaching out to embrace the entire rugby league community of clubs which had been his career. "I thought I'd like to play a game with blokes from everywhere," he said. "Make it an attackathon, not this boring defensive stuff people complain about week after week." From that thought came the Wally Lewis Celebrity Challenge played on Saturday night, 19 September, at Seagulls Stadium. The proceeds went to five charities, primarily the Hear-And-Say Centre teaching Jamie-Lee to speak, then Camp Quality, Make-A-Wish, Sporting Wheelies and the Tweed Heads Hospital.

Wally chased the players he wanted to invite. He excluded those from Brisbane, St George and Illawarra — the three clubs still in the premiership finals — as well as those players in the World Cup squad. He checked with Bobby Fulton just to make sure. "You don't want your blokes to play, do you Boze?" he asked, because Wally fully understood the risk of injuries. Ken Arthurson had given the game the all-clear and now Fulton surprised him, "Mate, it's fine." Wally got excited. Now he had some stars to promote.

For past champions he wanted Kerry Boustead and Eric "Guru" Grothe on the wings. He knew Bowie was trim and fit and well loved by Queenslanders, but heard that Grothe was way overweight. He rang Grothe and said tentatively, "Guru, you carrying a few pounds?" No, said Grothe, puzzled. "I heard you were as big as a house," said Wally. Grothe got indignant. "Bullshit! About half a stone at most." Wally had his wingers.

Next he secured the champion backs: Brett Kenny, who would be the other captain; Michael O'Connor, playing his very last match, and Peter Sterling. Wally reassured Sterlo that the dicey shoulder which had forced his untimely retirement would not be at risk in this type of game. Wally always had an ironic friendship with Sterling. "Similar hair styles, Sterlo and me," he told me. But Sterlo kept his

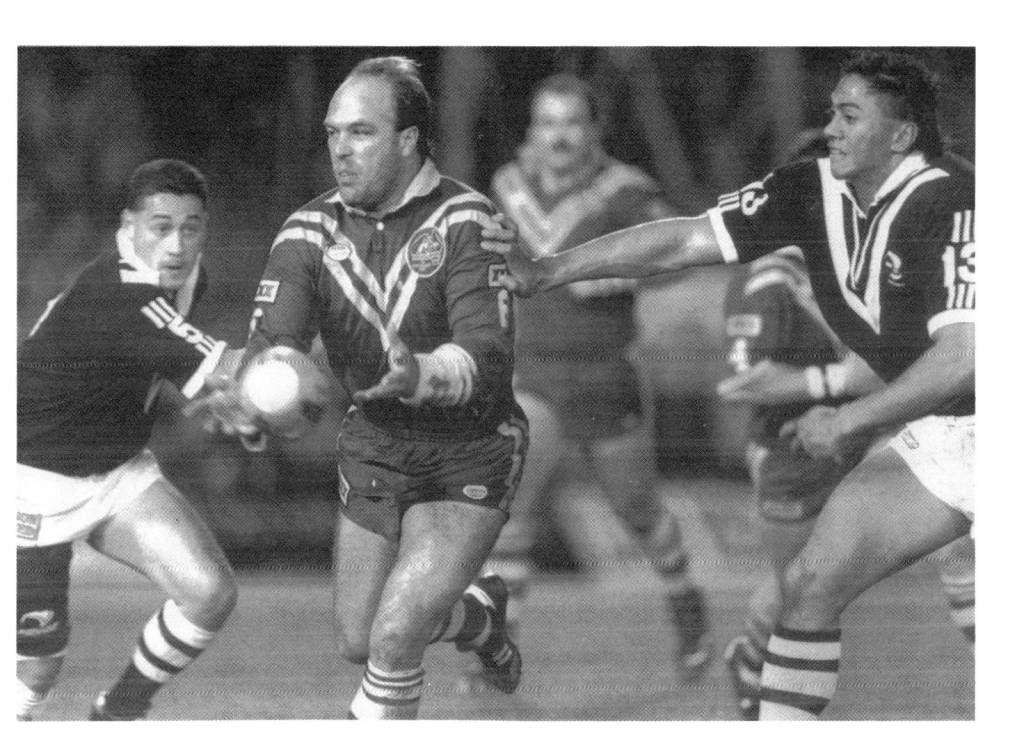

1991. First Test against New Zealand. Wally's good form evading Kiwis Jason Williams (left) and Tawera Nikau did not save his Test place

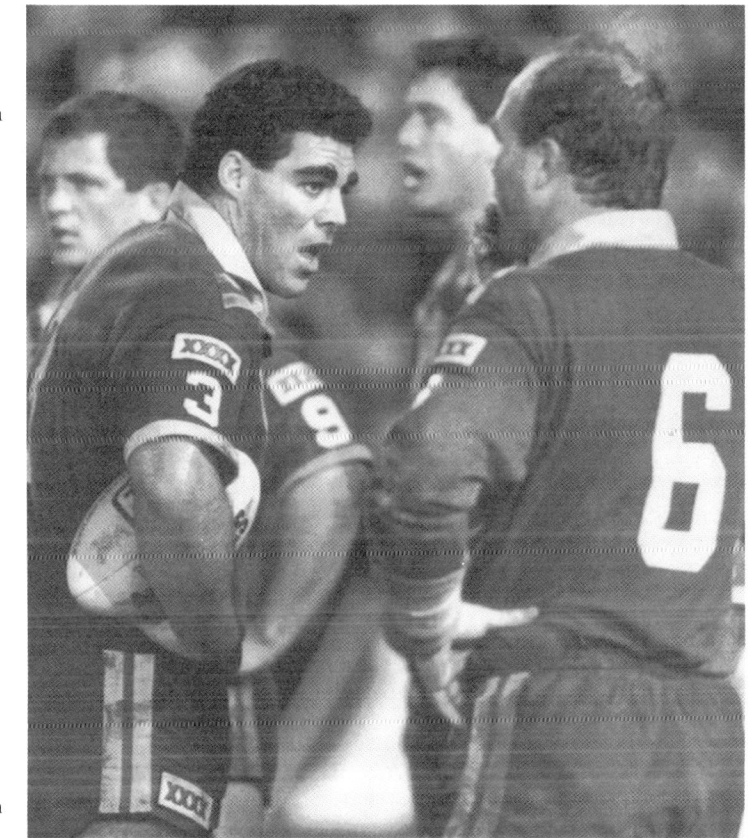

1991. First Test against New Zealand. Mal Meninga and Wally, present and past Australian captains in a losing Test

1992. Bronzed Aussie with Origin shield in safe-keeping

1992. The man behind the mask for the bronze sculpture

1992. Jacqui and Jamie-Lee — "Up, up, up" — as Wally's statue is unveiled.

1992. Wally with the Sea-FM morning crew; Suki has the long hair and no cap

1992. Mathew Devins, the 9-year-old Tamworth boy with leukaemia who touched Wally's heart. (Photo courtesy Tamworth *Northern Daily Leader*)

1992. In captain's pose, mouth-guard in hand, Wally asking the question

1992. A friendly farewell in his last game against Mal Meninga

1992. Not so friendly towards Kerrod Walters in his last match against the Broncos at Lang Park

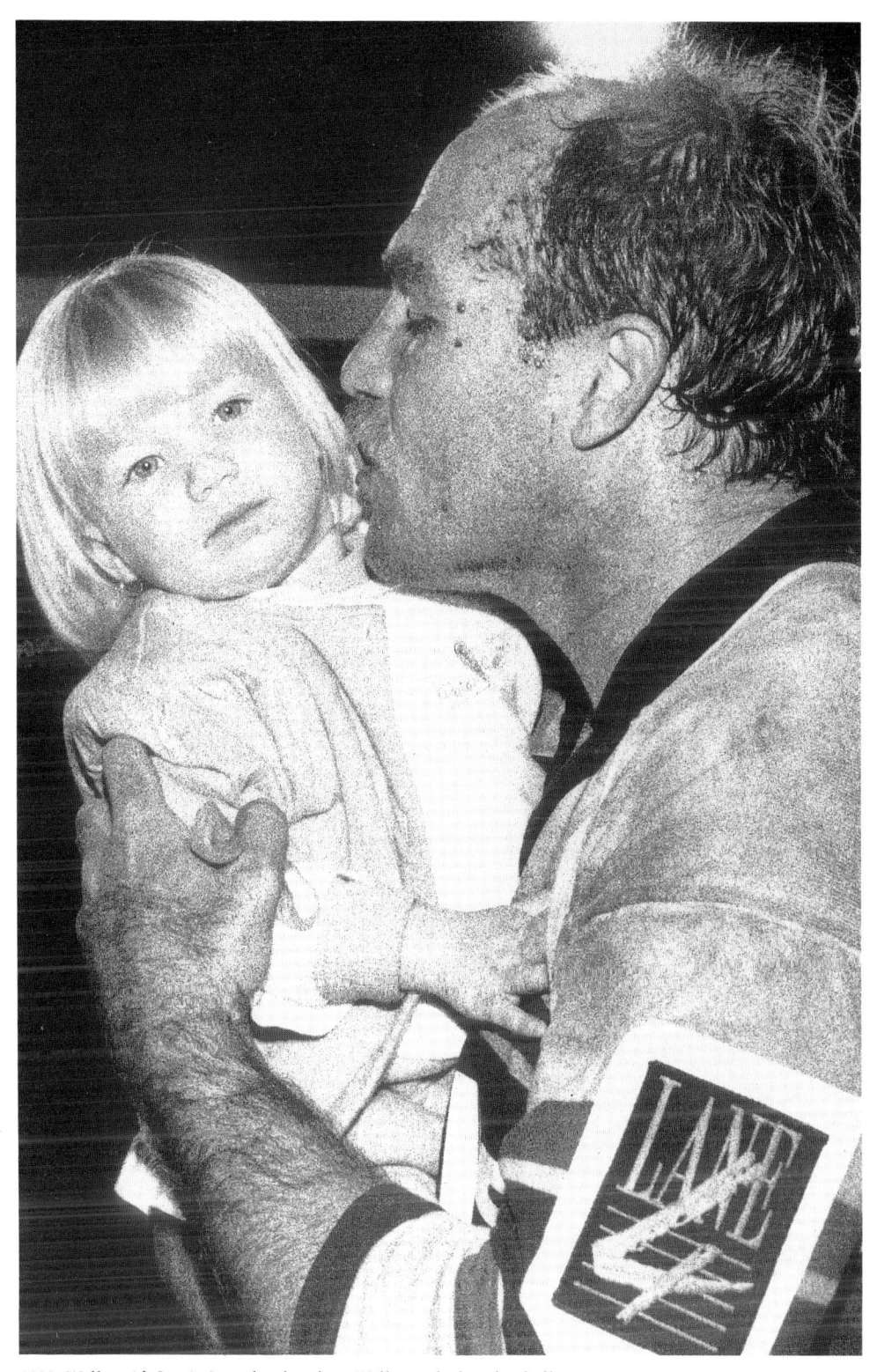

1992. Wally with Jamie-Lee, the daughter Wally put before football

1992. Triumphant to the last — Wally holds aloft the symbol of Australian Rugby League supremacy, the State of Origin shield, depicting Wally and his great friend and rival Brett Kenny

hair long, I said. "Yeah, he's still trying to keep it long, but it's going short in the wrong place!" Wayne Pearce came out of retirement to complete a quartet of champions of the past decade.

In the final 34-strong line-up Wally ended with an impressive 24 current or former internationals plus two State of Origin players. Included also was one ring-in, former Aussie Rules star Robert "Dippers" DiPierdomenico who had arrived to cover the match with fellow "Ray Martin" show comic Paul Vautin. Initially Wally was doubtful about Dippers, fearing the match could develop into a circus. But when he met the Victorian star at the airport he changed his mind. "I've never seen a bloke so eager to play a game of football," said Wally. "He kept saying, 'Mate, I was born in the wrong state. I like your game, the way you get in there and smash each other. I like that physical part instead of our game where you grab-tackle.'"

The galaxy of stars that gathered in each dressing room produced exactly the atmosphere that Wally intended — respect, enthusiasm, and fun. When Fatty Vautin entered the toilet Wally chided him, "Big game, Fatty! You're not having a spew are you?" Everyone had some advice for Dippers about the rules. Wally brought the room down when he quipped, "Dippers, if you don't know anything don't worry, Fatty played the game for 15 years and he never knew anything anyway!"

The new celebrity concept had caught on with the public. Wally's first match with the Seagulls in 1991 set a ground record of 13,189 and this last match set another record, 13,900. Many wore special Sea-FM gold cardboard crowns in Wally's honour. Wally and Brett Kenny descended to the field by helicopter, another Peter Hickey idea — Wally's manager was strong on choppers. When the chopper landing was delayed a few minutes Dippers exclaimed, "Don't tell me Wally's late! Here I am, bundle of nerves, ready for my first game of rugby league and I'm waiting for the King to arrive by chopper!"

The players laughed and when they heard the chopper overhead they shouted, "The Emperor Has Landed!" As Wally and Brett alighted Fatty led the players in the royal genuflect, bowing with both arms above their heads.

The match exceeded Wally's attacking expectations, the ball whipping about in 80 minutes of sheer exhilaration. It was not touch football, tackles were made, but line kicks were rare and penalties were always taken as taps. It was a semi-serious game in which past stars showed their skills. Seagulls' speedy Craig Weston made a break and looked certain to score until he was mown down from behind by a hurtling Eric Grothe. Wally turned to Sterling and Kenny, amazed at Guru's speed. They said, "Wal, he could play tomorrow if he wanted to." Sterling scored a try, displaying once more his deceptive sidestep. "The thing that amazes me about a bloke like Sterlo, I mean grasshoppers have got longer legs than he has, yet he sidesteps from one side of a big bloke to the other," said Wally.

Sledging became the order of the day; not the opposition — their own team-mates. Fatty Vautin told rookie Terry Hill, "Mate, I'll get you some of that stuff if you like." What stuff's that? asked Hill naively. Said Fatty, "Glue remover! So we can get the bloody ball off you!"

With the score tied 52-all, 1 minute 21 seconds still remaining, Wally signalled to the timekeeper to ring the bell. The keeper, not a man to have his job slighted, hesitated. Wally insisted. He did not set out to organise a draw, but it seemed a fitting end. Besides, the game had been played at such a hectic pace everyone was wilting. As Sterling said, "I'd have liked it a tad more fair dinkum. It was too quick for me, it was greased lightning." All voted it a success. "Take a look at the crowd, they loved it," said Vautin. Brett Kenny enthused, "If it's on again next year, you can count me in." Mick O'Connor exclaimed, "I didn't think league could be so much fun." The scoreboard blinked its last message for 1992 — "Wally, Still The King".

A week later Wally flew to Sydney for a Kangaroo reunion and next day joined a parade of retiring champions in the preliminaries to the grand final at the Sydney Football Stadium. As loud as the cheers were for Steve Roach, Michael O'Connor, Peter Sterling and Chris Walsh, they didn't match the roar that greeted Wally; "And here comes the Emperor!"

Wally's prime emotion at the Broncos grand final win was pride in having been part of the formation of the first Queensland club to win the Sydney premiership. "Didn't even cross my mind that it might have been me," he said. He congratulated Wayne Bennett and would have left except a Powers official pulled him into the dressing room. "I stood to one side, against a wall, said goodday to Alfie and a couple of the blokes. Only stayed 15 minutes. I felt like an alien. I just wasn't part of the place any more."

A few days later, back home, June Lewis walked into Paul Morgan's Mansfield hotel and congratulated him. Said Morgan, now Broncos chairman, "The only shame was that your eldest son wasn't able to sufficiently control his ego to lead that team onto the field." It was a curious comment. Did the Broncos actually regret jettisoning Wally? June accepted Morgan's remark as well intentioned words of peace. The truth, as Gene Miles remarked to me, was that it would have been difficult for the Broncos to have won the title with the Old Guard — him, Wally and Greg Dowling. "We were held in awe by the younger players and if things weren't going right, instead of lifting as a team, they all expected one of us to be the game breaker," said Gene. "When we left they all took a bit more responsibility and did it by themselves."

Wally played one more match, in Adelaide in November, as part of the Grand Prix festivities, the Seagulls giving an invitation team known as the Grand Prix Aces a 50-10 hiding. It was a strange place to end up but it wasn't as though he was severing all contact with the game. He was already playing matches from his lounge chair — the World Cup final at Wembley and the Broncos world club challenge against Wigan. "The left, the left Alfie! Not that way!" Wally whispered to himself, leaning helpfully in that direction. Said Jacqui, "He directs everything. He's a born coach."

15

Jacqui — Proud Partner

In the early 1980s Jacqueline Green and Wally Lewis had moved in vaguely the same school-football-surf club social circles on Brisbane's eastside. Jacqui remembers passing him on the beach one day and thinking, "I know you. Where do I know you from?" When she sat down a friend ribbed her, "Check out Wally Lewis. He was perving on you so hard he nearly fell over!" Ah! That's who he was. Jacqui, an effervescent blonde with twinkling blue eyes, had won a Miss Personality contest. Wally was about to become a household name. They met again soon after, with friends at a city hotel one evening. Jacqui had parked her car near the darker part of the Botanic Gardens and wasn't keen on walking there alone. She said to Wally, "If you walk me to my car, I can give you a lift home." As they walked Jacqui wondered, "I hope he doesn't think I've asked him for some other reason." She was so keen to disabuse him she nearly drove over his foot in her haste to escape after she dropped him off. She thought, "What's he got? He's baldy, he's quiet, I'm 21, fancy-free, I'm going to have a good time!" They were married about a year later.

That innocent girl could never have imagined what lay in store for her over the next decade as wife to the single most controversial character in Australian sport. It might be said she required the patience of Job and the saintliness of Mother Theresa. By the time Wally retired she had become central to the home resistance movement which buoyed Wally during his darkest hours.

She may appear a princess bride but Jacqui belies her innocent image. Once, at a Sydney match, when spectators behind began chanting their anthem "Wally's A Wanker", she turned on them and declared vehemently, "That's definitely one thing he's not, I can assure you!" On "The Midday Show", Ray Martin asked Jacqui, "Tell me, what's he like away from football?" Jacqui brought a blush to Wally's face when she replied, "Well Ray, I didn't marry him for his football ability, I can guarantee you that!" Jacqui laughed when I reminded her of that. She said, "I love him differently now, not like I did at first. I understand him. We can argue but we don't hang onto it, we're good mates."

Wally agrees they have grown together since moving to the Gold Coast. "She's my closest friend and supporter," he said. "We haven't had time to get bored with each other. I've been away so much, and when I'm home I get involved with everything. So when we do get time to relax and spend some time together we appreciate it all the more." He tried to keep football problems to himself, he said. "Jack's got enough burdens as it is. But if something goes wrong invariably she's the first to know."

Jacqui's way of coping is truly magnificent. In moments of crisis her effervescence becomes still, deep water. Traumas, confusions, stresses and pain rush at the Lewis household and subside under her passive strength. She says Wally is the strength, and so he is when called upon. Whenever he told her of some new defeat in his life it was Jacqui who would voice their rage or shed a tear for both of them. "Some of it was water off a duck's back to me," said Wally. "But it would upset Jack. And by sharing the disappointment she made it a lot easier for me to bear." In that way Jacqui set the tone of their marriage, providing the buffer and renewing the optimism when things fell apart. She was the oasis that sustained Wally through his barren year.

Said manager Peter Hickey, "If there ever was a woman behind a man, she's it. She's an incredible lady. I've seen Wally come home sometimes like an enraged bull and she'll just maintain this serenity. And all of a sudden he'll just melt into her frame of mind. She's irresistible. It's unbelievable how she does it."

Jacqui idolises Wally. "There have been four lovely occasions in my life — my wedding and the birth of my three children," she told me. Friends say they have never heard her, despite severe provocation from Wally in his blacker moments, use a sharp tone towards him or put him down in his absence. Indeed they wonder whether

her unquestioning loyalty always served him best — whether a more impartial opinion might have been more useful when he was butting up against the brick walls of authority. Jacqui's answer is that Wally was a big boy, she didn't have to ride shotgun on his career or decisions. She was there to offer unfettered love and support.

Her loyalty was not confined to the home. She once smacked a man over the head for abusing Wally at a match. "You, shut up!" she commanded the astonished spectator. She told me, "I don't mind them criticising his play, but abusing him, especially if my boys are there, I won't cop that."

She was well used to the awed murmurs which followed them down supermarket aisles — "There's Wally Lewis." But one day she was shopping with Wally near her home when she heard a shop assistant whisper, "Oh Wally Lewis? He's a wanker." Jacqui followed the girl. "I wasn't going to have that," she told me. "If I want to hear that I can go to Sydney. I don't need it in my own backyard. I explained that to her and I don't think she'll say it again."

Increasingly, when Wally's former managers were not vigilant, it was Jacqui who chased cheques in payment for Wally's attendance at functions. Both Billy J. Smith and Peter Hickey found the more they liaised with Jacqui, the more reliable Wally became. It was easy for Jacqui to act as Wally's advocate. She believed in him and he began to consult her more and more when making important decisions, not just because of the family but because he valued her opinion. Peter Hickey noticed that he'd say, "Oh, I want to ask Jacqui about that."

In October 1992, Wally rang Jacqui just before he was about to announce on air that he was accepting the State of Origin coaching. "We'd already discussed it," said Jacqui. "He knew it was fine with me but he just wanted that last-minute approval. He said, 'I'm going to, is that all right?' I said, 'Yes.'"

Few Australians, short of prime ministers, premiers and pop stars, have experienced the degree of loss of privacy that Wally has. "You've got to feel sorry for him," said Peter O'Callaghan. "He can never be the bloke next door that comes and has a drink in the pub with you. Yet when he was younger that's what we used to do all the time. You go out with him now and people queue up for autographs. If he tells them no, they say, 'Well you are what everyone says you are, arrogant, stuck up, too good for the common people!'

If he starts signing he ruins his outing. He got abrupt with them a few years ago but now he's more tolerant. He realises he has to do it."

Jacqui of course has witnessed it more than anyone. When the family prepares to go out where she knows Wally will be bombarded, Jacqui says, "You, you, you AND you, be good! Whoever asks you for an autograph, smile at them." Usually Wally is happy to oblige but sometimes the approaches catch him by surprise and he is unsure whether people are having a go at him or are delighted to meet him.

Pacific Fair, Broadbeach, is his local shopping place and regulars and shopkeepers have become used to him. One day a woman glimpsed him and shouted at the top of her voice, "WALLY LEWIS!" Jacqui felt sorry for the woman because it was an involuntary exclamation, she was simply shocked to see him up close. Said Jacqui, "She shouldn't have done it, but he was embarrassed and he gave her the death look."

The catch is, Wally often craves anonymity and loves to shop with Jacqui. She warns him, "If you want to come, bear with it. Don't do it to me. If you get the slightest bit angry ..." But equally she is happy to rescue him from bores who harrass him with lengthy conversations. "They don't know when to drop off and because I've told Wally to be polite he gets stuck," said Jacqui. "So I'll step in and say, 'Wally, I need you, NOW.' " Once, desperate to go out with friends, Wally told Jacqui, "I'll wear a hat and sunglasses." She said, "Great! Your physique stands out like a neon light. You won't get away with it just hiding your head. They'll recognise your body."

After the Test against Great Britain at Lang Park in 1992, Wally was swamped when he approached the dressing rooms. "My girlfriend was amazed," said Jacqui. "She couldn't believe it. He didn't even play. That's why I let him get away with being arrogant because it's fair enough sometimes. The other guys don't get nearly as much as that. Geno and Greg Dowling don't, they can walk the streets. Even Alfie doesn't get as much."

Wally likes to take the family to the Brisbane Exhibition. "You have to understand the rights of people to approach me," said Wally. "Someone asked could they get a quick photo and I said, 'If you'll just pardon me this one day, this is my kids' outing. If you come over to where the rides are I'll be with you when the boys are on the ride.'

Then Jacqui got onto me to be polite. I told her, 'You know what's it's like, it won't stop with one.' Anyway I stopped and within seconds there was a queue. I got over to the rides 45 minutes later and I reckon I got off light. I shook my head and Jacqui said, 'I'm sorry, I should have known.' "

After observing that incident Jacqui's father, Bruce Green, told Jacqui, "He must be the most recognised bloke on earth!" It wasn't just the autographs, it was the stress of the conversations and praise which went with them. "When people keep putting wraps on you, you run out of things to say," said Wally. "I say, 'Oh thanks, but plenty of other players helped along' or 'Rugby league is a team game' and they say, 'Yes, but you're this and that.' You can only say thanks so many ways and after 40 or 50 in half an hour you start thinking, 'I don't deserve all this. It's too much, it's unreal.' And I start getting angry with myself for not being grateful. Then I have to go right back to zero and start again and not let it get to me so I don't get shitty again."

Then there were the ridiculous requests which accompany an autograph. At that Exhibition stint someone said to him, "My brother would like to meet you. You played football with him at Valleys in 1955." Before Wally was born! Another asked, "Could you write me a reference please?" and "Can you come and talk to our social club?"

The boot was on the other foot one day at Hamilton Island. Wally was bending down examining a cabinet of gifts and yanked Jacqui by the slacks to get her attention. "What do you reckon about these?" he said. He heard a muffled laugh, looked up and found he had tugged George Harrison's trousers. For once Wally was speechless as he looked up at the ex-Beatle. Jacqui giggled later, "Don't you dare ever get annoyed with anyone if they're lost for words with you."

At private functions guests aren't sure how to treat Wally. He generally sticks close to Jacqui and her girlfriends. "They all tend to shelter him because he's just Wally to them now," said Jacqui. "He'll stand around and listen and occasionally they'll say, 'Wally have you ever ...' and he'll come into it. But they don't expect him to chatter on. Talking, socialising tires him. Nor can he mingle at a party. He can't just go up and say, 'Hi!' because people around him stop to listen. If he goes to get a plate of food, everyone's eyes follow him.

The room sort of watches. What's the King going to eat? What's he going to do next? He can't relax."

Wally found sanctuary with Jacqui's close friends after Broncos football matches while Jacqui was taking the children to her parents before returning to the club. "I'd say, 'If you like, the girls will drive you to Red Hill.' He could have gone with any of the team but he'd tell them, 'Jack's organised me to go, I'm right.' He'd come out and stand beside them and wait. Wouldn't say anything. It's amazing how quiet he is like that." It took Jacqui a while to get used to Wally's silences. She said, "He'd ring me from, say, England, three times a day and I could count the words he said to me. He says, 'I'm listening'. Even my family had to learn that he doesn't yack on."

Wally's work commitments have meant he is constantly in company he would not necessarily choose for himself and in which he is not always comfortable. He's expected to charm businessmen as easily as football fans but in truth he is as lost at a corporate dinner as any stranger in their midst. "It comes back to one-sided conversations again," said manager Peter Hickey. "He's a good storyteller and that gets him by. But obviously he's more at home with footballers. That's the only time I see him relaxed and having a laugh." Hickey amuses himself watching Wally at functions, surveying the surroundings as though he is evaluating a new football pitch. "It takes him 20 minutes, shifting in his seat, looking around the room," said Hickey. "He can't relax until he's got it all sussed out and then suddenly, Bang! he'll settle."

He has an instant rapport with other sportsmen of equal stature, especially cricketers. Footballers are open, gregarious types, whereas cricket isolates players and turns them into solitary independent individuals, much more Wally's type.

A particular friend has been former Test batsman Greg Ritchie. "He was a real good supporter, 'Fat Cat'," said Wally. "When I switched to the Seagulls he used to get a few of his mates, hire a limo for the night and drive down the coast to watch the game. That used to mean a hell of a lot to me."

Wally is an avid swapper of sporting apparel. Once he walked into the West Indies dressing room at the 'Gabba and Viv Richards saw him. "Worl! How are you mun!" said Viv. Wally swapped an Origin jumper for a Windies World Series shirt. He has an Allan Border Aussie one-day shirt and an Ian Botham Test sweater as well.

Botham joked to him, "I believe you're the bloke the media likes to write about and give as much trouble to as they give me?"

Though the Lewises have a silent phone number any new outbreak of publicity always attracts nuisance calls. During an Origin camp abusive messages were left on the Lewis' answering machine. "Hideous they were, effing this and that," said Jacqui. "They were young girls and a man. I called police and they took the tape away and somehow traced it." Wally's sacking from the Australian team caused a new outbreak of strange, sometimes incoherent calls, neither abusive nor in praise. One caller pretended to be *Courier-Mail* journalist, Steve Ricketts. Could he speak to Wally? He's mowing the lawn, said Jacqui. Oh, I'll ring back later, said the caller. "That's when I knew it wasn't Steve," said Jacqui. "Steve would have said, 'Get him!'"

When the family moved to the Gold Coast, they experienced a minor case of the infatuated fan syndrome which plagued Australian champion surf iron-man Trevor Hendy. "She was a young girl, maybe 15, short and chubby," said Jacqui. "She rode her bike and sat outside our unit at Burleigh and watched us for hours. In the school holidays it was worse, she'd be there all day until 7 p.m.. Went on for months. You'd look out the window and there she was, morning and afternoon. Then one day she slipped through the electronic gates. I was hauling groceries up the stairs and she said, 'Are you Wally Lewis' wife?' She somehow got our number from the unit manager and began talking to me on the intercom. As soon as she saw Wally come home she'd call and ask if she could come up. Wally didn't want to know. One day she sent us chocolates and flowers and said it was because I was so nice to her. I did feel sorry for her. But I felt uneasy and it got weird, this constant surveillance, it worried me. So when we moved, we just went, left no forwarding address. Just disappeared. We haven't seen her since."

The Lewises learned that the best way to cope with Wally's fame was to go to the same place again and again until the owners, at least, grew used to his presence. That way they could relax at a selected steakhouse or cinema without the owner offering them freebies. At airports Wally heads for the Golden Wing lounge and reads. He knows better than to sit in any public place and look unoccupied.

He surrounds his home with a high brick fence for privacy, though that doesn't stop sightseers cruising slowly by for a peek at the rich and famous. Wally is well off rather than rich. If he sold every asset he owned down to his toothbrush he might just reach the million mark, but anybody who owns a solid home in Sydney's eastern suburbs would match that. Still, he is only 33, a young man in the business world.

The Lewis children have not yet felt the full impact of having Wally as a father. It may hit the boys when they enter high school and they're expected to perform up to the standards of the Lewis name. Heath Lewis, though of first grade standard himself, never quite shed the burden of being Wally's younger brother.

When Wally enrolled his older son Mitchell in school, word quickly spread through the playground that Wally Lewis was on the premises. "By the time we left kids were lined up along both sides of the school driveway waving to us," said Jacqui. "My boys thought it was wonderful. The schoolkids were yelling out 'Jamie-Lee, Jamie-Lee' and she's waving back, grinning everywhere, can't hear a thing but loving it all." Mitchell's popularity was sufficient to cause one teacher to tell older children not to single him out for attention. What impressed Wally about the school was that pupils were taught manners. If boys approached for an autograph it was, "Excuse me, Mr Lewis, would you mind?" not, "Hey Wally, sign this!" But Wally will never be able to help out at the school fete. He'd destroy it because of queues to his booth.

Wally enjoys his children, fatherhood providing him with an uncluttered sense of priorities. Apart from his clockwork morning calls from Sea-FM, he will not leave on a trip without saying goodbye, even if it means driving out to the school in the middle of the day. He adores being asked father-son, "How do you do this?" questions. The boys say, "Dad's smart." Not because of football, but because he can play Nintendo computer games with them. Both boys could have begun junior football already but Wally can't bear being around the sideline mothers with the killer instincts.

Mitchell does not share June Lewis' athletic Ballinger ability and has evinced no interest in playing football. He shows academic promise, however. Lincoln has Wally's competitiveness but not his build. Both boys identify the split persona of their father. When playing football in the yard Mitchell will sing out to Lincoln, "I'll be Dad and you be Wally Lewis." Being Dad is the better choice of the two. After Wally's relaxed charity match night Mitchell told Jacqui,

"Dad won't be sore tonight. It was a real good match that one." The boys know that after hard matches they can scarcely touch their father for fear of worsening his aches and pains. Jamie-Lee is pure Ballinger-Lewis, strong, athletic, fights with Lincoln tooth and nail and will shine in any sport where her deafness is no impediment.

Jacqui Lewis began marriage thinking about Wally as her "head man". Her father had been that once and then she transferred to Wally. She is no feminist, comes from a traditional family backround. The years have changed her, though. "I'm my own person now," she said. "Wally was away a lot, I had children then came the troubles and Jamie-Lee. I became independent and when the off-season came I had to adjust to having him around the house again. I had to stop myself getting cranky with him because I was used to doing things my way. I can see it's a relief for him to be home with me. Friends say, 'He must be bugging you, getting under your feet.' But I think to myself, 'Never once will I complain, because there'll be times when I want him and he won't be there'.

While Wally attracted all the media attention in the past, it focused equally on Jacqui during the Jamie-Lee saga. Only Ray Martin has realised so far but Jacqui has the priceless ability to project herself on television. In a different life she could have been a show hostess on looks alone. She's naturally telegenic. But one star in the family is probably enough for now.

16
The Greatest Ever

What manner of man has rugby league bequeathed us? He's not a big drinker, he doesn't smoke inside the house or in front of the children, which, given his lifestyle, scarcely qualifies him as a smoker at all. He doesn't limp, he has no visible scars, and his nose, though broken several times, has never taken a crooked turn like Geno's or been flattened like Greg Dowling's. His looks however, belie the damage he has suffered. Football has broken, cracked and dislocated so many bones and so damaged his joints that Wally's hospital ward card reads like that of a survivor of a head-on highway collision.

Seagulls physiotherapist Mike Pahoff admires Wally's defensive power even more than his attacking skill. "His front-on defence is amazing," he said. "He knocks them silly. The impact is unbelievable. He can pick up a forward running at him at full speed and drive him backwards. It's almost a miracle because forwards these days are not only huge, they're nimble, can change speed and change direction. Wally nails them just the same." At a price.

In the four years from 1988 to 1991 Wally underwent general anaesthetics for surgery on his limbs in Holy Spirit Hospital, Brisbane, on no fewer than eight occasions — an average of once every six months. The surgeon who has supervised most of Wally's operations is Brisbane orthopaedic specialist Dr Peter Myers. He understands football, because he was a reserve rugby union half-back for Queensland in the Mark Loane era. Wally was first referred to him shortly after Myers returned from an extended working stint overseas. "The name didn't mean an awful lot to me and he sat for an hour in the waiting room," said Dr Myers. "He was a bit uptight — I'd say he was fuming by the time I did see him. He's never waited since." He joked, "Today he pulls up here and says, 'Can I see Peter, I'm double-parked?' "

Starting at the top, Wally's injury roll call begins with the inner walls of his eye sockets — technically the medial wall of the orbit — both fractured by elbow blows, both serious injuries, right eye in 1989, left in 1991. Each required treatment and rest but not surgery. In 1980 New Zealand forward Mark Graham broke Wally's jaw in a punch-up and in the same season paralysed Wally's larynx in a tackle. Wally needed mouth-to-mouth to halt the spasm. In 1987 he jammed his chin on his chest in a tackle, straining the ligaments in his neck, resulting in hospitalisation and a neck brace.

In 1977, as a schoolboy rugby union international, he dislocated the acromioclavicular joint — commonly known as the AC joint, where the collarbone meets the shoulder — in his left shoulder. In 1982 he dislocated his right AC joint, did it again in 1986 and a third time in 1988. Eventually that right clavicle, protruding into and irritating the skin, caused bursitis. In 1989 Dr Myers operated on the joint, cut off the damaged outer centimetres of the clavicle and stabilised the joint by transferring a ligament around his shoulder. In his final seasons Wally was careful, as much as is possible in football, not to land on the point of either shoulder.

He fractured his right forearm in 1988 and his left forearm in 1990, in each case the radial bone. Dr Myers inserted steel nails 20 cms long — called Rush pins — through the marrow of each radius to help mend the fractures. The pins were used to avoid the experience of Mal Meninga who had an arm fracture repaired with a conventional steel plate. When Meninga returned to football his arm fractured on several different occasions at the holes in the bone where screws held the steel plate to the arm.

"Nails are a real fiddle because you have to pre-bend them to exactly the right shape of the bone," said Dr Myers. "A lot of older surgeons used nails before plates came along. Professionally, the safest thing for me to do would have been to use plates because of the controversy that would have ensued had the pins failed. I bit the bullet because I wanted to avoid any re-fracture." The second arm was slower to heal than the first. "As soon as you've got two, one's faster than the other," he said.

Both pins eventually backed out a little. Dr Myers knocked the right pin back in again. That sounds simple, but it required a general anaesthetic. When the pin in the controversial left arm, which caused him to miss the 1990 Kangaroo tour, backed out in 1992, Dr Myers removed it. Wally kept it as a wry memento. As with his shoulders, after his arms were repaired Wally tried to avoid direct blows to them. If he missed a tackle, likely as not he was instinctively protecting his arms.

Repeated arthroscopies have been necessary to repair worn or torn cartilage in both Lewis' knees. In the left knee arthritic deterioration is painfully evident. Wally has a patch, about the size of a one cent piece, where the contact is bone upon bone — there is no surface joint cartilage left at all. If he sits in the wrong position for long periods it starts to ache. Occasionally it locks painfully and he can't walk. As his surgeon Dr Myers told me, "The overall joint isn't terrible but it doesn't have a happy future. It's significantly worse than the right knee."

These major injuries don't include the restricted rotation of his neck. Wally is known for setting up play, which means he invites a tackle in order to send other players into the clear. The result is that he is off balance as he passes the ball and in the resultant tackle — collision — his head is violently flicked, producing repeated minor whiplash neck injuries. If you spend enough time in his company you will see him absently place one hand on his head and the other under his chin and sickeningly wrench his head sideways in a chiropractic manipulation. The sight makes strong men pale.

The preceding list does not include the half-dozen CAT scans and scores of X-ray visits, or the concussions, black eyes, repeatedly broken nose, deaf ears from blows in tackles and hundreds of stitches to his mouth, forehead and eyebrows. Nor does it include the soft tissue injuries, such as his chronic hamstring tears requiring physiotherapy daily for weeks. Then there is the blunt trauma — corked thigh, calf and arm muscles. Wally bruises significantly and his body after a weekend game was often a chequerboard of black and blue marks.

Nor does that list include all the injuries Wally ignored. "I went to slip his wedding ring back on after his bath one night and he yelled," said Jacqui. "The joint was so swollen from a dislocation it wouldn't fit. Then I noticed his thumb was sticking out sideways and I said, 'That's got to be broken.' But he played next week." Wally never slept well the night after a game. "He was always pretty restless from the aches and pains. Or he'd be up wandering around in the middle of the night looking for ice or washing soda. I was so grateful after his final game that it was the last time I'd have him moaning and groaning in his sleep beside me."

The washing soda was a trick passed onto Wally by some old-time footballers; it was used to reduce swelling in injuries. "You put washing soda in an old sock and tie it to your knee or whatever and it absorbs the fluid during the night," said Wally. "When you get up in the morning the powder has set like a brick from the fluid it draws from the swelling. I've told a few young physios about it and they've laughed but then I've heard them later telling blokes, 'If you want to reduce the swelling, get a bag of washing soda …' "

Wally played right at the threshold of fastest, strongest and hardest, among those who risk injury the most. He did it for 15 years and towards the end it showed. In 1988 he missed only four matches and that was one of his worst ever season for injuries, yet by 1990 he scarcely took to the field owing to a combination of crook knees, torn hamstrings and a broken arm.

Team-mates often bagged Wally as a hypochondriac. It was true that as the team doctor moved around the players checking for injuries after a match, Wally usually had something to report — he was usually injured. "Some players never say boo, and then turn up midweek and say something's sore," said Dr Myers. "I ask, 'Why didn't you tell me after the game?' and they say, 'Oh I thought it would get better.' I preferred Wally's awareness. He looked after injuries, sought help and worked hard at repairing himself."

Said Seagulls physiotherapist Mike Pahoff, "What really struck me about Wally was that he would come to you for advice, listen and heed it. Not in full view of everyone, but at home exercising, stretching or icing." Pahoff said people did not give Wally credit for his courage. "He's a hard, tough man, and he always put his body on the line," he said. "He'd have a significant injury, I'd know it, but he wouldn't carry on too much about it, just let you know after the game when the fuss had died down."

Reading Wally's psychological health card is not as easy as his physical history. Deciphering the Lewis personality is like examining a Rubics cube — it has just as many facets and few people know the answer. Depending upon the person to whom you last spoke, Wally has the capacity to become a successful businessman or he will end up talking to the pigeons in the park. Most people are confident he will translate his vast experience as a player into an excellent coaching career. Others say he's just an ex-footballer and there's a truckload of them dumped every season. Such is the broad spectrum of Wally's admirers and critics. Therein lies the explanation of why Wally's career, after such a long period of success, plummeted as it did towards the end.

It could be argued that Wally's complex personality was formed in childhood; that Wally owed both his gifts and his hindrances to his parents. Both were first-class athletes without ever proceeding to stardom, Jim as a first-grade footballer and coach, June as a Queensland netballer. They knew what success required and ensured that nothing, neither self-doubt nor self-discipline, stood between Wally and his destiny.

Jim Lewis provided the relaxed expertise, teaching Wally the importance of defence. Then, when Wally had a perfect defensive game, Jim would ask, "Yeah, but how'd you go in attack?" That's how he kept Wally's ego earthed. June believed in sport as an educator and Wally inherited her fiercely competitive spirit. Wally could do little wrong in her eyes, and this built up his confidence.

Some family friends saw Jim and June's joy in Wally's achievements as being adoration approaching ecstasy, parental love allied to vicarious pleasure. There are parallels — the parents of Pat Cash, John McEnroe — except in those instances the father was paramount, whereas with Wally it was more June. Wally admired both those tennis rebels and their approach to sport, as well as another controversial sportsman, West Indian batsman, Viv Richards. "I loved the way he used to walk out with that arrogant look on his face, chewing gum, looking as if nothing ever worried him," said Wally. In the role models chosen we see the student revealed.

It was always a fine line for his parents, governing their headstrong eldest son without restricting his freedom to express his talent. Even if they erred on the side of too much freedom and too little discipline, they laid the groundwork for Wally to blossom eventually into Australia's best known footballer.

Wally didn't need to be pushed into the ring. He leapt in. He was good at everything he tried, be it sport, cards, drinking beer, driving fast cars or chasing girls. Everything always fell into place. He carried his gift lightly in his younger years, always doing just enough to nurture his natural athleticism. He also had the knack of being in the right place at the right time. When first grade lock John Ribot left Valleys to play for Newtown, in Sydney, the Valleys reserve grade lock had just retired. It left an opening for the lad with the long, thick blond locks in his first year out of high school.

Wally often used to wonder whether he would make it to the top, even after playing Brisbane first grade and representing Queensland. Then he was selected in the first Origin side. Said Wally, "I looked at Arthur Beetson in the dressing room and thought, 'I can either go on from here or bugger it up. So make up your mind, do you want success or not?'" He did. But during those years neither home nor school, and certainly not football, instilled in him a work ethic. He was rarely employed and so never had to bow to authority. He never learnt to be discreet when he should have, to discern good advice from bad, and never to trust the silver-tongued without first examining their motives.

From that 1980 Origin on, Wally's future was sealed. He was chosen by the QRL — Senator Ron McAuliffe more precisely — to lead Queensland football back to equality with NSW. As so often happened with Wally when he was given a challenge, he produced more than they could have hoped. He gave Queensland supremacy. With that single act he actually altered the self-image of the Queensland populace. You didn't have to follow State of Origin football to be infected by the confidence which bubbled from the media. He knocked the chip off Queensland's shoulder, but the weight of such parochialism doesn't disappear. It is merely transferred and Wally carried it away with him. For a decade on the football field Wally acted out Queensland's most basic prejudices, hang-ups, paranoia and zenophobia. His influence on the population worked a catharsis. The more he strutted, argued and gesticulated ... and won, the more he freed Queenland of those long-held grudges for alleged and real discriminations perpetrated by NSW. Spectators left Lang Park elated, usually by victory, but always by having vicariously experienced Wally act out a payback for them against the southern tribe. Wally took upon himself the burden of Queensland's sporting past. He has it still. Maybe Alfie Langer, if he's got the right stuff, can pick up the baton. Maybe nobody can. We'll see.

They called him the King and the Emperor yet the power he gave Queensland was more spiritual than material. Wally led the renaissance of rugby league in Queensland and with every passing season he grew in stature and in fame. Through his leadership and brilliance he consistently confounded NSW and turned predicted failure into victory. Powerful men, even premiers and prime ministers, sought to associate with him. I remember meeting a prominent city businessman who, upon learning I was Wally's biographer, said in awe, "I shook hands with him once." He could have been speaking about the Pope. Women fawned upon him.

In rugby league the uncritical approval went as high as ARL chief Ken Arthurson, under whose patronage Wally led a charmed life, making mistakes but rarely being punished. Arthurson once said, "He's always had a remarkable propensity to get people's backs up and he certainly got them offside. For anyone to say differently they'd be having themselves on." Rugby league has its share of top players who have been drunks, thugs and druggies — all forgiven. Wally had only to spit and the media never forgot, which made it difficult for the public to forgive. Arthurson's proudest boast was that he had stuck up for Lewis when others would have had his head. Arthurson made allowances for Wally because he liked him, because Wally was charismatic and because, faced with the Australian Rules challenge from the Sydney Swans and the Brisbane Bears, two powerful states of rugby league were better than one. Wally's continued reign was vital to the game. As Arthurson said, "If Wally had been born in Sydney the Origin score would be reversed. He was the difference." It was popularly said around this time that Wally became bigger than the game. It is a fatuous statement. He was never that. He was merely too important, too useful to rugby league to be knocked off at that stage.

It was remarkable, such was his genius, how Wally's star climbed and climbed, from 1981 to 1988, with scarcely a setback. From State of Origin to the Broncos became a natural progression. Where McAuliffe built the state's resurgence around him, the Broncos built a club. Once more he was feted, this time by the Broncos directors. His fame bankrolled the Broncos as surely as Marilyn Monroe bankrolled films for Hollywood. No single footballer had reached his prominence within Australia before.

He didn't play matches, he delivered performances. The football stadium was his amphitheatre, the field his stage. He bestrode the game with a passion unequalled before or since. Coaches might scheme but as captain he was writer, director and lead player and he altered the script at whim. His soliloquies to referees were as much part of his repertoire as his solo skills. He didn't perform brilliantly every game, no artist does. But the greater the occasion the larger he grew, reserving his best for State of Origin at Lang Park.

There he captured the air like Judy Garland or Elvis Presley. He communed with the crowd, projected himself like a hologram, departing the physical field and giving himself to the stands. The people rose and roared, privileged to have witnessed another masterful performance. Nobody short of a prophet should instill 33,000 faithful with such euphoria, but Wally did. He added a new dimension to the game. As letter writer Mr Tom Ramsay of Broadbeach, put it so lyrically to the *Courier-Mail* one day, "He was able to amplify the inaudible whisper of discontent in the Queensland soul. Nothing else matters. Except the score."

He was, however, likened to Charles de Gaulle, or Gough Whitlam, who were so blinded by their own magnificence that they failed to observe their rudeness to others. Arrogance was the word most often used to censure Wally, but he was loved far more than he was hated. In a country which put a rogue like John MacArthur on its banknotes, and where to call someone a "bastard" is a term of endearment, Wally's larrikinism made him admired. He had a working-class self-effacement; despite being hailed as a hero, he was reluctant to stand out in the crowd. It was accepted as modesty but it was more likely rooted in Wally's instinctive understanding of the twin cliches in Australian culture, that the only thing worse than failure is too much success, and that it is more important to avoid making enemies than to make friends.

If you reach such heights there's always someone trying to bring you down by fair means or foul — a jealous club director, an envious team-mate, anyone who felt they'd been offended. Whether the Broncos executives liked Wally or not they could console themselves with this: that although there were plenty of other five-eighths around who didn't have egos, who would train the house down and never give the coach the slightest trouble, they wouldn't draw a dime at the Lang Park turnstiles.

Then suddenly Wally was 30. Though still King of the Origins, his two years with the Broncos hadn't produced a Sydney premiership. In the eyes of those who mattered, Wally was like those other phenomenons of the exuberant 1980s, Bond, Skase and Elliot — he hadn't delivered.

Wally will remember the events of 1990 for the rest of his life. He fought his fall every inch of the way. But the fingers on which he thoughtlessly trod on the way up, fastened around his throat on the way down.

In his formative years Wally never learned any mechanism for coping with adversity of such magnitude. He had never had to. Then it overwhelmed him. Those who might have given Wally wise counsel, but who had instead given him adulation, discarded him. Nobody ever said, "You're doing the wrong thing by yourself. Don't think that because you're Wally Lewis you can crash through all the time." Who would tell the King he had no clothes? Not that Wally would have taken such advice kindly anyway. He had been as seduced by his robes as everyone. Realism could only return when the humiliation was complete.

By the time he was stripped of all offices he was a shaken man. He had lost his self-esteem, his confidence, his trust in friends. He was bewildered. He was a victim, of course, of the era in which he played which permitted one man to so dominate. It can't happen again. As in American football, coaches now take top billing. He was a victim of his own greatness because inevitably there had to be a decline, yet nobody could have been prepared for the speed with which he fell. He was a victim of the renaissance of rugby league in Queensland. We've got Wally Lewis, the QRL trumpeted, and year after year he dared not fail them. The image sustained him but the responsibility sapped him, eventually distorted his thinking and affected his behaviour.

He was a victim of the media — not necessarily of the media's messengers, the journalists — a distinction Wally didn't always make. His critics say he manipulated the media but the reality was the reverse — he was just too easy to bait. He told me, "They reckon I shouldn't react. Well pig's arse! I'll never sit there and pretend nothing has been said." He was often justified. He once received a letter from a Sydney solicitor offering to represent him in an action against a newspaper over excessive use of that scornful "wanker" title.

Wally's relations with the media fluctuated to such a degree that he became a contradiction — he could be the best communicator in the world and the worst. Yet anyone who spent an hour in Wally's company at the height of his fame would understand that the sheer volume of calls meant he could only deflect media interest rather than orchestrate it. The *Courier-Mail*'s Robert Craddock wrote in a farewell column about Wally, "The demands on his time were incredible. No wonder top sportsmen such as Don Bradman, Greg Chappell and Greg Norman gained a reputation for being aloof. If any of these had tried to give time to everyone who approached them they would have turned themselves inside out mentally." Greg Norman lives outside Australia and in cricket Greg Chappell never had to deal with rugby league's corrosive interstate jealousy. Bradman is the only true comparison and nobody ever accused the Don of being humble. He eventually became such a private man he was almost a recluse. Wally likewise withdrew.

If the debacles of 1990 sent him into his shell, the discovery of Jamie-Lee's deafness winkled him out again. For months, during his career decline, Wally refused to believe that things wouldn't fall into place once more. He never imagined he was bigger than the game, nor even bigger than a club, but he thought he directed his own fate. "With the help of people like McAuliffe and Arthurson, Wally used to control his career," said Jacqui. "When that went bad we still had our two sons and daughter, and everything seemed perfect. But after Jamie-Lee he realised he couldn't control everything at all, not even in his own family." So a tiny blond toddler finally cut him down to normal proportions.

Jamie-Lee changed not just Wally's priorities but his way of thinking. At first he took her news almost as another punishment, more of the same being dealt out by clubs, medicos, selectors and now the hand of fate. He took it as a judgment upon himself. But then he asked himself questions he had never needed to ask before. Where was he going? What was important? How should he live? These were metaphysical questions he could answer only if his mind was free of a lifetime's humdrum habits. His life had been a frenetic round of playing and training, appearances and promotions, day and night, weekends as well, dashing between work, airports and home. Sometimes even his superb cool failed him and the stress was almost too great. Against Jamie-Lee's needs everything else subsided. For the first time since he was a boy, rugby league was challenged in his affections. The game had arrested an area of Wally's personality in his childhood, never allowing him to mature fully because his phenomenal success meant he had no need to. But as football subsided beneath Jamie-Lee's demands, so too did the child in Wally.

He had already lost the Australian and Broncos captaincies. Jamie-Lee's deafness released him from the superhuman image in which the public had falsely imprisoned him for so long. He could stop pretending he had ever been anything but imperfectly human. He wasn't Queensland's captain anymore.

His football demotions reverberated through his family. His parents were shocked — no, they were devastated. The pain showed in their eyes for months until they came to terms with the truth that their son's brilliant football career was over. Spectators and commentators alike still longed for the romance of Wally, however the loss of football freed Wally forever from the call of "Blondie".

Acquaintances noticed him coming out of himself. "He was just a different person in 1992," said a Sea-FM staffer. "He came to station lunches where we take out a group of listeners every month. Generally it turns into a great big party. We usually didn't ask Wally along because we assumed he wouldn't come. But now he does and has a good laugh. He's a good sport."

When Peter Hickey first took over as Wally's manager he occasionally copped the usual wisecracks about Wally's arrogance, just as I have as his biographer. None of them knew Wally, because few people do; they had merely formed opinions from scuttlebutt, which was founded upon Wally's moodiness.

According to Hickey, Wally used to be unpredictable. "Sometimes I'd ring up and he'd be in a real shitty mood. Or I'd arrive with a stack of business to deal with and he'd say, 'Oh mate, I've got to go and play golf now.' I thought, 'I'm not going to let this bloke beat me.' Then next time he'd be good as gold and I worked out that his mood changes were directly related to stress. He's the same as you and me." Another acquaintance recalled how when he called to discuss business, Wally wearily ate Jamie-Lee's lollies and kept one eye on the television. He was simply too tired to pay full attention, the friend finally realised.

Both Jacqui and Seagulls marketing manager Ron Morris believe Hickey is the best thing that has happened to Wally's business life. Jacqui says that Wally didn't know who to trust anymore until Hickey came on the scene. Morris was puzzled when he heard Wally have a shot at Hickey. "That was his problem," said Morris. "He'd been ripped off that many times in his life, he'd lost respect for everyone, even those helping him. But in his second season with us he mellowed. You wouldn't go to him when he was tense before a game, that's just putting your head in the lion's mouth. You deserve to be snapped. But I've never seen him so mellow as during that charity game. He was very responsive to everyone, appreciative of what we did. He was good."

In 1992 Hickey found that occasionally the phone would ring. "It'd be Wally and I'd be looking through my paperwork thinking 'What have I forgotten?'" said Hickey. "And he'd say, 'Oh, just checking how things are going.' That pleased me no end because it was a breakthrough. We're not great mates, don't have to be. But I feel I'm a lot more accepted now and he'll give me a ring just for a chat. When that career pressure was lifted he changed. He's less and less moody. Wally would be the hardest guy ever to manage, but I respect the guy. A great bloke."

The testimonial committee also noticed a marked difference in Wally's attitude between their first meeting in January 1990, soon after he had been sacked as Broncos captain, and their last when they presented him with his cheque. "He was a bit shell-shocked around the time of the first meeting; he'd copped a lot," said one committeeman. Indeed when Wally first heard of his testimonial's plight, he was so distressed that Jacqui took one look at him and said, "If I drank, I'd have one with you right now." The committee remarked how well Wally seemed to have adjusted to the loss. Wally shrugged and told them, "There's not a lot I can do about it now." Later everyone at the table commented on how his demeanour had changed. It was almost as though, through having to cope with the disasters that had befallen him, he had reached deep into himself and discovered a resilience he never knew he had.

If Wally went to those businessmen for help today he would be welcomed. "The football setbacks were not failures," said one committee member. "They should be the catalyst for change. Nothing else. He's never been a failure, no reason to be one now."

Was Wally the greatest player ever? Not according to *Rugby League Week*'s list of the Top 100 all-time greats published in 1992. Wally was ranked seventh after Churchill, Raper, Gasnier, Messenger, Langlands and Fulton. It might seem churlish to point out that six of the seven judges were from NSW. The sole Queensland judge, Box Bax, told me, "I rated Gasnier first but after I saw the results I was sorry I didn't put Wally first." I could fill another book with tributes to Wally but a select few from distinguished judges gives some balance to the RLW rankings.

In Queensland former top broadcaster, George Lovejoy — credited with originating the phrase, "Rugby league, the greatest game of all" — always named forward Duncan Hall as Queensland's best ever player, until one night at Lang Park, after another Lewis triumph, Hall himself stood up and told Lovejoy, "The greatest Queensland player ever is out there." Another Queenslander, pre-war Kangaroo vice-captain and later Test selector, Jack Reardon, had no hesitation in writing that he had never seen a greater player than Lewis. Ron McAuliffe's way of putting it was, "Any team which has Wally Lewis must start odds-on favourite."

In Sydney Graham Lowe was responsible for the compliment — which was eventually employed by others as a criticism — that Wally was bigger than the game itself. "You don't want too many like him coming along," said Lowe. "But when they do, you just have to accept it." Respected coach and commentator, Alan Jones, said, "You talk about Bradman, Walter Lindrum, Dawn Fraser and I think you can talk about Wally Lewis. He's up there among the immortals." ARL chief Ken Arthurson saw in action all the players ranked ahead of Wally, except of course Dally Messenger. I have Arthurson on record, after the first State of Origin at Lang Park on 23 May 1989, as saying, "He might just be the greatest player I've ever seen." Perhaps the most telling comment of all came from Arthur Beetson, a contemporary of nearly all those ranked ahead of Wally in that RLW list. Said Beetson, "I have no reservation in saying he's the greatest player I've ever seen."

Can he match his playing record as a coach? "He could," said Great Britain assistant coach Phil Larder. "Wally's challenge will be passing on his strategies to players not as gifted as him. Because what he did was innate and frequently not coachable." Larder also warned against expecting too much too soon. "Wayne Bennett coached a lot of teams before he won with Brisbane," he said. "Malcolm Reilly was a good coach in 1985 and he's a far better coach now. But he still hasn't won the Ashes."

Wally himself is under no illusions about coaching. "If I don't succeed I want to be able to stand up and say I tried," he told me. "If I'm not good enough I'll join the queue who had a go. There's nothing wrong with failing as long as you give it your best shot. Winning is wonderful, having the courage to admit you're beaten is the other half of the lesson."

The next five years of his life will be Wally's test as he makes the difficult transition from player to coach and seeks a future business career. Vultures lurk in the world of entrepreneurs, ready to rip him off if he pays no heed to past lessons. "People tell me I won't have much to do with Wally now he's retired," said Peter Hickey. "But I reckon I'll be more busy. I'd prefer to have him right now. Arthur Beetson was a giant in his day, Alfie Langer reached hero status with his field goal in 1992. But Wally is about to become Queensland's only true legend, the man who never had to leave the state to prove himself the best."

Like most classic legends Wally's career has traversed heroism, disaster and triumph. "Football has been my life, it's my first love and probably be my last love," he told me. "You just don't get games like that out of your blood. It's too hard." Not out of his blood, but under control. Wally appreciated what rugby league brought him. "I've travelled the world through football and I've been fortunate to represent what I believe is the greatest country of the lot," he said. Ken Arthurson knew that. Said Arthurson, "He was so proud to pull on the green and gold and for that I admire the man more than anything else."

Wally Lewis experienced moments in rugby league which were his alone, when he was swept to heights of valour usually the preserve of men at arms. The sensual sound wave of massed adulation rippled over him, the lights blazed, the rockets cascaded overhead, the anthem soared into the night sky. It was heady stuff. At the height of this fame his love of rugby league became so intoxicating, was such an obsession, that it took over his life. All rational existence for him and his family subsided beneath the game's insatiable demands. Trapped in this terrible symbiosis he drifted further and further from the reality of his self identity and his family. He lost himself. And when this great love suddenly spurned him he was inconsolable. To have given so much, for so long and be cast aside.

Painful though it was, it is a universal experience, as old as history, the true significance of which may be the acquiring of wisdom. Wally came of age and was restored to Jacqui and the boys, and the daughter who needed a father capable of his great depth of affection. The fires of indignation still burn within Wally, it's his natural condition, fuelling his need to compete and win. But I see him today like a soldier returned from the front — beyond bitterness, glad to have survived, appreciative of the things that remain, ready to move on and share his knowledge. In the immediate future it will be as State of Origin coach. But the analogy goes far deeper than that. Through the dust, noise and chaos of his conflict with rugby league, Wally Lewis may have found the path to himself.

Wally Lewis Picks His Players

Wally agreed to name the top players of his era but stipulated that he would only judge those he played with or against in Origin or Test football. Too many had retired or were past their best before he played in the Sydney competition. Comparing players from past eras was impossible.

Best player of my era

I break it down to four I've played with and against — Brett Kenny, Peter Sterling, Gene Miles and Mal Meninga. Brett's speed off the mark was sensational, his acceleration to join the line tremendous. I had to be at my best if I wanted to be at all competitive with him on the night. I always had to ensure I was in the right frame of mind, which was difficult sometimes with him pulling faces at me at the first scrum!

I always admired Sterlo from my side of the five metres. I'd look at his size and ask myself how could he control a game the way he did? He tackled big guys as easily as little guys, structured his attacking line, threw cut out passes, had a great kicking game, set play up — just the complete footballer.

Injuries meant Geno and Mal took it in turns to be the world's number one centre. Two huge blokes, as happy to run over you as around you. I can remember the early Origins when they played against two of the greatest centres of all time, Mick Cronin and Steve Rogers. It became obvious as each game progressed that the two established blokes were about to be overtaken by the two young guys. Mal has produced magnificent Test football longer than us all.

If I'm forced to narrow it down to one player, it would probably be Sterlo.

Best ever NSW team

Fullback: Garry Jack gets the nod because he dominated NSW teams for so long. Very strong, quick, good timing in defence, had an elusive step and such a good runner of the football. Graham Eadie is the other who springs to mind, but Wombat only played one Origin game and I didn't see enough of him to appreciate his talents.

Wingers: Eric Grothe would be a runaway for one wing, because he was just so powerful. He was one of those blokes who if you were going across in cover defence you knew you'd have to put an extra 25 per cent effort into the tackle to stop him. His speed was phenomenal. At Lang Park one night I put Colin Scott away on the halfway and when Scotty reached the 22 metre line he was 10 metres in front of everyone else. Three metres out Guru caught him. No one could believe it. Amazing. The other winger? A fight between Chris Anderson who was a very good finisher and Andrew Ettingshausen. They were two different styles of wingers. ET's biggest problem was some games he'd play fullback, some centre, some winger, whereas Anderson was trained in wing play all his life. We won one game at Lang Park 43-22, I think we led 33-0 and Anderson ended up scoring three tries for NSW in their comeback. I'll go with him.

Centres: I've got Mick O'Connor down as one. You'd pick him first because of his elusive running, goal-kicking and his importance to any NSW side. Mick Cronin played six Origins and Steve Rogers four. They'd battle out the other position. Most people would normally say you'd pick both, but they were in the twilight of their careers when I played them and we won nearly all those matches against them. Both magnificent centres. Rogers went on the 1982 tour but Cronin didn't. I never got to see the best of Mick. I'll give the nod to Rogers.

Five-eighth: Brett Kenny and daylight second. Not even a close one there. That's no disrespect to the other five-eighths at all. Terry Lamb was a bit unlucky to strike Bert.

Half: Peter Sterling, just in front of Steve Mortimer, even though Mortimer played his best football at Origin level. Turvey tended to be very much a team man for NSW and he inspired them. Sterlo produced more as an individual and his kicking game was an advantage. He played sixteen games to Mortimer's seven. I've chosen Sterlo as one of my top four so he gets the vote.

Lock: I would probably pick Ray Price even though he retired in 1984 and NSW hadn't won a series up until then.

Second rows: I'd put in two other locks, Wayne Pearce and Bradley Clyde, because they both had some experience there for NSW. To put them in I have to leave out Les Boyd and Paul Sironen. Boyd played under different rules. He could go and clout someone as hard as he liked and probably not get sent off. That made him a feared man but his form of aggression wouldn't work in today's game. I like Sirro because of his size and mobility but then again Junior's not that much smaller than me and Clyde's a big bloke. So, I'd put Clyde and Pearce in second row to just edge out Boyd and Sirro.

Props: I'd pick Steve Roach first because he was inspirational for NSW for so long, and have the other prop spot shared between Craig Young and David Gillespie. Young in the early years and Gillespie in the later years. Cement played more Origin games so he gets it.

Hooker: Very hard to split Benny Elias and Royce Simmons. Again Simmons was in the early years and Elias later. Max Krilich too. All had good reigns as NSW hookers and all were good at various jobs. Do I vote for them because NSW was successful that year? Simmons if I'm forced to choose.

Best Queensland team

Queensland changed players far less often so there is less debate.

Fullback: Gary Belcher. Colin Scott played more games but Badge would just have the edge on him.

Wingers: Kerry Boustead and Dale Shearer. Bowie was just electric, fast, could step, loved knocking over blokes twice his size, in a class of his own. Rowdy was a big match man. Current wingers Willie Carne and Mick Hancock miss out because I didn't get to play many games with them. Otherwise they'd be putting pressure on the other two.

Centres: Gene Miles and Mal Meninga. Chris Close just gets squeezed out. After that you can put up anybody but it's not even close.

Five-eighth: I'll vote for myself because in a team like this I want to be in it.

Half: Allan Langer. His latter day football explains why he's in the team. Alfie has gone on in the last couple of years to bigger and better things. Until then I'd have picked Mark Murray and I'd choose him as first reserve because of the great games he played for Queensland.

Lock: Bobby Lindner or Paul Vautin — Lindner I think, he played there more often.

Second rows: Vautin one spot and for the other I find it hard to split Wally Fullerton-Smith, Trevor Gillmeister and Brian Niebling. All did very well for Queensland. Maybe Fullerton-Smith, his career spanned eight years.

Hooker: Greg Conescu. I played the majority of matches with him rather than Kerrod Walters. Great team man, Turtle, and probably the most underrated footballer I've ever seen.

Props: Greg Dowling gets the first vote and the other would be from Dave Brown, Martin Bella or Sam Backo. People would say it's strange to put Brown's name in but his performances for Queensland were superhuman. The way he psyched himself up for a match was unbelievable. I can never ever remember him playing a bad game for Queensland. People might say, what about Arthur Beetson and Rod Morris? But I only played one game with Arthur, and only four with Rod, so it's not fair to the other blokes who I played with so often. Maybe Martin Bella half a nose in front of Brown and Backo, but that would be it.

Australia

For Australia, and again it goes on Origin or Test form, I'd choose:

Fullback: Garry Jack. He held out Gary Belcher then, so he does here.

Wingers: Boustead and Grothe for the previous reasons.

Centres: Miles, Meninga and Kenny. Whatever combination you'd have an outstanding pair. I think Geno for one. Mal missed a fair few Origins with his arm. Then on the 1986 tour Brett played centre and Mal had to sit on the line. He eventually got a

start in the forwards, played second row. Brett kept him out of it the whole tour. Brett played genius football over there. That's the hardest choice of the lot.
Five-eighth: I've put Brett in the centres so I'll choose myself here.
Half: Langer or Sterling. Sterlo did a little bit more at Australian level than Alfie who did it at Origin level. But now Alfie's about to hit his straps at Test level. Sterlo for now.
Lock: Price, narrowly over Bob Lindner. Their careers hardly overlapped. Only played a couple of Origin games against each other. Bob always had enormous tours to England. Price took a great amount of pride in playing for Australia. I'll give him that, as often as we argued.
Second row: Pearce and Clyde, just over Fatty Vautin because of the number of Tests they played. Fatty never seemed to get the Test selectors' tick. It was hard to understand why he never got accepted. To me he was a real big match player. I never played against him much at club level, but he captained Manly to a Sydney premiership which is a fair recommendation. He'd be my first reserve.
Props: Dowling and Roach, two hard but creative forwards.
Hooker: Simmons. Max Krilich tended to play more of a captain's dig at that level and I used to think it affected his game a little. He played a kind of "I'll go down with the ship" type of role. Benny Elias was always highly rated by the Poms because they could never contain him. But Royce at international level was first class.

Great Britain

Great Britain had some good players who didn't necessarily produce their best in matches against me.
Fullback: Joe Lydon was their best. Paul Loughlin and Steve Hampson weren't a touch on Joe. George Fairbairn was vastly overrated.
Wingers: Des Drummond, John Joyner, Henderson Gill. Garry Schofield was wasted out there. Martin Offiah only came on the scene late. He played here in 1988 and we'd heard so much about him, how quick he was, but he did nothing on tour. Now he's proven his worth. But I'd go for Drummond one, and a bloke called Basnett. He was a big, strong bloke from Widnes and we

could never work out why they didn't pick him more often. He played against us in the third Test in 1986 and played very well.
Centres: Paul Loughlin first up and I'd put Ellery Hanley in there. Ellery was another player, like Offiah, who didn't always play well against us. In 1984 we heard what a great player he was and they picked him on the wing for the tour. He scored one good try and that was it. In 1986 we toured and again he didn't do a thing. Our centres embarrassed him. Ellery didn't show his best form against Australia until 1990.
Five-eighth: Garry Schofield and daylight second.
Half: Andy Gregory. It's between him and Schoey as their best player. Andy showed an immense amount of pride in representing his country and was just such a hard bastard. He was built like a brick outhouse, rolled his pants 45 times up his leg and he'd be the first to admit he was never going to star in a Hollywood movie, but when he went out on a football field he always played the lead role.
Lock: Andy Goodway. Not a strong era of Pom forwards.
Second row: Mike Gregory. In 1988 Great Britain came out and in that tight first Test it was Gregory who got them going. Paul Dixon as the other.
Front row: Kevin Ward every time. One of the strongest blokes you could imagine. He was the British bulldog. If they'd had two like him things might have been different. Lee Crooks as the other even though he never lived up to his promise against us.
Hooker: Kevin Beardmore. No outstanding candidates.

All my coaches

Ross Strudwick (Valleys): He knew what he wanted to achieve and whether he made friend or foe didn't make any diference to him. I used to take a lot of notice of him early and people said that's the reason I gained so many enemies. The Rat taught me a lot of good and bad things along the way.
Des Morris (Wynnum and Origins): I enjoyed my time under Des. We won the Brisbane premiership with him as a player in 1984. The next year he coached us and we just lost the grand final 10-8.
John McDonald (Origins): I only had him one year of Origin in 1980. I was so nervous I can't remember what he was like.
Arthur Beetson (Origins): Arthur was just the perfect bloke for the

crime. To everyone in the team he was a legend and they wanted to play to a standard to suit the man's reputation. He was totally inspirational, had a lot of technical knowledge in the forwards, less so in the backs. But as he said, unless the forwards do it, the backs can go home. He pulled out after 1984 and when he came back in 1989, to the younger blokes like Hancock and Carne, suddenly he was the legend all over again.

Frank Stanton (Kangaroos): A very strict disciplinarian, Frank. He realised the 'Roos were away in England and France for three months and you couldn't let up. On the 1982 UK tour, I believe, as the incumbent Test five-eighth, I should have played the Test in New Guinea on the way overseas. Instead Stanton chose Brett Kenny and that gave Brett the edge when we arrived in England. But I should say, in all honesty, that in the lead up to the first Test, Brett showed superior form to me. Contrary to most beliefs I got on fine with Stanton after our initial blow-up.

Rocky Turner (Wakefield Trinity): Great bloke, former legend. Training was a game of touch and go home. He tried to inspire you ten minutes before the game and at half-time. Not really enough.

Bob McCarthy (Brisbane): Applied himself to the modern game. His coaching in 1984 was perfect, fitted the team well, we used to get together before, during and after training. Knew all the moves, what patterns to adopt. I got on with him 110 pc. A wasted talent not coaching in Sydney.

Terry Fearnley (Kangaroos): He was said to be a "brains" coach. I honestly believe he didn't like me from the start. Not that he had to. He thought I ran things too much and he was there to affirm his dominance. If I put one foot out of line he was there to make an example of me. I often think back to that 1985 Test series and to be honest I couldn't give a damn in that last Test we lost in New Zealand. Terry Fearnley had completely split the touring party in two.

Don Furner (Kangaroos): Got on terrific with Donny. He said. "Listen mate, you've got the reputation as a bloke who's not going to run marathons in training. But we're over here to do a job, if you do yours and I do mine we'll get on very well." He didn't get blokes up at 7 a.m. for a walk around town, but when they got on that bus at 10 a.m. everyone had to be on time and he put the work in at training. He was the coach I enjoyed being associated with most. Results showed it worked.

Wayne Bennett (Origins and Broncos): I enjoyed being associated with him in the Origin series but later, well this book says it all.

Bob Fulton (Kangaroos): Bozo and I got on pretty well. We didn't end up being together too long. One year in New Zealand. He adopted the modern beliefs more than anyone else, made sure the players were happy and we were. Made us train hard but not ridiculous. Very balanced man.

Graeme Lowe (Origins): Terrific, very good. Came along when Beetson was given the sack, and people automatically put up the no-thanks sign. He was the most hated man in Queensland before the first Origin in 1991 but after the third he could have been elected Premier. Used to be very inspirational. He'd say, "Alfie, you can do it, you can do it. You're a great player and you can do it." After he walked from the room the blokes used to have a bit of a giggle. They'd sit and whisper just loud enough, "Great player Alf, great player." But by the time we got to game time everyone believed in themselves.

Malcolm Clift (Seagulls): Shifty had a big reputation as a coach. He was only there one year and in all fairness we didn't have the best team in the world. Despite the results we had some good times.

Career Statistics

Origins:
Played 30, 29 as captain, won 19 lost 11, was man-of-the-match a record eight times. He scored seven tries (two when tries were worth only three points) for 26 points, kicked two field goals and one goal for four points, a total of 30 points.

Club football	Matches
Valleys (1978-83)	135
Wakefield Trinity (1983-84)	10
Wynnum-Manly (1984-87)	76
Brisbane Broncos (1988-90)	50
Gold Coast Seagulls (1991-92)	37
Total	308

Queensland	Matches
State of Origin	30
Origin (L.A. exhibition)	1
Interstate	4
Agst touring sides	2
On tour	5
Total	42

Australia:	Matches
Tests	33
World Cup	1
Rest of the World	1
On tour (UK and NZ)	19
Total	54

Other	Matches
Oceania v Europe	1
All up total	405

Index

Abbott, Bob, 100-102, 104, 183
Adidas World Ratings, 3
Alcatraz, 42, 44
Alexander, Greg, 21, 143-144, 180, 182
Annesley, Graham, 74
Archer, Ron, 107
Artbusters, 172, 175-176
Arthurson, Ken, 7, 9, 15, 19, 84-85,
    87, 99, 102-103, 106-107, 112,
    115-117, 142, 144, 147, 150-151,
    157, 180, 183-184, 203, 209-210
Australian Airlines, 108
Australian Grand Prix, 137-139
Australian Rugby League, 7, 37, 84,
    99-100, 102, 104-107, 112,
    116-117, 146, 150, 158-160, 183,
    203, 209
Australian, The, 171

Backo, Sam, 4, 23, 27, 50, 56, 57-58,
    126, 136, 151
Bagnall, Geoff, 120
Baker, Neil, 5
Ballinger, 149, 196
Bangkok Post, 81
Bax, Bob, 54-55, 73, 209
Beattie, Dud, 171
Beetson, Arthur, 17, 20-21, 23, 24, 62,
    81-86, 167, 202, 209-210
Belcher, Gary, 20, 143

Bella, Martin, 19, 23, 156
Bennett, Trish, 41
Bennett, Wayne, 4-6, 10, 12-13, 16-18,
    85-86, 123, 134, 180, 182, 186, 210
    Balmain bogey, 32-34
    Gene Miles, 66-68, 78
    Lewis's arm, 95-98
    Lewis cut, 88, 90-92,
    Lewis, five-eighth, 70-74,
    Lewis's hamstring, 76-77
    Lewis sacked, 36-41, 46-47, 50-52,
        54, 57, 59-64,
    Seagulls derby, 141-142,
Bennettization, 50-51
Bond, Alan, 108, 128
Bookworld, 113
Boon, David, 125
Border, Allan, 33, 109, 193
Botham, Ian, 193-194
Boustead, Kerry, 184
Boyd, Les, 146
Brereton, Dermot, 137, 172
Brisbane Bears, 34, 119, 203
Brisbane Bullets, 110, 119
Brisbane Exhibition, 191-192
Broncos
    World Club Challenge, 187
    Grand Final (1992), 62, 186
    Final (1990), 95-97
    Semi-final (1990), 95

Index

1988, 4, 34
  v. Balmain, 50
1989
  v. Balmain, 32, 33
  v. Cronulla, 34
  v. Easts, 10,
  v. Gold Coast, 7, 8
  v. Illawarra, 13-16
  v. Manly-Warringah, 5
  v. Newcastle, 34
  v. Parramatta, 12-13, 34
  v. Penrith, 5
  v. Souths, 13, (Panasonic Cup) 136
  v. St. George, 10
1990
  v. Canberra, 95-97
  v. Balmain, 74
  v. Manly, 78, 95
  v. Norths, 77
  v. Wests, 73
  v. St George, 86
1991
  v. Gold Coast, 141-142
1992
  v. Gold Coast, 168-69
Clubhouse, 4, 10, 16, 36, 47, 49, 57, 91, 97, 99, 193
Directors, 33, 35, 40, 50, 61-64, 91-92, 98, 119, 203-204
Brown, Dave, 66
Burns, Tom, 114
Butler, Jack, 107

Callinan, Ian, 75
Camp Quality, 128, 184
Canavan, Brian, 52-53, 63, 71
Carne, Willie, 53, 158
Carroll, Tom, 140
Carter, Steve, 182
Cartwright, John, 181-182
Chappell, Greg, 206
Churchill, Clive, 99-100, 159, 209
Clift, Malcolm, 134
Close, Chris, 120, 135
Clubs
  Brisbane

    Grand final (1990), 104
    Norths, 68
    Redcliffe, 7, 8, 48
    Souths, 51, 75
    Valleys, 9, 28, 38, 40, 52, 169, 181, 202
    Wynnum-Manly, 7, 8, 38, 51, 65, 164
  NZ
    Mangere East Hawks, 126
  Sydney
    Grand finals (1987) 25; (1988) 50; (1989) 36; (1990) 88; (1992) 62
    Balmain, 7, 32, 33, 71, 74, 114
    Canberra, 4, 12, 50-51, 66, 71-72, 95-97, 105, 171, 178
    Canterbury, 4, 47, 50, 183
    Cronulla, 34, 167
    Eastern Suburbs, 10, 82, 88
    Illawarra, 10, 13, 14-16, 169-170, 178-179, 184
    Manly-Warringah 5-7, 25, 32, 40, 47, 65-66, 78, 86, 88-89, 95, 119, 141
    Newtown, 202
    Newcastle, 34
    North Sydney, 47, 77, 88, 98
    Parramatta, 12, 34, 81, 114
    Penrith, 5, 71, 179-180
    South Sydney, 13, 136
    St. George, 10, 86, 114, 184
    Wests, 159

  UK
    Featherstone Rovers, 88
    Widnes, 88, 106
    Wigan, 69, 164, 167, 187

Clyde, Bradley, 17, 22, 50
Collins, Chris, 121
Collins, Kate, 61
Colman, Mike, 2, 42, 81
Conescu, Greg, 4
Connor, Dennis, 27
Conti, Dick, 75
Cooper, Russell, 47

Cornelson, Greg, 165
Corowa, Larry, 180-181
Courier-Mail, 1, 82, 113, 158, 171-172, 194, 204, 206
Cowell, Jim, 7-9
Coyne, Gary, 20-21, 145-146
Craddock, Robert, 82, 206
Cross, Dr Merv, 101-103, 106
Currie, Tony, 4, 10, 13, 15, 20, 35, 46, 50-51, 56-58, 77, 81
Curry, Lisa, 164-165

Daily Mirror, 9, 23, 88
Daily Telegraph, 9, 10, 85, 87
Daley, Laurie, 17, 19-20, 22, 50, 142, 160, 177
Denyer, Craig, 122
Devins, Mathew, 129-132
DiPierdomenico, Robert, 185
Disneyland, 36, 42-43, 55
Donnelly, James, 57-58
Donnelly, John, 58
Dornan, Dimity, 162-163
Dowling, Greg, 3, 4, 8, 12, 14-16, 32-33, 37-38, 40-41, 46-47, 51-58, 60, 66, 68-69, 71-72, 82, 87, 90-91, 95, 97, 136, 144, 164, 187, 191
Dowling, Rhonda, 41
Dreamworld, 131

Eadie, Graham, 179-182
Eastlake, Darrell, 140, 182
Earthquake, 44-46
Elias, Benny, 74, 85, 112, 145, 147, 156
Elias, John, 74-75
English Rugby League, 111-112
Ettingshausen, Andrew, 20, 143

Fenech, Jeff, 21
Ferrato, Anne, 161
Ferguson, John, 18, 20
Fordham, David, 6, 16, 36, 39, 43, 46-48, 59, 62, 75, 77, 103, 107, 110, 120, 160
Forsythe, Linda, 161-162
Fourex, 108, 127-128

Frail, Holly, 3
French, Gary, 34
Frilingos, Peter, 9, 23, 88, 144
Fulton, Bobby, 3, 25-27, 29-31, 34, 43, 62, 73, 75, 87, 99-100, 159, 164, 184, 209

Gardiner, Frank, 141
Garnsey, John, 107
Gasnier, Reg, 99-100, 159, 209
Gee, Andrew, 145
Geyer, Mark, 145-147, 159
Gibbs, Dr Nathan, 100-104, 106, 112
Gibson, Jack, 13, 16-17, 23, 28, 81-82
Giles, Kelvin, 71, 76-77, 81, 86, 94-96, 169, 179
Gillmeister, Trevor, 20-22
Gold Coast Bulletin, 133, 135
Gold Coast club, 7, 8, 88, 97, 109, 114-115, 118-119, 130, 133-135, 164, 166, 178
1991
 v. Broncos, 141
 v. Canterbury, 133-34
 v. Manly, 141
 v. Wests, 135, 139
1992
 v. Broncos, 167-169
 v. Canberra, 171,178
 v. Wigan, 69, 167
 v. Illawarra, 169-171
 v. Penrith, 179-182
Gold Coast Indy, 116, 135, 139-141
Gomersall, Barry, 8
Goss, Wayne, 1, 2, 175-176, 184
Gould, Phil, 171
Graham, Mark, 198
Grauf, Craig, 72
Green, Bruce (father) 192, (son), 15
Gregory, Andy, 13-14, 16
Grothe, Eric, 184, 186
Gympie incident, 57

Hagan, Michael, 19, 22
Hall, Duncan, 209
Hammerton, Ernie, 3

Hampson, Steve, 13-14
Hancock, Michael, 13, 17-18, 20-21, 23, 53, 58, 95
Hanley, Ellery, 177
Harding, Jeff, 30, 56
Harrison, George, 192
Hatcher, Bruce, 107, 111
Hauff, Paul, 95, 143-144, 146, 158
Hawaii, 45-46
Hawke, Bob, 1, 2, 61
Heads, Ian, 147, 158
Hear-And-Say, 162, 184
Hendy, Trevor, 124, 194
Herring, Ray, 120
Hewson, Dr J. 138
Hickey, Peter, 53-54, 124-125, 127-131, 135, 165, 185, 189-190, 193, 207-208, 210
Hill, Terry, 186
Hilton, (Brisbane) 114, (Sydney) 116
Hohn, Mark, 75
Holmes, Paul, 26-27
How To Play Rugby League, 113
Howes, David, 110, 112
Hughes, Graeme, 15, 177
Hyde, Frank, 108

Izzard, Craig, 170

Jack, Garry, 17, 22
Jackson, Peter, 4, 13, 30-32, 41-43, 50-51, 56 57, 59, 61, 73, 98, 146, 151, 160, 176
Jackson, Siobhan, 43
Johns, Chris, 18, 23, 35, 41, 56-57, 95, 144
Johnson, Dick, 141
Johnstone, Billy, 135
Jones, Alan (driver), 140
Jones, Alan (coach), 85, 154, 209

Kangaroos
 1982 (UK), 17, 18, 65
 1985 v. NZ, 26
 1986 (UK), 102-103
 1989 v. NZ, 25; (1st Test) 27-28; (2nd) 28; (3rd) 29
 1990 (UK), 68, 87-88, 93, 95, 99, 104-105, (1st Test 105, 112), 111-112, 116
 Reunion, 186
Kavanagh, Lawrie, 158, 171-172, 175
Kelly, Hugh, 171
Kelly, Peter, 43
Kennedy, Terry, 26-27, 120-121
Kenny, Brett, 69, 142, 178, 184-185
Kenny, Grant, 137-138, 140
Kilroy, Joe, 13

Langer, Allan, 3, 10, 13, 17, 19, 21, 32, 34, 47, 56-57, 69, 71-72, 83-84, 109, 112, 171, 177, 180, 187, 191, 202, 210
Langlands, Graeme, 159, 209
Larder, Phil, 209 210
Lattin, Mike, 107, 110
Lawrence, Laurie, 114
Lazarus, Glenn, 71, 83
Leahy, Darryl, 164-167, 179
Leech, Guy, 165
Le Man, Brett, 14, 47, 50, 55, 74
Lewis, Hayley, 109
Lewis, Jacqueline, 10, 94, 123, 129, 132, 183, 199-200, 206
 And Wally, 188-196
 Bennett, 64, 77, 85
 Broncos, 4, 15-16, 89, 98-99, 120
 Broken arm, 87
 Earthquake, 43-46, 54,
 Gene Miles, 67-68, 70,
 Green, Jacqueline, 65, 188
 Jamie-Lee, 149-156, 159-163
 Kangaroos, 101, 103-106, 112
 Rumours, 60-62,
 Sacking, 38-41, 46-48
 Seagulls, 118
 Statue, 175-176
Lewis, Jamie-Lee, 87, 149-155, 158, 160-163, 176, 195-196, 206-207
Lewis, Jim, 182, 201

Lewis, June, 149, 168, 182, 187, 195, 201
Lewis, Heath, 195
Lewis, Lincoln, 42, 131, 195-196
Lewis, Mitchell, 42, 101, 120, 131, 157, 163, 176, 183, 195
Lewis, Scott, 90, 104
Lewis, Wally
  And fans, 10, 42-43, 80, 104-105, 112, 119, 126, 171-176
  As lock, 5, 34, 72-75
  Birthday, 67
  Bungie, 30-32, 50
  Captain-coach, 134, 164, 167
  Captaincy, 3, 7, 9-12, 20, 24, 26, 28, 30, 105, 144, 148, 151, 158-159, 178
  Captaincy
    Sacking, 36-44, 46-64, 67-70, 86
  Celebrity Challenge, 184-186
  Charity, 52, 124, 128-129, 184
  Coach, 86, 209-210
  Conspiracy, 105-106, 116-117
  Contracts, 88-92, 97, 133
  Crowds, 12, 14-15, 28, 85, 96-97, 133, 168, 171, 178, 182, 185, 191, 202
  Diet, 17, 165
  Drinking, 39, 56, 98
  Driving, 52, 135-141
  Drugs, 169
  Fines, 9, 13, 75, 84
  Gouging, 74
  Helicopters, 43, 125-126, 135, 185
  Hospital, 48, 86-87, 128-129, 149-152, 197
  Injuries
    Annotated, 197-200
    Arm, right, 3, 5, 55
    Arm, left, 86, 88, 94-106, 165
    Eye, left, 122, 143
    Eye, right, 24-25
    Hamstring, 74, 76-77, 80-81
    Head, 134
    Knee, left, 34, 36, 48, 55, 119
    Knee, right, 55
    Nose, 141
    Shoulder, right, 36, 48, 55
  Judiciary, 6-7, 9, 75, 170
  Last match (Lang Park) 168, (Premiership) 179-184, (Adelaide) 187
  Man-of-the-match, 19, 23, 144
  Rumours, 59-62
  Sent off, 5-6
  Spitting, 7-10, 13-14, 50
  State of Origin coach, 190, 211
  Statue, 158, 171-176
  Strength, 166
  Tackling, 14, 29, 83, 86, 177, 182
  Testimonial, 107-115, 208
  Training, 3, 4, 10, 54-55, 71, 74, 90, 94-95, 134, 153, 164-167, 179
  Tries, 12, 22, 182
  UK trip, 112, 114
  Work, 4, 57, 92, 120-128
Lindner, Bob, 21, 23
Livermore, Ross, 65, 81-82, 84, 86, 142, 156-158
Loane, Mark, 31, 197
Long Live the King, 147
Los Angeles, 42-43
Love, Jackie, 109
Lovejoy, George, 209
Lowe, Graham, 75, 86, 142, 146, 149-151, 153, 159, 171, 209
Lukas, Brendan, 10
Lyons, Cliff, 142, 160

Mayfair Crest, 109
McAuliffe, Ron 44, 100, 116, 142, 202, 209
McCallum, Greg 5-6, 83-85
McDermott, Craig, 124
McLachlan, Bruce, 99
McLean, Mike, 170-171
Make-A-Wish, 184
Malone, Paul, 2
Maloney, Larry, 88, 133
Manson, David, 145-147
Maranta, Barry, 3, 50, 63, 91
Martin, Ray, 19, 123, 185, 189, 196

Martin, Steve, 75
Masters, Roy, 9-10
Mathers, Sir Robert, 107
Matterson, Terry, 5, 18, 72
Maurice, Ian, 15
Mayfair Crest, 108
Meir, Rudi, 179
Melbourne, 82-84
Meninga, Mal, 17, 19-21, 42, 66, 68, 94, 96, 99, 112, 142-144, 156-159, 171, 178, 198
Messenger, Dally, 209
Miles, Debbie, 41, 66, 67
Miles, Gene, 3, 4, 7, 10, 12-13, 17, 24, 32, 38, 40-41, 51-53, 55-57, 65-72, 77-79, 90, 95-98, 109, 136-137, 144, 164, 187, 191
Mohr, Clinton, 170
Moore, Peter, 25-26, 115, 183
Morgan, Paul, 87, 91, 98-99, 187
Morris, Ron, 109, 114-115, 181, 208
Mortimer, Chris, 22
Mortimer, Steve, 18, 109
Muir, Barry, 75, 144
Murray, Mark, 66, 82
Myers, Dr Peter, 24, 36, 86-87, 97, 102-103, 165, 197-199, 200

National Acoustic Laboratories, 161
Neller, Keith, 120
Nelson, H.G., 171, 175
Nobbys, 118
Norman, Greg, 206
North, Sam, 171
NSW Leagues Club, 7
NSW Rugby League, 9, 13, 16, 75, 88, 90, 100, 105, 146-147, 158, 170
NSW Rugby League Yearbook, 3
NSW TAB, 18

O'Callaghan, Peter, 40, 62, 103-104, 119, 190
O'Connor, Michael, 3, 144-145, 158-159, 178, 184, 186
Old Trafford, 111
Olympic Park, 83

Packer, Kerry, 65, 119
Pahoff, Mike, 119, 179, 197, 200
Pan Pacific Hotel, 130
Panasonic Cup, 4, 10, 12-13, 15-16, (1984) 13
Parkroyal Hotel, 47, 57
Paul, Barry, 107
Pearce, Wayne, 17, 102-103, 108, 117, 185
Penthouse, 7, 9, 74, 122
Peters, Peter, 101
Pickering, Larry, 110, 140
Plowman, Brett, 71
Potter, Mick, 86
Power, Bernie, 108, 110, 127-128
Power Brewing, 104, 108, 116, 127, 186
Power, Jan, 81
Price, Ray, 18, 33-35, 75, 87-88

Quayle, John, 16, 147
Queensland Newspapers, 107
Queensland Rugby League, 84-86, 107-108, 110, 113, 128, 142, 146, 172, 176, 202, 205

Radio ABC, 180
3ZM-FM, 27
Sea-FM, 118, 122-124, 127, 133, 185, 195, 207
FM-104, 32
Radliff, Ron, 119
Ramada Renaissance, 112
Ramsay, Tom, 204
Raper, Johnny, 23, 47, 73, 99, 108, 159, 184, 209
Raudonikis, Tommy, 144
Reardon, Jack, 209
Reilly, Malcolm, 210
Renouf, Steve, 53
Ribot, John, 6-7, 32, 40-43, 46-47, 50, 62, 82, 88-92, 95, 202
Richards, Ron, 107
Richards, Viv, 193, 201
Ricketts, Steve, 194
Ritchie, Greg, 193

Rix, Grant, 72
Roach, Steve, 27, 75, 83, 126, 143, 178, 186
Roberts, Ian, 78
Roberts, Tom, 2
Roberts, Wayne, 115
Robinson, Clint, 164
Robinson, Jon, 139-140
Rodwell, Brett, 13
Rollers, Gold Coast, 119
Rorke's Drift, 21
Rosie's Tavern, 151
Rowe, Normie, 138
Royal Hop Pole, 111
Rugby League Week, 7, 209
Russell, Ian, 13
Ryan, Doug, 107-108
Ryan, Glenn, 5-7
Ryan, Warren, 159

Samios, Milton, 111
Sands, John, 109-110, 113
San Francisco, 43-45
Sawrey, Hugh, 176
Schofield, Garry, 177
Scott, Colin, 41, 66
Schifilliti, Dean, 13
Seaworld, 124, 126
Sengstock, Larry, 119
Shearer, Dale, 20, 95, 157
Shepherd Centre, 161-162
Simmons, Royce, 75
Sironen, Paul, 27
Smith, Billy J., 15, 47, 52, 88-92, 103, 107-115, 120, 124, 190
Smith, Wendy, 161
Smith, Wayne, 2
Spillane, Debbie, 171
Sporting Wheelies, 52, 184
State of Origin
  1980, 120
  1984, 19
  1985, 42
  1988, 16, 28
  1989 (1st) 10, 13, 16, 18-19, (2nd) 9, 19-24, (3rd) 23, 209
  1990 (1st) 76, 80-82, (2nd) 82-85, (3rd) 85
  1991 (1st) 142-144; (2nd) 144-148, 150; (3rd) 69, 147-151, 153-158
  1992 (1st) 171; (2nd) 171, 175, 177
Sterling, Peter, 3, 12, 17, 18, 109, 184, 186
Stewart, Jackie, 139
Stewart, Sam, 28
Stone, Mick, 28
Strudwick, Ross, 9, 28, 169
Stuart, Ricky, 145
Suki (Susan Mead), 122
Sun, Brisbane, 49, 104, 144
Sun-Herald, 10
Sunday Mail, 1, 49, 61
Sunday Sun, 147
Sydney Swans, 203
Sunday Telegraph, 2, 23, 42, 73, 81
Sydney Morning Herald, 9, 85, 147, 158-159, 171

Tamworth Leader, 130
Tamworth Truck Drivers' Club, 129
Telegraph Mirror, 142, 144
Television
  NZ, 26
  Queensland
    ABC, 16, 62
    Channel Nine, 22, 69
    Channel Ten, 4, 6, 16, 26, 36, 43, 47, 52, 57, 59, 75, 83, 92, 98, 107-108, 110, 112-113, 120-121
  Sydney
    Channel Nine, 116, 140
    Channel Seven, 160
    Channel Ten, 15
TV Week, 34
Tennant, Ray, 27, 28
Tests
  1914, Aust. v. GB, 21
  1986, Aust. v. GB, 6
  1988, Aust. v. GB, 4
  1989, Aust. v. NZ, 17, (1st Test) 26, 27; (2nd) 28; (3rd) 29
  1990, Aust v France

1991, Aust v NZ, (1st) 159; (2nd) 160; (3rd) 160,
1992, Aust v GB, 177, 191
Thomas, Alan, 22
Thompson, Col, 111
Thuys, Dwayne, 140-141
Todd, Brent, 168-170, 181-182
Tronc, Scott, 47
Turner, Dick, 81, 83, 85, 107, 142, 147, 149, 153, 155-57
Tuuta, Brendon, 27, 28
Tweed Heads Hospital, 184
Tyrrell's Wines, 108, 113

Underwood, John, 172

Vagabond Motel, 43
Vautin, Kim, 150
Vautin, Matthew, 150
Vautin, Paul, 6, 12, 20-21, 24-25, 29, 32, 38, 40, 68, 73, 81-82, 86, 89, 100, 109, 123, 160-161, 182, 185-186

Walsh, Chris, 186
Walsh, Ian, 34, 66, 75, 142, 144
Walters, Kerrod, 4, 13, 17, 21, 58, 72, 168-169
Walters, Kevin, 72-74, 98, 168, 171
Walters, Steve, 72, 145
War games, 71
Ward, Eddie, 9
Wells, Jeff, 171
Wembley, Cup Final, 69
Weston, Craig, 186
Williams, Darrell, 29, 35
Williams, Steve, 91
Wishart, Rod, 13
Wolf, Bradley, 163
World Cup
1988, Aust. v. NZ, 3, 25, 36, 55, 87
1992, 184, 187
World Sevens, 69, 167
Wright, David, 83

More UQP SPORTS

King Wally
by Adrian McGregor

Wally Lewis was the undisputed King of Australian Rugby League, a player of awesome skill and power. He was also League's most gifted captain, who led the victorious 1986 Kangaroo tour of Great Britain.

Prize-winning feature writer Adrian McGregor has put together all the inside stories, the drama, disasters and triumphs of Wally Lewis's eventful life, from working class son to the country's highest paid footballer. For sports fans, this was the most talked about book of the year.

"After Australia narrowly held off New Zealand in a violent Test clash, I watched a compassionate Wally Lewis move slowly around the dressingroom, quietly talking to each of his bruised and bleeding players. They'd been through hell for him. I decided to find out more about the special qualities of such a champion."

Adrian McGregor

"A fascinating and brilliant insight into the life of Australia's Test captain."

Neil Cadigan, *Rugby League Week*

Greg Chappell
by Adrian McGregor

"If a film was taken of a long innings by Greg Chappell and then, for some reason, the game of cricket was lost to civilisation, the entire art of batting could be deduced by a future generation from that film."

Henry Blofeld

Greg Chappell is the greatest Australian batsman since Sir Donald Bradman. His records are endless and his achievements unique. But Greg Chappell was an enigma. During his career he was a hero one moment, a renegade the next.

In this new edition of his landmark biography, Adrian McGregor, one of Australia's most respected journalists and sports writers, reveals the personality behind the public performer.

It's the story of a boy whose love for a game took him to the pinnacle of Australia's most popular sport. And it reveals the high points, and the low, of Greg Chappell's career: his relationship with Bradman; his first test, captaining Australia; and the infamous underarm incident.

"It makes captivating reading for the cricket fan of all ages."

Courier-Mail

"Well written...a significant contribution to both the history of the game and its literature."

Weekend Australian

"When I put the book down for the second time I considered that never again could I possibly read such an accurate and honest description of this giant among his fellows."

Canberra Times

"One of the best biographies of a contemporary Australian cricketer."

Sydney Morning Herald